COMMUNICATION PROBES

PROBES

Second Edition

Brent D. Peterson
Brigham Young University

Gerald M. Goldhaber
State University of New York at Buffalo

R. Wayne Pace
University of New Mexico

SCIENCE RESEARCH ASSOCIATES, INC.
Chicago, Palo Alto, Toronto, Henley-on-Thames, Sydney, Paris, Stuttgart
A Subsidiary of IBM

Photograph Credits

p. 4: Nick Pavloff; p. 40: Nick Pavloff; p. 72: George B. Fry III;
p. 102: Tom Tracy; p. 144: Tom Tracy; p. 170: Nick Pavloff; p. 196:
Tom Tracy

Library of Congress Catalog Card Number: 73–93238

ISBN 0-574-22550-1

Contents

Communication is a process in which people interact to achieve an effect on one another. As editors, we occasionally enjoy face-to-face or written interactions with our readers, but more often, we rely upon sales figures to indicate the understanding and acceptance of our written messages. In its brief life span of just over three years. *Communication Probes* has been read by over 130,000 students on over 400 college and university campuses. Although we gratefully accept the popularity of *Communication Probes,* we openly acknowledge its drawbacks.

We have coupled the formal opinions of the 20 reviewers of our book with the many unsolicited letters we received from current and former users. This input allowed us to identify the major strengths and weaknesses and make appropriate changes, additions, and deletions. The result, in our opinion, is a greatly strengthened *Communication Probes,* Second Edition that retains the conceptual framework and innovative format of its predecessor while increasing its instructional usefulness in the classroom.

Major changes in the second edition include:

I. *New or expanded topics* on sex roles and language, assertiveness traning, the environment, serial and speaker-audience relationships.
II. *More structure* by using essays to introduce each major section; adding new probes for each major article and sequentially numbering them throughout the book; adding an index to help locate important people and subjects; and preparing two tables of contents, one highlighting the major articles and probes and the other (at the back of the book) restricted to the supplementary material.
III. *Dramatic format* including 20 new songs, cartoons, newspaper/magazine stories, poems, advertisements, quotes and comments, and more than 50 photographs, including 20 in full color.

Definition of a Probe

A PROBE is a key topic or main idea about communication that is stated, explained, and illustrated by combining scholarly articles with popular works. For example, the Message Component (2) of this book has five PROBES, the first of which is *Appropriate verbal and nonverbal symbols are essential to effective communication.* This PROBE (and the other four) first appear on the cover sheet introducing Component 2. Later, each PROBE appears inside the component, set aside in special type near an illustration of a comet, to introduce the article(s) that explain and illustrate the PROBE. Thus, in the example above, this PROBE is immediately followed by a scholarly article and a cartoon. To make your task easier in locating a particular PROBE, we have consecutively numbered the 34 PROBES appearing in the book. Taken as a whole, the PROBES provide a set of propositions that best explain how people communicate in an environment by sending messages to establish relationships.

During the completion of the Second Edition of *Communication Probes,* we relied heavily upon the advice, guidance and love of several persons whom we now acknowledge: first, again, our wives Arlene, Marylynn and Gae, for their tolerance of our work and appreciation of our success; May Polivka for her expert typing and clerical assistance; Al Lowe for his editorial guidance; Judy Olson for her highly creative layouts; Gretchen Hargis for her diligent copyediting; our reviewers for their thoughtful and most helpful comments and criticisms; Richard Browning, Donald G. Clark, John E. Crawford, Mary V. Crowley, Ronald Cummings, R. G. Finney, Claude C. Fuller, William Gorden, Roger D. Haney, Albert Lewis, Thad P. Lindsey, Thomas Lower, Stacy Myers, Donald Shields, Charles B. Summers, Julie Ann Wambach, Lew Wilson, and David R. Wright; the entire SRA sales staff for their incredible, tireless and enthusiastic efforts to market our first edition; and finally, since no book could succeed without readers, we thank the more than 130,000 student readers of *Communication Probes*. It is to you students that we dedicate *Communication Probes*, Second Edition.

McLuhan on Probes

A Probe is just noticing an effect of any kind of development, especially where it relates to innovation. You Probe by studying what effect it is having upon me or upon the situation I'm working on. And by simply noticing the new relation it has between you and the clouds, between you and the library, and between you and the textbook, you identify a Probe, the study of effects. Simply noticing these effects, stating them as challengingly and as extremely as possible—stingers, you know—I call them Probes. Most people never study the effects of anything.

So, for example, you may ask what is the effect of the copy machine on my teaching? It has, for example, created some position papers which make committees possible. The committee is one of the big effects of the copy machine. It enables everybody to participate by having a complete agenda and a complete ability to know what is going on in the group.

Now the computer's effect on, for example, bookkeepers, or on the world of the credit card, or the world of finance is fantastic. The thought of inflation is very closely tied to the enormous speed-up in transactions as the result of the computer.

These are what I call Probes; they sound very exaggerated. You tend to push them all the way to a high point of penetration, where they really bite you. So many of my Probes about the effects of printing on people over the centuries— for example, print makes everybody a reader, the copy machine makes everybody a publisher—(these are probes) simply study the effects, with no point of view involved at all.

Well, you see, many of the *New Yorker* cartoons are a world of Probes in which all sorts of social situations are revealed as ridiculous. There are many kinds of Probes. Anything that highlights or intensifies awareness of something tends to be a Probe, I think.

From an interview with Marshall McLuhan conducted by Gerald M. Goldhaber on January 24, 1976, at the Centre for Culture and Technology at the University of Toronto.

40

Ric Masten

i have just
wandered back
into our conversation
and find
that you
are still
rattling on
about something
or other
i think i must
have been gone
at least
twenty minutes
and you
never missed me

now
this might say
something
about my
acting ability
or it might say
something about
your sensitivity

one thing
troubles me tho
when it
is my turn
to rattle on
for twenty minutes
which i
have been known to do
have you
been missing too?

The Beginning

The missing person is the bane of effective communication. Whether the absence is altogether physical or merely a silent slippage into a netherworld of misty memories and daydreams, the isolation of lonely message-sending grips the hearts and minds of most of us. Nobody likes to talk to the "brick wall." What can be done? Wander back with us. Join our conversation and listen to our plans.

Our *ability* to communicate is based on our understanding of HOW people communicate and WHY they fail. Effective communication may produce success in gaining understanding from and influencing those with whom we wish to establish personal relationships. Through practicing the principles of communication, we may express love, help others, get information, and develop profound relationships. No other human ability offers so much for both good and evil.

Through communication people find, establish, and foster close relationships; world powers negotiate treaties and make decisions that affect millions of people; industrialists coordinate the efforts of thousands to produce goods and services; protests are expressed; clubs are formed and sustained; civilization is created; wars are waged and civilizations destroyed; people are hurt and helped, and love is created and crushed. Clearly, communication—especially effective communication—matters.

What are the essential building blocks to help us understand communication? What is the essence of communication? There seems to be somewhat general agreement among professionals that communication occurs when a person makes sense out of something. Making sense means that one sees some connection among aspects of a situation. Communication is, therefore, a wholly human activity performed by people. When two people come together, each of them tries to make sense out of one another and out of the environment into which they have come together. Making sense is helped by what we call symbols.

A symbol is something that stands for something else. A word, for example, is a symbol when it refers to an object. To communicate, a person must be able to evolve a mental picture of something (create a concept), give it a name, and develop a feeling about it. Effective communication with another person implies that the concept, the name, and the feeling are similar to what that person has in mind. In other words, effective communication means that you and I refer to the same things when we talk. We share understanding. If we are communicating effectively and I say, "Meet me at 7 o'clock near the gym," you visualize the same gym as I do, you fix the same time of day as I do, and you identify the same relationship associated with meeting people as I do.

What kinds of clues help us know what people mean when they talk to us? What kinds of clues can we give others so that they can know what we mean? I can ask you directly, "What do you mean?" or "What are you referring to?" If you can physically point to what you are talking about, I have a good chance of finding out what you mean. Many things that we talk about, however, are difficult to point to phys-

PROBE 1. **Effective communication occurs through a process of human transaction in which PEOPLE share symbolic MESSAGES in complex ENVIRONMENTS for the purpose of achieving useful human RELATIONSHIPS.**

ically: feelings, hopes, plans, experiences. How can we determine what a message means when we cannot look at what is being referred to? In such a case we need to describe to each other the concepts we have inside ourselves.

We ought to remember, however, that communication is a process in which events are not controlled to any great extent. As I say something to you, for example, I interpret your behavior; you react nonverbally to some parts of what I say and verbally to others. While you are reacting, you are also formulating what you will say when I finish. You might even interrupt me. At the same time, I might react to a concept inside of me that sprang to prominence by some movement you made and that is somewhat unrelated to our immediate conversation. The moments when we respond directly to what each of us means are few and precious. Effective communication depends in part upon our abilities to sense and respond to these fleeting revelations at just the right moment.

We can say that communication among humans begins when some source has a purpose, when a person has a reason for communicating. A person's purposes are expressed through symbols—verbal or language symbols and nonverbal or behavior symbols—which, when combined into units, become messages. A source's messages are interpreted by a receiver. Recent thinking by communication theorists suggests that the parties to a communication event are engaged in a *transaction*. That means simply that both sender and receiver are engaged in simultaneous and continuous production of and response to each other's messages. In communication, it is the person—in fact, both persons in dyadic relationships—that is the

focus of understanding. Thus, the first component of this book is called THE PERSON. Communication, in this sense, really represents persons in transaction.

Although the persons are of primary importance in a study of communication, their relationships are mediated by their transactions through messages. Therefore the second major component is called THE MESSAGE. It is through sending or receiving messages that persons make sense of one another.

The third major component is called THE ENVIRONMENT. Developments in methods of producing messages for distribution over the mass media have created what some have called a symbolic social environment. This suggests that people communicate with one another in a social setting. A symbolic environment dominates the atmosphere in which human transactions take place. Much of the environment is influenced by mass-produced messages. Even our most personal conversations are greatly influenced by electronic modes of communication. Therefore the third component explores the modern environment as it is affected by television and newspapers, computers and copy machines.

When these components merge, they create a communication event. Although such communication events may be rather individual and quite personal, with interpretations taking place internally, the presence of others imposes demands on the people so as to create a unique situation. People combine in ways that produce dyads (two persons), serial chains, small groups, and formal audiences. We refer to these combinations as RELATIONSHIPS. Four basic communicative relationships are identified:

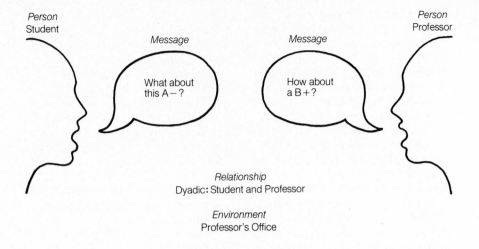

Diagram of Communication

dyadic, serial, small group, and speaker-audience. Each of these relationships is treated in separate sections in this book.

The accompanying diagram illustrates that effective communication occurs through a process of human transactions in which PERSONS share symbolic MESSAGES in complex ENVIRONMENTS for the purpose of achieving useful human RELATIONSHIPS.

Information about each of the components and relationships can help you to better understand the process of communication and how to communicate more effectively with others. Within these pages you will find out how to prepare messages and how to interact with people in order to establish personal, intimate relationships; how to participate in small groups; how to reduce the loss of information that occurs when a chain of communicators reproduce messages; and how to prepare and give a public speech.

Communication Probes, Second Edition seeks to do more than introduce the basic theory of human communication and demonstrate its application. This book raises questions and encourages you to answer them. Selections may also be viewed as types of PROBES. A PROBE is anything that highlights or intensifies your awareness of something. PROBES are investigative tools; they initiate further comment. In this book, we are attempting to provoke you, to probe you, to highlight and intensify your awareness of communication.

At the end of each component and relationship are PRODS— questions, problems, and exercises that relate back to the PROBES and urge you to apply them to your own life. We want you to take responsibility in communicating with other people and to analyze your own behavior to find out how you can improve your own communication. Take a PROBE. Respond to a PROD.

THE PERSON

PROBE 2 Your values and attitudes are part of your personality and serve as guidelines for how you behave and what you perceive.

PROBE 3 Your self-concept develops through contact with others.

PROBE 4 Imagination can change your self-concept as you reflect upon your interactions with others.

PROBE 5 Self-disclosure and feedback can help you form close relationships with others.

PROBE 6 Your perceptions may be a prime obstacle to effective communication.

PROBE 7 Active listening requires perceiving situations from the point of view of the sender.

PROBE 8 We listen more carefully to things we want to hear and tend to blot out things we do not want to hear.

Component 1: The Person

Human communication, by definition, has people as its core. As simple as that may seem, we cannot overemphasize that people are the keys that unlock the mysteries of communication. Of fundamental importance is one clear conception: that which makes us human is that which also facilitates and hinders communication. To comprehend communication, we must discover what human factors affect the creation of meaning.

The Person Component discusses and analyzes several aspects of human behavior that affect the way communication takes place. Included are contributions dealing with the types of personalities of both senders and receivers of symbols. Personality involves regularized patterns of behavior determined or at least highly influenced by beliefs and values. Self-concept is another important determinant of how we communicate and behave. Perceptions of self and, especially, others are both cause and effect in communication. The quality of communication is often a function of our ability to perceive ourselves accurately and to reveal that self to others. What we imagine others think of us and what we imagine about ourselves may set the stage for fanciful bouts of meaningful and meaningless dialogue with ourselves as with others.

Factors such as personality, self-concept, and perception meld into a communicative style that establishes a personality receptive or resistant to interaction with others. The result is a predisposition to listen or not to listen. Defensiveness, resistance, and hostility choke off the expression and reception of feelings, undermining the understanding of others through active and effective listening.

We cannot escape our human condition. Our perceptions, self-concept, imagination, listening attitudes and behaviors, personality, and inclinations toward disclosing and hiding information affect our ability to communicate effectively, and they constitute The Person Component in communication. Consequently, if you understand that individuals perceive events differently and understand also that differences are a source of resistance, you may be able to discover where the differences lie, why they have developed, and how they might be changed to help an interaction continue.

Naturally, much of the information in this component should be considered for purposes of self-enlightenment—to comprehend our own personality more clearly, to sense how we perceive ourselves and others, to call attention to how we self-disclose, to assess our own tendencies toward active listening, to reveal to ourselves aspects of personality, attitudes, and values that might interfere with our own communication efforts. Through self-understanding we make the initial step toward evaluating the quality of our own contribution to a communication relationship. Through self-understanding we begin the process of understanding others to accommodate, encourage, support, and help both parties in the relationship. Through understanding The Person Component in communication, we begin to chart attitudes, feelings, beliefs, and values that make communication feasible, enduring, viable, profound, enlightening, and to the benefit of all concerned.

The Responsibility of Communicators

The Role of Human Values in Communication

Virgil L. Baker
Professor of Speech, University of Arkansas, Fayetteville, Arkansas

A value, we learn, is a concept of the desirable. The Greeks had no word for value, but they did have a close synonym, *axios*, meaning worth. A value thus is anything of worth. Values, as we define them, are the goods of life, life resources. Values are all those things both objective and subjective without which we cannot be human beings.

What are the chief human values and how may we structuralize them for use in our communications? While we might well trace all human values to their first origins in our primitive ancestors, we now look to the Western World for our modern, more highly developed value system. From the Greek civilization of the fifth century B.C. came that classic value triad: the good, the true, and the beautiful. From the Hebrew-Christian cultures come the values incorporated in the Ten Commandments, the seven virtues (faith, hope, charity, prudence, justice, fortitude, and temperance), and the seven mortal sins (pride, wrath, envy, lust, gluttony, avarice, and sloth). Finally, modern scientific technology has added a host of values ranging all the way from the scientific method itself to better health, longer life expectancy, and to technology that fills our homes with labor-saving devices and comforts, including electronic communications that make incidents from any spot on earth "no sooner done than said."

Perhaps no more realistic way of structuralizing a human value system can be found than that of indicating the values our institutions gather, nurture and disseminate. Says Harold Lasswell, "Values are shaped and shared in patterns that we call institutions." Here we classify human values in tabular form adapted from Speech in *Personal and Public Affairs*, a textbook recently published by myself and my colleague Dr. Ralph T. Eubanks.

These we believe to be typical human values. They are universal life resources, characteristic of those sought for by human beings in all cultures, all civilizations. Says Sumiti Kunai Chatterji, "The mainsprings of human culture are the same—they are universal: and certain ideals, values, attitudes or behaviors, whether good or bad, have always been found to be transmissible. These ideals, values, attitudes or behaviors form patterns comparable to language." Indeed, these values make up human

PROBE 2. Your values and attitudes are part of your personality and serve as guidelines for how you behave and what you perceive.

Abridged from "The Role of Human Values in Communication: The Responsibility of Communicators" by Virgil L. Baker—a speech delivered to the Communications Seminar sponsored by the General Extension Service for Red Cross Volunteer Workers, April 2, 1965, and published in *Vital Speeches of the Day*, May 1, 1965. © 1965 City News Publishing Company. Used by permission.

Human Value System	
Typical Functioning Institution	Typical Value Clusters *Positive/Negative*
Home	Love/hate
School	Enlightenment/ ignorance
Church	Rectitude/immorality
Library	Literature/trash
Government	Freedom/bondage
Court	Justice/impartiality
Hospital, clinic	Health/illness
Prison	Reform/punishment
Occupation	Wealth/poverty
Social organization	Respect/disgrace
Leisure organization	Recreation/boredom
Welfare organization	Charity/miserliness
Pressure organization	Dissent/conformity
Museum, gallery	Beauty/ugliness

nature itself. Let a carpenter from our country meet one in Israel, or India, or Africa, or Mexico, or Japan. He will be able to communicate in large measure with each, and each with him, through the language of universal human values. Erich Fromm makes this doubly clear when he says: "The universal symbol is rooted in the properties of our body, our senses, and our mind, which are common to all men and, therefore, not restricted to individuals or to specific groups. Indeed, the language of the universal symbol is the one common tongue developed by the human race. . ."

How do we, as communicators, speak this universal language? We speak it secondarily by non-verbal symbols of meaning: by our actions, attitudes, and appearance. Others read our values first in the appearance of our possessions: the style, cleanli-ness, orderliness of our dress, study desk, or interior of our cars or homes. Next they read them in our gestures, facial expressions and body movements. They then hear them in the nuances of vocal tones whether they be tones of joy or anger, love or hate, fear or hope, melancholy or optimism, sympathy or jealousy, pity or envy.

But these are all secondary ways that we communicate our set of values. The primary way, of course, is by our use of words in the sentences we speak or write. By words we express our set of values when we make as-sertions, demands, requests, pleas, declarations, contracts; when we ask or answer questions or give commands; or when we state opinions, decisions, judgments, and commitments.

Values are the goods of life, without which we cannot be human beings.

Our words are stimuli, stand-ing in or substituting for our values. "The wonderful thing about language," says M. Mer-leau-Ponty, "is that it promotes its own oblivion." Words are fleeting signs and symbols, as quickly gone as heard or seen, but as they go they probe deep into our set of values, feeding out and feeding back exchanges of value meanings. The ultimate referent of the word is to values. Communication redefined means to exchange values.

It now becomes clear why communications between peoples so easily break down, for no two individuals have precisely the same set of values.

Our value systems differ first of all as we differ in age. The child's set of values shifts as he becomes a teenager; the teenag-er's values shift as he goes to high school, and again when he goes to college and even during college they may shift, making of him a good student or a dropout; they may change when he leaves college, again when he marries, again when he takes a job, and so on throughout his life as he becomes a father, a grandfather or a great grandfather.

Our value systems differ also according to the particular daily roles we take as afforded by our functional institutions: the home, school, church, library, hospital, occupations, social institutions, and the like. In a single day one may take a dozen or more func-tional roles, each with its distinc-tive value patterns. Let me enu-merate some of the typical roles taken in a day by an average citi-zen. He takes the role of a son, a husband, a father, worker, wor-shiper, student, committeeman, philanthropist, friend, voter, dis-senter, writer, speaker, creator of beauty, to mention but a few. And furthermore, we find that every role one takes is hedged about with rules, regulations, customs — communal performance rites — all of which must be observed as one performs the role. As we worship we follow the minute details of the ritual; as we play the role of say a golfer we follow the minute details of the performance rites as set forth in the rules and com-mon practices of that game; and as we take the role given us by our occupation, as a teacher for instance, we follow through the long sequences of communal performance rites and regulations connected with teaching class after class and meeting student after student in conference.

Since each individual's set of values differs from another's, may not such differences account

Age 7

Age 14

On Seeing a Policeman

From "MAD's Lifetime Chart of Attitudes and Behavior," written by Frank Jacobs and illustrated by Paul Cokes, Jr., Reprinted from MAD Magazine. © 1974 by E.C. Pub-lications, Inc.

largely for the breakdowns that occur in communications? Breakdowns occur daily between peoples of different races and colors speaking different languages; between peoples whose forms of government are unlike; between peoples participating in different religious rituals; between individuals belonging to different political parties; between management and labor, teacher and student, executive and subordinate, and even between brother and brother, sister and sister, and husband and wife.

With individual value systems being as varied as they are, it is little wonder that breakdowns occur resulting in speakers shouting hate names: "Nigger," "Wop," "Chink," "Dago"; or writers hoisting hate signs screaming "Whites only," or "Yankee Go Home."

Peoples with highly specialized value clusters find difficulty in communicating with those whose sets of values are less specialized. Individual specialization is highly necessary in our complex industrial society. Yet highly specialized value clusters may stand in the way of effective communications between individuals. For example, teachers may communicate at their best only with teachers, executives with executives, scientists with scientists, doctors with doctors, lawyers with lawyers, and architects with architects.

Probably most breakdowns in communications occur between individuals who have developed extremely lopsided value clusters. As indicated by our chart, the values of life include both the good and the bad – the positive and the negative. Both positive and negative values are found in everyone's set of values, for both are part of our life experiences. We cannot, for instance, know the fuller meanings of love without having experienced hate, nor enlightenment without being conscious of ignorance, nor rectitude without knowing immorality, nor can we experience freedom to the full without having experienced bondage or servility, nor justice without partiality, health without illness, wealth without poverty, or beauty without ugliness. Thus positive and negative values are counterparts like the two sides of a coin. Love completely divorced from hate, envy, jealousy, and anger, would be a love so thin, anemic, idealistic and lopsided that it would be realistically meaningless. Hate completely divorced from love, trust, pity, and brotherhood would be a monstrous, lopsided figment of the imagination.

What we seek in our sets of values is balance, proportion, harmony, norms. The Greeks brought the concept of The Golden Mean into our Western Communications. Newton in his laws of action-reaction gave us an equation of equilibrium that is basic in our star and earth sciences. W. B. Cannon noted that the human body had built into its structures a number of energy governors to maintain physical, mental and emotional health. He called this self-governing propensity homeostasis or "The Wisdom of the Body." Homeostasis as we now know is extendable beyond man's physiological and psychological self-governing propensities to a kind of governor in social relationships. There is a tendency toward maintaining relative stability in social conditions among forces with respect to various factors, such as food supply, competing tendencies, and powers within the body politic, and thus to society as a whole and even to culture among men. Only as we succeed in keeping a sane balance between positive and nega-

tive values can we find the normal clusters that make for human survival.

Age 20

Age 35

PROBE 3. **Your self-concept develops through contact with others.**

The Search for Self-Identity

Kim Giffin and Bobby R. Patton

We all have ideas about who and what we are; taken together these beliefs are our self-image or identity. Some persons, particularly adolescents, seem to be desperately struggling to define themselves. Other persons seem to know what they are, but are most concerned about what they might hope to become.

With respect to this identity-formation, it is useful to note the contribution of G. H. Mead; perhaps more than any other theorist he viewed the development of self-identity as the product of social interaction. Mead emphasized the importance of face-to-face interpersonal communication—how we respond to others and they in turn respond to us. In this way we learn about ourselves; each interchange gives us cues about how others see us and this shapes our view of ourselves. From the time we are small children this process goes on; virtually all communication to us gives us indications of our importance, capabilities, and potential, as well as our inadequacies.[1]

The following description of the process of identity formation has been given by another very well-recognized theorist on self-identity, Erik Erikson:

> . . . identity formation . . . is a life-long development largely unconscious to the individual and to his society. Its roots go back all the way to the first self-recognition: in the baby's earliest exchange of smiles

there is something of a self-realization coupled with a mutual recognition.[2]

The process of identity-formation via interaction with others, suggested by Mead and Erikson, is largely a reflection of the perception of us by others. Cooley coined the phrase "the looking-glass self" and Sullivan spoke of "reflected self-appraisal." These are graphic labels for this process.

Of course, not all beliefs about ourselves are formed by social interaction. Direct sensory perception tells us when we are tired, hungry, or burn our finger. Also, Festinger's social-comparison process tells us when we are as tall as our parents, weigh more than "the average," or work arithmetic problems "faster than most" persons. Even so, *the choice of persons with whom we make such comparisons* is largely shaped by social interaction with persons in close relation to us.[3] There are some indications that as we pass from childhood into adulthood, more and more of our beliefs about ourselves are formed through feedback about ourselves from others and employed by us for comparing ourselves with norms, averages, and members of reference groups.[4]

As children we like to have our parents give us things, but most of all we want them to *communicate* with us. We do not know for

Age 50

Age 70

certain what we are until others (significant to us) tell us. We even prefer mild punishment to total indifference; in later life we can tolerate hate better than we can accept total neglect.[5]

Even in the pain of being hated we can at least know that we really exist. Socrates, condemned to death, faced condemnation with pride and honor; he believed that his death would affect important future acts of his countrymen. But if no one responds to our acts or thoughts, while yet we cannot live without thinking and acting, the incongruity between our needs and our world becomes unbearable. Under such circumstances children aggress against their parents and teenagers test authority by violating rules. In extreme circumstances a person may behave in extreme ways in order to obtain a response —any response— to establish his *existence*, regardless of the degree of antagonism or hostility his behavior will produce.

An unprovoked attack upon another person can never be condoned; however, the terrible sense of loneliness, neglect, and the need for some kind of attention from others which instigates such an attack is pertinent to the study of interpersonal communication. Attempted destruction of oneself may be a call for "help"—attention from and consequential interaction with others; it may also be the despondent conclusion that this need will never be met, that rewarding human interaction for such a person is impossible.

The important point to be understood is that almost every time we initiate communication, even on a nonverbal level, we are making an implied request: "Please confirm my viewpoint." Sometimes this request is actually spoken; usually, however, it is implied on the unspoken, nonverbal

They, the Jury

Every trial lawyer knows that jurors often start out with prejudices against the defendant or plaintiff. By using his rights to challenge prospective jurors, a lawyer can try to obtain a jury with as little prejudice as possible against his client. To help lawyers assess prospective jurors, a research team working under the auspices of New Jersey's Fairleigh Dickinson University persuaded some 500 persons of varied backgrounds to take an elaborate test designed to reveal prejudices that might affect their judgment as jurors. The test was set up to detect both "overt" and "covert" prejudices. The findings, released this week, include a lot of surprises about who is, or is not, biased toward whom.

RACE.   In view of the national turmoil about discrimination against Negroes, it is remarkable that the study uncovered very little anti-Negro prejudice. Negroes showed detectable biases against the successful and the established— business executives, for example. Negroes also show biases in favor of the young, the poor and the unemployed.

RELIGION.   The people tested revealed, as prospective jurors, almost no prejudice against Roman Catholics, Jews, or any of the old, established Protestant denominations. In contrast, many people in many diverse walks of life showed at least covert prejudice against "Adventists/Jehovah's Witnesses" (the researchers lumped them together as a single category).

OCCUPATION.   The occupational groups against which prejudice is most widespread are government officials and labor union executives. The most prejudiced occupational group among those covered in the study: salesmen, by far. The salesmen, as a group, showed virtually no overt prejudices, but they revealed secret prejudices against the unemployed, people with low incomes and people of Latin or Eastern European origins. The findings also indicate that, as jurors, salesmen tend to be prejudiced in favor of women.

INCOME.   Those with low incomes are often prejudiced against the highly prosperous, and vice versa; so people in the middle, earning from $7,500 to $15,000, are less likely to meet with prejudice than those above or below them in the income scale.

SEX.   Women stand somewhat less chance than men of getting a fair verdict from a jury, because two large groups tend to be biased against women: 1) men earning less than $5,000 a year and 2) women.

AGE.   People in their 30s are less prejudiced than those younger or older. The most prejudice-prone of all the categories covered by the study: the retired.

NATIONAL ORIGINS.   While discovering much less racial and religious prejudice than might have been expected, the study also revealed remarkably pervasive biases against people who trace their origins to Eastern or Southern Europe. Of the 14 nationality groups covered in the test, the one that aroused the most widespread prejudice of all was "Rumanians/Hungarians" (the study grouped them in a single category). It would appear that if a Rumanian-born woman who is a Seventh-Day Adventist gets involved in a damage suit, she would do well to settle out of court.

From "They, the Jury" in TIME, August 9, 1963. Reprinted by permission from TIME, The Weekly Newsmagazine; Copyright Time Inc.

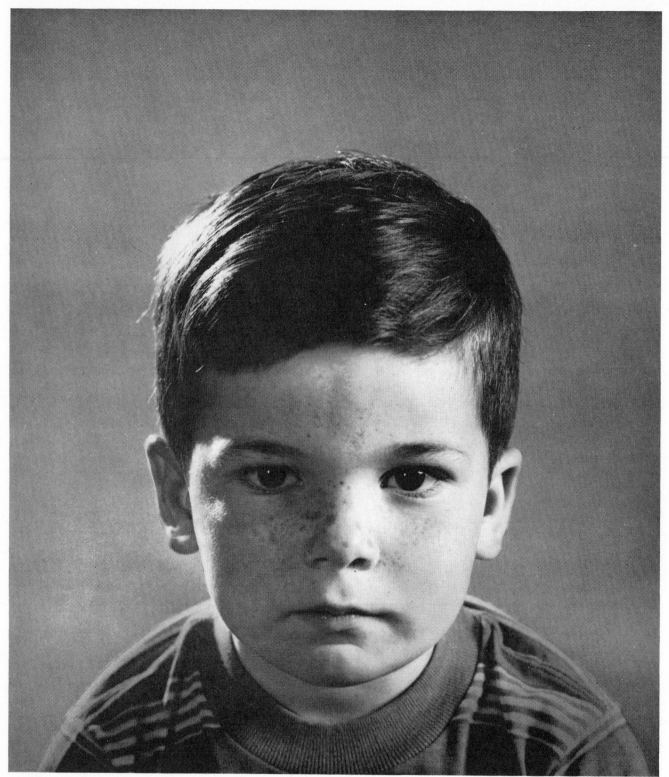

SEAGRAM-DISTILLERS COMPANY, NEW YORK, N.Y.

Two unquestioning eyes. Wherever they look, they learn. Whatever they behold, they believe in. Two shining reasons for every father to exercise judgment, wisdom, and moderation in all things...including the use of the products we sell.

Nineteenth in the series of Father's Day messages from THE HOUSE OF SEAGRAM *Fine Whiskies Since 1857*

level. Sometimes it concerns our understanding of factual data or information; frequently, it involves confirmation of an opinion. Always there is an implicit request for evaluation of us as a person. We can summarize the point thus: *every time we initiate communication or respond to it, we also make this request: "Please validate me—confirm my viewpoint and indicate my value as a person."* In this fashion we use interpersonal communication to form an impression of our self-identity.

The maintenance of a self-image, once it is formed, is a continuing process. Our self-image is confirmed anew whenever another person responds to us. Mutual recognition of such self-image provides confirmation and maintenance.

If there is consistent social confirmation, a strong and integrated self-identity will be developed and sustained. In such a case there is less need to seek confirmatory responses or to shield ourselves from possible disconfirmation. This condition provides greater freedom for the individual to be spontaneous, creative—to live; there is no great need to be concerned about every little criticism or evaluation of one's behavior. Such a person can dare to hear feedback about who and what he is, and can frequently test the validity of his beliefs about himself.

On the other hand, a person whose self-image is frequently disconfirmed will almost continually seek information about it; he will need to hear feedback, but will fear it; he will seek it, and at the same time try to avoid it. His self-image will suffer either way: if he hears negative evaluation no matter how slight, he will likely feel anxiety; if he avoids evaluation he will derogate himself for

---

Why Communications Falter

Sydney J. Harris

I receive many letters from wistful and well-intentioned correspondents who want to know "why people can't communicate better with one another." Whenever I hear this complaint, it reminds me of the pertinent fact that William James pointed out a half-century ago in one of his psychological texts.

James said that in any dialog between two persons there are six participants; it is not merely a dialog between Jones and Smith, which would be simple, but between three aspects of each personality.

First of all, there is Jones as he appears to himself, Jones as he appears to Smith, and Jones as he really is; the complementary triad, of course, is Smith as he appears to himself, Smith as he appears to Jones, and Smith as he really is.

It is within this multiplicity of identities that the communication gets lost. It is not merely that Jones says one thing, and Smith thinks he means another thing. It is that Jones himself is divided into the man as he appears to himself, and the man he really is. Even before the listener is involved, the communicator himself may be confused, or contradictory, or self-delusive.

We can see the difficulty most clearly in domestic disputes of the sort that happen every day. A wife complains about a certain attitude or activity of her husband—but she is really complaining about something else. Only neither of them is aware of the nature of the true complaint.

Thus, an argument begins on a false basis, and can have no good or final ending. The wife, as she appears to herself, is saying one thing; as she appears to her husband, she is saying another; and as she really is, she is expressing some different and deeper grievance locked within her unconscious and allowed to trickle out only in this distorted form.

Likewise, the generally poor communication between parents and growing children is largely based on differing self-conceptions. The parent, as he appears to himself, is asking only "what is for the child's good." But the child sees it differently; to him the parent is serving his own private needs.

If persons cannot genuinely communicate, how can societies, communities, governments communicate with one another? The answer is that they cannot, except on a formal, superficial level; and even such a communication breaks down in a crisis. Mankind has not even begun to tackle seriously the prime problem of sending, receiving, and decoding messages.

---

being a coward—he's "damned if he does and damned if he doesn't" seek self-image confirmation. Someone very wise once said, "To him who hath shall be given, and from him who hath not shall be taken away." This principle very much applies to the maintenance of one's self-image. To a very large extent theories of non-directive counseling developed by Carl Rogers are attempts to break this vicious circle of need, fear, and avoidance of possible image-building feedback.[6]

There is little question of the importance to the individual of the continuing need for interpersonal communication which confirms one's self-image. Once is never enough. Men have developed elaborate social rituals to reduce the probability of disconfirmation. Children are taught to become "tactful," responding to other people in a way that does not challenge the validity of the self-image they present in public. . . .

The Development of Self-Esteem

The self-image one desires must be achieved in his own eyes. Confirmation of this self-image by feedback from others gives a person the feeling that he is entitled to have this image of himself. Continuing confirmation helps him to maintain and to clarify the image. In this sense the desired self-image is improved—it is perceived as more real, its wearer feels that it fits more comfortably, and the shadows of self-doubt are dispersed.

A desired self-image is the basis of self-esteem. A person acts and in doing so intentionally or unintentionally exposes his view of himself. Another person responds to this behavior; very fre-

quently this response conveys approval or disapproval, acceptance or rejection. This simple unit of interpersonal communication is the basis of self-esteem. We tend to note and to increase our acts that elicit rewarding responses; those actions producing undesired responses are used less and less frequently. To a large extent, the ratio of satisfactory to unsatisfactory responses is the index of our self-esteem.

Communication senders seek to build and defend their self-identities and self-concepts.

Many responses from others are not easily interpreted as clear approval or disapproval. Most of us who are parents set an impossible task for ourselves: we want our children to believe that we love them unconditionally—without reservation; we also want them to behave in a reasonably acceptable way. To accomplish this we must respond approvingly to some of their behavior and disapprovingly to other actions. This will be communicated to them as *approving of them as persons* some of the time, and *disapproving of them as persons* at other times. For a child to interpret our responses as unconditional acceptance of him is almost impossible; therefore, our love will be viewed as conditional. A child learns that certain of his behavior is acceptable and some is not; he will learn to like parts of himself, and parts he will not. His self-esteem will reflect the amount of himself that he likes or accepts; to increase self-esteem he will tend to repress those parts of himself which he does not like.

Interpersonal communication is the hinge upon which this process swings. If a child cannot distinguish between (1) strong approval of himself (and his potential) and (2) disapproval of a few specific behaviors, then his self-esteem will not be congruent with the attitudes expressed by his parents and others toward him. Accurate communication of approval and disapproval of him is imperative to his appropriate development of self-esteem.

The maintenance of self-esteem is as important and complex as its development. Many of our attempts at maintenance are successful; some are self-defeating. *We should look first at those which are least likely to be successful because they are used altogether too much.*

There are three self-defeating approaches to maintenance of self-esteem: (1) trying to hide parts of ourselves from others, (2) acting as if we were something we are not, and (3) following only the "straight and narrow" ritualized patterns of interaction. Our interest in this discussion will center upon the ways in which interpersonal communication is related to the success or failure of such attempts; improving one's own communication habits through new insights should be the reader's goal.

When we perceive that parts of ourselves are eliciting disapproval, we may attempt to hide those parts—if we think it can be done. We then relate to others as "part-persons" rather than whole persons. For example, we may attempt to hide our anger when aroused. Or we may attempt to show no fear except when we are alone. Generally such attempts are ineffective: people usually see nonverbal signs of tension which are beyond our control; these are communicated to persons close

to us despite our efforts to "say nothing." However, there are two considerations which are very important when we are successful at hiding such parts of ourselves. The first is that our anger or fear is stored up inside us, possibly influencing our later responses to communication from others. These feelings may break out in ways we don't understand and which are not understood by others. Such breakouts (or outbreaks) may not even be perceived by us but are easily seen by others.[7] In this fashion, later communication not related to the focus of our anger or fear may be influenced in such a way that others (and we) are confused. At best, such internalized anger and fear contribute to our problem of fighting off an early ulcer.[8] Improved habits of being open and frank in our interpersonal communication can be personally helpful.

A second possibly damaging effect of hiding parts of ourselves is that we cause apprehension in those persons with whom we relate. Suppose as your employer, I must tell you that you have failed to do your job in an adequate manner; suppose I tell you, and you show no reaction—you smile, remain calm, say nothing, and go your way. My interpretation is that you are a cool one, that you maintain your calmness through stiff self-discipline, and do not easily go out of control. But I also wonder if you'll "lay low and stab me in the back" when I'm not expecting it—I become suspicious of you! I wonder how many emotional stimuli you can take before you react; do you remain calm under stress until at a certain point you "break" and cannot be depended upon at all? The point is this: you have given me no way to assess your emotional behavior—I perceive only part of you

and suspect there is more. I have experienced you as only a "part-person," and as such you do not seem to be real. I am confused and will be suspicious until I learn more about you. In the meantime, this attitude will tend to distort my perceptions of even your ordinary, everyday communications which may be totally unrelated to the earlier event. In such fashion interpersonal communications and personal relationships are distorted by attempts to hide part of ourselves.

A second ineffective approach to maintaining our self-esteem is to pretend that we are something we are not. This approach includes attempts to communicate false messages about ourselves—to wear masks or to erect facades. This game can be carried to incredible extremes; we can even put forth a little of that part of ourselves which produces undesired responses and then deride, derogate, or castigate such behavior! . . .

Dishonesty with self and others undermines the self-concept.

A number of points may be made about pretending to be what we are not. In the first place, it takes much energy and concentration—while focusing on our performance, we may miss many clues to the way people are perceiving us. Goffman makes the point that many times people eventually discover that nobody is really watching these performances and in reality could not care less.[9] Such performances, when ignored, can amount to a severe loss of time and effort—

THEN AS I GREW A LITTLE OLDER AND LEARNED DISAPPOINTMENT I DEVELOPED THE NEW FEELING THAT WHEN I ENTERED A CROWDED ROOM—

—I WAS THE ONLY PERSON WHO WASN'T THERE.

time during which a genuinely rewarding interpersonal relationship might have been achieved.

In the second place, such play-acting must be good. Many a television comedy is based upon a character's pretense to be something he is not, with himself being the only member of the group who does not know that all others see through his facade. We may laugh at a comic character in a play, but we hardly want people laughing at our silly performance in real life. We'll mention more damaging effects later, but it seems bad enough to have people meet us and go away saying to themselves, "What an ass!"

A more damaging effect of another person's penetration of our "cover" is that he cannot further depend upon anything we do or say—suspicion haunts his every observation of our behavior—"What a phony!" He may never give us a very *obvious* clue of this suspicion, while his *subtle* show of a clue is lost by us in our concentration on our "performance." But when we need his confidence most—when we very much want his real trust and accurate estimate of our potential, when we ask him sincerely to give us a try—he will try others first, and we may be left alone with our pretenses, a lonely phony.

In our estimation, the most severe consequence of pretending to be something we are not is that it becomes a way of life. The more we pretend, the better we become at "playing a part." And the better we are at "playing parts," the more we will try to solve our problems of interpersonal relations *by pretense* rather than by honestly facing issues and working out solutions based upon reality. One phony bit of behavior thus produces another, and even if we convince many

other people, we will be faced with the problem of trying to find our real self. "Who are you?" is the basic question asked of persons thought to be mentally disturbed. Unlimited pursuit of pretense in life can produce the seeds of madness.[10]

The final disadvantage of pretense which will be mentioned here is that it seldom works for most people. Most of us are incapable of carrying it off on the non-verbal level. By tone of voice, facial expression, modified posture, jerkiness of gesture, and other elements of metacommunication usually beyond our control, we signal our anger, grief, fear, surprise, elation, and other real feelings and attitudes.[11] Few of us are adept at maintaining "poker faces" in our interactions. People may tolerate our pretense but they usually know it for what it is if they care at all to look. . . .

A third ineffective approach to the maintenance of self-esteem is to be very cautious, to pursue only the ritualized, common, "tried and true" forms of interpersonal behavior. "I can't receive negative feedback if I only do as everybody else does." This process is one of deliberate hiding of unique parts of ourselves, responding to the fear that they may be discovered. The effect on the other person is one of appraising you as only a "part-person"—too cautious, unnatural, and somewhat unreal. In some cases the other person becomes somewhat apprehensive, wondering when your real self may show and what it will be like—and to what extent it may prove to be a threat.[12]

All three ineffective approaches to maintaining self-esteem discussed, hiding, pretending, and cautious adherence to ritualized responses, have been shown

in one way or another to be a sham—unnatural, artificial, and to some extent damaging to our interpersonal interactions. Some of the time we may fool other people, and to some extent they may even succeed in helping us to fool ourselves. These approaches project a view of life which is superficial and lacking as to solid foundations, and thus ineffective in maintaining genuine self-esteem. The basis of a strong self-image is eroded.

Effective *maintenance* of self-esteem requires the same kind of behavior that developed it in the first place—exposure, feedback, and honest attempts at desirable change. The cycle must constantly be repeated. Maintaining self-esteem is a lifelong concern for most of us. Few persons appear to receive complete confirmation of perfection. As we expose new parts of ourselves and gain feedback, we see additional need to change; as we try to change, we receive new feedback evaluating these attempted changes. Thus, new exposures produce new change attempts, and so on as the cycle continues.

The Facilitation of Personal Change

Increasing self-esteem requires positive reevaluation of oneself. This reevaluation requires exposure plus awareness and honest responses on the part of another person. As pointed out, it is very difficult for a person to achieve change in interpersonal behavior without interaction with other persons.[13] The helpful relationship is one in which there is unconditional acceptance of a person (or his potential) combined with honest, direct feedback. Some persons achieve this relationship. It

begins when people trust themselves and each other enough to start exposing more and more of their thoughts, ideas, and feelings. Each exposure is tentative; it comes in small increments and the response is noted. A disapproving response may stop the interaction temporarily or even permanently. When exposures are met with acceptance, interpersonal trust and self-confidence start to build. Each interacting party is mutually reinforcing: when one person trusts enough to expose himself more, trust is generated in the other person.[14]

In order to establish a relationship in which interpersonal communication of this order can be achieved, we may have to go out of our way to find persons who are open and frank and accepting toward us. There is increasing evidence that such relationships can be obtained if sought, with consequent benefit to both of the interacting persons.[15] Such relationships are to be prized and protected with great care and caring.

We have given extensive consideration to the development of self-image and the achievement of self-esteem. We have done so deliberately because, in all of the areas in which interpersonal communication influences people, we can think of nothing which is more important. We believe that these elements are fundamental to most if not all human interaction.

1. G.H. Mead, *Mind, Self and Society*, Chicago, Univ. of Chicago Press. 1934, pp. 144–64.

2. E. Erikson, "The Problem of Ego Identity," *Psychological Issues*, 1 (1959), 47.

3. B. Latane, "Studies in Social Comparison—Introduction and Overview," *Journal of Experimental Social Psychology Supplement*, 1 (1966), 1–5.

4. R. Radloff, "Social Comparison and Ability Evaluation," *Journal of Experimental Social Psychology Supplement*, 1 (1966), 6–26.

5. H. Duncan, *Communication and Social Order*, New York, Oxford Univ. Press, 1962, pp. 271–73.

6. C. Rogers, *On Becoming a Person*, Boston, Houghton Mifflin, 1961.

7. Ibid., pp. 338–46.

8. S. Jourard, *The Transparent Self*, New York, Van Nostrand Reinhold, 1964, pp. 184–85.

9. E. Goffman, *The Presentation of Self in Everyday Life*, Garden City, N.Y., Doubleday Anchor, 1959.

10. H. Deutsch, "The Imposter: Contribution to Ego Psychology of a Type of Psychopath," *Psychoanalytical Quarterly*, 24 (1955), 483–505.

11. P. Watzlawick, J.H. Beavin, and D.D. Jackson, *Pragmatics of Communication*, New York, Norton, 1967, pp. 62–67.

12. E. Goffman, "On Face-Work: An Analysis of Ritual Elements in Social Interaction," *Psychiatry*, 18 (1955), 213–31.

13. W.G. Bennis, et al., *Interpersonal Dynamics*, rev. ed., Homewood, Ill., Dorsey, 1968, pp. 505–23.

14. J. Gibb, "Defensive Communication," *Journal of Communication*, 11 (1961), 141–48.

15. D. Barnlund, *Interpersonal Communication*, Boston, Houghton Mifflin, 1968, pp. 613–45.

IM NOT SURE ANY OF US ARE THERE.

Imagination—The First Key to Your Success Mechanism

Maxwell Maltz

Imagination plays a far more important role in our lives than most of us realize.

I have seen this demonstrated many times in my practice. A particularly memorable instance of this fact concerned a patient who was literally forced to visit my office by his family. He was a man of about forty, unmarried, who held down a routine job during the day and kept to himself in his room when the work day was over, never going anywhere, never doing anything. He had had many such jobs and never seemed able to stay with any of them for any great length of time. His problem was that he had a rather large nose and ears that protruded a little more than is normal. He considered himself "ugly" and "funny looking." He imagined that the people he came into contact with during the day were laughing at him and talking about him behind his back because he was so "odd." His imaginings grew so strong that he actually feared going out into the business world and moving among people. He hardly felt "safe" even in his own home. The poor man even imagined that his family was "ashamed" of him because he was "peculiar looking," not like "other people."

Actually, his facial deficiencies were not serious. His nose was of the "classical Roman" type, and his ears, though somewhat large, attracted no more attention than those of thousands of people with similar ears. In desperation, his family brought him to me to see if I could help him. I saw that he did not need surgery . . . only an understanding of the fact that his imagination had wrought such havoc with his self-image that he had lost sight of the truth. He was not really ugly. People did not consider him odd and laugh at him because of his appearance. His imagination alone was responsible for his misery. His imagination had set up an automatic, negative, failure mechanism within him and it was operating full blast, to his extreme misfortune. Fortunately, after several sessions with him, and with the help of his family, he was able gradually to realize that the power of his own imagination was responsible for his plight, and he succeeded in building up a true self-image and achieving the confidence he needed by applying creative imagination rather than destructive imagination.

"Creative imagination" is not something reserved for the poets, the philosophers, the inventors. It enters into our every act. For imagination sets the goal "picture" which our automatic mechanism works on. We act, or fail to act, not because of "will," as is so commonly believed, but because of imagination.

A human being always acts and feels and performs in accordance with what he *imagines* to be *true* about himself and his environment. This is a basic and fundamental law of mind. It is the way we are built. When we see this law of mind graphically and dramatically demonstrated in a hypnotized subject, we are prone to think that there is something occult or supra-normal at work. Actually, what we are witnessing is the normal operating processes of the human brain and nervous system.

For example, if a good hypnotic subject is told that he is at the North Pole he will not only shiver and *appear* to be cold, his body will react just as if he were cold and goose pimples will develop. The same phenomenon has been demonstrated on wide-awake college students by asking them to *imagine* that one hand is immersed in ice water. Thermometer readings show that the temperature does drop in the "treated" hand. Tell a hypnotized subject that your finger is a red hot poker and he will not only grimace with pain at your touch, but his cardiovascular and lymphatic systems will react just as if your finger were a red hot poker and produce inflammation and perhaps a blister on the skin. When college students, wide-awake, have been told to *imagine* that a spot on their foreheads was hot, temperature readings have shown an actual increase in skin temperature.

Your nervous system cannot tell the difference between an *imagined experience* and a "real" experience. In either case, it reacts automatically to information which you give to it from your forebrain. Your nervous system reacts appropriately to what "you" *think* or *imagine* to be *true*.

Nowhere Man

John Lennon and Paul McCartney

He's a real Nowhere Man,
Sitting in his Nowhere Land,
Making all his nowhere plans for nobody.
Doesn't have a point of view;
Knows not where he's going to.
Isn't he a bit like you and me?

Nowhere Man, please listen,
You don't know what you're missing,
Nowhere Man. The world is at your command.

He's as blind as he can be;
Just sees what he wants to see.
Nowhere Man, can you see me at all?
Doesn't have a point of view;
Knows not where he's going to.
Isn't he a bit like you and me?

Nowhere Man, don't worry.
Take your time; don't hurry.
Leave it all till somebody else lends you a hand.

He's a real Nowhere Man,
Sitting in his Nowhere Land,
Making all his nowhere plans for nobody,
Making all his nowhere plans for nobody,
Making all his nowhere plans for nobody.

Invisible Man

Ralph Ellison

I am an invisible man. No, I am not a spook
like those who haunted Edgar Allen Poe;
nor am I one of your Hollywood-movie
ectoplasms. I am a man of substance, of
flesh and bone, fiber and liquid—and I
might even be said to possess a mind. I am
invisible, understand, simply because people
refuse to see me. Like the bodiless heads
you see sometimes in circus sideshows, it is
as though I have been surrounded by
mirrors of hard, distorting glass. When they
approach me they see only my surroundings, themselves, or
figments of their imagination—indeed, everything
and anything except me.

Excerpted from *Invisible Man* by Ralph Ellison. Copyright, 1947, 1948, 1952, by Ralph Ellison. Used by permission of Random House, Inc.

Why Not Imagine Yourself Successful?

Realizing that our actions, feelings, and behavior are the result of our own images and beliefs gives us the lever that psychology has always needed for changing personality. It opens a new psychologic door to gaining skill, success, and happiness.

Mental pictures offer us an opportunity to "practice" new traits and attitudes, which otherwise we could not do. This is possible because again—your nervous system cannot tell the difference between an actual experience and one that is vividly imagined. If we picture ourselves performing in a certain manner, it is nearly the same as the actual performance. Mental practice helps to make perfect.

In a controlled experiment, psychologist R. A. Vandell proved that mental practice in throwing darts at a target, wherein the person sits for a period each day in front of the target, and imagines throwing darts at it, improves aim as much as actually throwing darts.

Research Quarterly reports an experiment on the effects of mental practice on improving skill in sinking basketball free throws. One group of students actually practiced throwing the ball every day for twenty days, and were scored on the first and last days. A second group was scored on the first and last days, and engaged in no sort of practice in between. A third group was scored on the first day, then spent twenty minutes a day, imagining that they were throwing the ball at the goal. When they missed they would imagine that they corrected their aim accordingly. The first group, which actually practiced twenty minutes every day, im-

proved in scoring 24 per cent. The second group, which had no sort of practice, showed no improvement. The third group, which practiced in their imagination, improved in scoring 23 per cent!

Practice Exercise

Your present self-image was built upon your own imagination pictures of yourself in the past which grew out of interpretations and evaluations which you placed upon *experience*. Now you are to use the same method to build an adequate self-image that you previously used to build an inadequate one.

Set aside a period of thirty minutes each day when you can be alone and undisturbed. Relax and make yourself as comfortable as possible. Now close your eyes and exercise your imagination.

Many people find they get better results if they imagine themselves sitting before a large motion picture screen – and imagine that they are seeing a motion picture of themselves. The important thing is to make these pictures as *vivid* and as *detailed* as possible. You want your mental pictures to approximate actual experience as much as possible. The way to do this is pay attention to small details, sights, sounds, objects, in your imagined environment. One of my patients was using this exercise to overcome her fear of the dentist. She was unsuccessful, until she began to notice small details in her imagined picture – the smell of the antiseptic in the office, the feel of the leather on the chair arms, the sight of the dentist's well-manicured nails as his hands approached her mouth, etc. *Details* of the imagined environment are all-important in this exercise, because for all practical purposes, you are creating a *practice experience*. And if the imagination is vivid enough and detailed enough, your imagination practice is equivalent to an actual experience, insofar as your nervous system is concerned.

The next important thing to remember is that during this thirty minutes you see yourself acting and reacting appropriately, successfully, ideally. It doesn't matter how you acted yesterday. You do not need to try to have faith you will act in the ideal way tomorrow. Your nervous system will take care of that in time – if you continue to practice. See yourself acting, feeling, "being," as you want to be. Do not say to yourself, "I am going to act this way tomorrow." Just say to yourself – "I am going to imagine myself acting this way now – for thirty minutes – today." Imagine how you would feel if you were already the sort of personality you want to be. If you have been shy and timid, see yourself moving among people with ease and poise – and *feeling good* because of it. If you have been fearful and anxious in certain situations – see yourself acting calmly and deliberately, acting with confidence and courage – and feeling expansive and confident because you are.

This exercise builds new "memories" or stored data into your mid-brain and central nervous system. It builds a new image of self. After practicing it for a time, you will be surprised to find yourself "acting differently," more or less automatically and spontaneously – "without trying." This is as it should be. You do not need to "take thought" or "try" or make an effort now in order to feel ineffective and act inadequately. Your present inadequate feeling and doing is automatic and spontaneous, because of the memories, real and imagined you have built into your automatic mechanism. You will find it will work just as automatically upon positive thoughts and experiences as upon negative ones.

PROBE 5.   Self-disclosure and feedback can help you form close relationships with others.

Self-Disclosure

David W. Johnson

How well do I know myself? How well do other people know me? Am I an easy person to get to know? Do I feel free to tell others how I am reacting, feeling, and what I am thinking? These are important questions. To like you, to be involved with you, to be your friend, I must know who you are. In order for me to know you, you must know yourself. In order for you to feel free to disclose yourself to me, you must accept and appreciate yourself.

Without self-disclosure you cannot form a close personal relationship with another person. A relationship between two individuals develops as the two become more open about themselves and more self-disclosing. If you cannot reveal yourself, you cannot become close to others, and you cannot be valued by others for who you are. To become closely involved with another person, you must know him and he must know you. Two people who share how they are reacting to situations and to each other are pulled together; two people who stay silent about their reactions and feelings stay strangers. To like you, to be involved with you, I must know who you are. To like me, to be involved with me, you must know who I am.

Self-disclosure may be defined as revealing how you are reacting to the present situation and giving any information about the past that is relevant to understanding how you are reacting to the present. Reactions to people and events are not facts as much as feelings. To be self-disclosing means to share with another person how you feel about something he has done or said, or how you feel about the events which have just taken place. Self-disclosure does not mean revealing intimate details of your past life. Making highly personal confessions about your past may lead to a temporary feeling of intimacy, but a relationship is built by disclosing your reactions to events you both experience or to what the other person says or does. A person comes to know and understand you not through knowing your past history but through knowing how you react. Past history is only helpful if it clarifies why you are reacting in a certain way.

There has been a considerable amount of research on the effects of self-disclosure upon interpersonal relationships (Johnson, 1972). There is, for example, much evidence that indicates that healthy relationships are based upon self-disclosure. If you hide how you are reacting to the other person, your concealment can sicken the relationship. The energy you pour into hiding adds to the stress of the relationship and dulls your awareness of your own inner experience, thus decreasing your ability to disclose your reactions even when it is perfectly safe and appropriate to do so. Hiding your reactions from others through fear of rejection

---

and conflict or through feelings of shame and guilt leads to loneliness. Being silent is not being strong; strength is the willingness to take risks in the relationship, to disclose yourself with the intention of building a better relationship.

Healthy relationships are based upon self-disclosure.

Several aspects of a relationship influence self-disclosure. The more self-disclosing you are to another person, the more likely that person will like you. You are more likely to self-disclose to a person you know and like than to a person you do not know or do not like. The amount of self-disclosure you engage in will influence the amount of self-disclosure the other person engages in; the more you self-disclose, the more the other person will tend to self-disclose.

Willingness to engage in self-disclosure is related to several characteristics. The research done in this field indicates that a person willing to be self-disclosing will likely be a competent, open, and socially extroverted person who feels a strong need to interact with others. He is likely to be flexible, adaptive, and perhaps more intelligent than his less self-revealing peers. He is objectively aware of the realities of the interpersonal situations in which he is involved and perceives a fairly close congruence between the way he is and the way in which he would like to be. Finally, he views his fellowman as generally good rather than evil.

Communicating intimately with another person, especially in times of stress, seems to be a basic human need. Disclosing yourself to another person builds a relationship which allows for such intimate communication, both by yourself and by the other. If neither you nor the other feels free to engage in self-disclosure, you can be of little or no help to each other during periods of stress.

Being self-disclosing means being "for real." It is important that your self-disclosures are as honest, genuine, and authentic as possible. In this chapter we will focus upon some of the skills involved in effective self-disclosure, but the communication of the sincerity, genuineness, and authenticity of your self-disclosures is one of the most important aspects of building a relationship.

In addition to being *open with* other people, you must be *open to* others to build meaningful relationships. Being open to another person means showing that you are interested in how he feels about what you are saying and doing. It is being receptive to his self-disclosure. This does not mean prying into the intimate areas of another's life. It means being willing to listen to his reactions to the present situation and to what you are doing and saying.

In responding to another's self-disclosure, it is important to accept and support him if possible. Being accepting and supportive will increase the other person's tendency to be open with you. It will strengthen the relationship and help it grow. Even when a person's behavior seriously offends you, it is possible for you to express acceptance of the person and disagreement with the way he behaves. To be open with another person is to risk rejection; to self-disclose is to ask for support and acceptance in trying to build a better relationship. You

should be careful, therefore, to give the support and acceptance necessary for the relationship to grow.

Appropriateness of Self-Disclosure

Self-disclosure must be relevant to your relationship with the other person and appropriate to the situation you are in. You can be too self-disclosing. A person who reveals too much of his reactions too fast may scare others away; a relationship is built gradually except in rare and special cases. Certainly being too self-disclosing will create as many relationship problems as disclosing too little. Although you should sometimes take risks with your self-disclosure to others, you should not be blind to the appropriateness of your behavior to the situation. Self-disclosure is appropriate when:

1. It is not a random or isolated act but rather is part of an ongoing relationship.

2. It is reciprocated.

3. It concerns what is going on within and between persons in the present.

4. It creates a reasonable chance of improving the relationship.

5. Account is taken of the effect it will have upon the other person.

6. It is speeded up in a crisis in the relationship.

7. It gradually moves to a deeper level.

While relationships are built through self-disclosure, there are times when you will want to hide your reactions to the present situation from another person. If a person has clearly shown himself

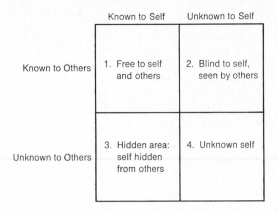

	Known to Self	Unknown to Self
Known to Others	1. Free to self and others	2. Blind to self, seen by others
Unknown to Others	3. Hidden area: self hidden from others	4. Unknown self

Fig. 2-1. *Identification of areas of the self*

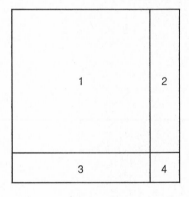

Fig. 2-2. *At the beginning of a relationship*

Fig. 2-3. *After the development of a close relationship*

to be untrustworthy, it is foolish to be self-disclosing with him. If you know from past experience that the other person will misinterpret or overreact to your self-disclosure, you may wish to keep silent.

Self-Disclosure and Self-Awareness

Your ability to disclose yourself to others depends upon your self-awareness and self-acceptance. You must be aware of your reactions in order to communicate them to others. Without accepting your reactions you cannot feel free to allow other individuals to hear them. In this section we will focus upon self-awareness. In a later chapter in the book we will focus upon self-acceptance.

You should be continually trying to increase your self-awareness in order to be able to engage in self-disclosure. In order to discuss how you may increase your self-awareness, it may be helpful to look at the models found in Figures 2.1, 2.2, 2.3 (Luft, 1969).

These models are named the Johari Window after its two originators, Joe Luft and Harry Ingham. It illustrates that there are certain things you know about yourself and certain things that you do not know about yourself. Correspondingly, there are certain things other people know about you and certain things they do not know. It is assumed that it takes energy to hide information from yourself and others and that the more information that is known the clearer communication will be. Building a relationship therefore often involves working to enlarge the free area while decreasing the blind and hidden areas. As you become more self-disclosing, you reduce the hidden area. As you encourage others to be self-disclosing

with you, your blind area is reduced. Through reducing your hidden area you give other people information to react to, which enables them to help you reduce your blind area. Through reducing your blind area, your self-awareness is increased; this helps you to be even more self-disclosing with others.

Constructive Self-Disclosure[1]

People rarely talk openly about their reactions to each other's behavior. Most of us withhold our feelings about the other person (even in relations that are very important or dear to us) because we are afraid of hurting the other person, making him angry, or being rejected by him. Because we do not know how to be constructively self-disclosing, we say nothing. The other person continues to be totally unaware of our reaction to his actions. Likewise we continue to be ignorant of the effect our actions produce in him. Consequently, many relations that could be productive and enjoyable gradually deteriorate under the accumulated load of tiny annoyances, hurt feelings, and misunderstandings that were never talked about openly.

The following points increase the chances that self-disclosure will improve a relationship rather than harm it.

1. Self-disclosure must begin with a *desire to improve your relationship with the other person*. Self-disclosure is not an end in itself but a means to an end. We are not open with people when we do not care about them. When you are trying to establish an open sharing of reactions with another person, try to let him know that

---

1. The material in this section was originally developed by J.L. Wallen.

this means you value your relationship with him and wish to improve it *because* it is important.

2. Try to create a shared understanding of your relationship. You wish to know how the other person perceives and feels about your actions. You want him to know how you perceive and feel about his actions. Each of you will then view the relationship from more nearly the same viewpoint.

3. Realize that self-disclosure involves *risk-taking*. Your willingness to risk being rejected or hurt by the other person depends on how important the relationship is to you. You cannot tell that the other person will not become angry or feel hurt by what you say. The important point is that you are willing to risk his being himself, whatever he feels, in the effort to make the encounter into a learning situation for both of you.

4. Although the discussion may become intense, spirited, angry, or tearful, it should be *noncoercive* and should not be an attempt to make the other person change. Each person should use the information as he sees fit. The attitude should not be "Who's wrong and who's right?" but "What can each of us learn from this discussion that will make our relationship more productive and more satisfying?" As a result of the discussion one, both, or neither of you may act differently in the future. Each of you, however, will act with fuller awareness of the effect of his actions on the other as well as with more understanding of the other person's inten-

tions. Any change will thus be self-chosen rather than compelled by a desire to please or to submit to the other.

5. Timing is important. Reactions should be shared at a time as close to the behavior that aroused them as possible so that both persons will know exactly what behavior is being discussed. For example, you can comment on behavior during the encounter itself: "What you just said is the kind of remark that makes me feel pushed away."

6. Disturbing situations should be discussed as they happen; hurt feelings and annoyances should not be saved up and dropped on another person all at one time.

7. Paraphrase the other person's comments about you to make sure you understand them as he means them. Check to make sure the other understands your comments in the way you mean them.

8. Statements are more helpful if they are
   Specific rather than general: "You bumped my plate," rather than "You never watch where you're going."
   Tentative rather than absolute: "You seem unconcerned about Jimmy," rather than "You don't give a damn about Jimmy and never will."
   Informing rather than ordering: "I hadn't finished yet," rather than "Stop interrupting me."

9. Use perception-checking responses to insure that you are not making false assumptions about the other's feelings. "I thought you weren't interested in trying to understand my idea. Was I wrong?" "Did my last statement bother you?"

10. The least helpful kinds of statements are those that sound as if they are information about the other person but are really expressions of your own feelings. Avoid the following:

    Judgments about the other: "You never pay any attention."

    Name-calling, trait labeling: "You're a phony"; "You're too rude."

    Accusations; imputing undesirable motives to the other: "You enjoy putting people down"; "You always have to be the center of attention."

    Commands and orders: "Stop laughing"; "Don't talk so much."

    Sarcasm: "You always look on the bright side of things, don't you?" (when the opposite is meant).

11. The most helpful kinds of information about yourself and your reactions are:

    Behavior descriptions. To develop skills in describing another person's behavior you must sharpen your skills in observing what actually did occur. Let others know what behavior you are responding to by describing it clearly and specifically enough that they know what you saw. To do this you must describe visible evidence, behavior that is open to anybody's observation. Restrict yourself to talking about the things the other person did.

    Examples: "Bob, you seem to disagree with whatever Harry suggests today." (*Not* "Bob, you're just trying to show Harry up." This is not a description but an accusation of unworthy motives.)

    "Jim, you've talked more than others on this topic. Several times you interrupted others before they had finished." (*Not* "Jim, you're too rude!" which names a trait and gives no evidence. *Not* "Jim, you always want to hog the center of attention" which imputes an unworthy motive or intention.)

    "Sam, I had not finished my statement when you interrupted me." (*Not* "Sam, you deliberately didn't let me finish." The word *deliberately* implies that Sam knowingly and intentionally cut you off. All anybody can observe is that he did interrupt you.)

    Descriptions of your own feelings. You should attempt to describe your feelings about the other person's actions so that your feelings are seen as temporary and capable of change rather than as permanent. It is better to say, "At this point I'm very annoyed with you," than "I dislike you and I always will."

Reach Out in the Darkness

Jim Post

*I think it's so groovy now
That people are finally getting together.
I think it's so wonderful and how that people are finally getting
    together.
Reach out in the darkness.
Reach out in the darkness.
Reach out in the darkness and you may find a friend.*

*I know a man that I did not care for;
And then one day this man gave me a call.
We sat and talked about things on our mind,
And now this man he is a friend of mine.
Don't be afraid of love.
Don't be afraid, don't be afraid to love.
Everybody needs a little love.
Everybody needs somebody that they can be thinking of.*

*I think it's so groovy now
That people are finally getting together.
I think it's so wonderful and how that people are finally getting
    together.
Reach out in the darkness.
Reach out in the darkness.
Reach out in the darkness and you may find a friend.*

Perception and Human Understanding

Raymond S. Ross

An understanding of the way people receive, decode, and assign meaning is critical. Listening is much more than hearing acuity. All of our sensory apparatus may be involved in helping us interpret even a primarily oral signal. The perception process is for our purposes identical to the communication process except that the emphasis is on receiving instead of sending. The receiver or perceiver is thought to posit hypotheses which he accepts or rejects. Postman calls this a cycle of hypothesis involving information, trial and check, confirmation or nonconfirmation.[1] The meaning then is supplied primarily by learning and by past experience.

Sensation and Interpretation

Have you ever been on a train which is stopped between other trains in a railroad terminal? Have you then felt, seen, and heard all of the signs indicating movement, only to find that it is the other trains that are moving? Perhaps you discovered this when the other train was actually gone, or perhaps you fixed your gaze on something you *knew* was not moving, such as the ceiling of the station, a roof support, or the ground itself.

The point is that perception involves essentially two acts: (1) the *sensation* caused by the stimulation of a sensory organ, and (2) the *interpretation* of the sensation. . . . It is primarily through our knowledge and experience that we interpret or attach meaning to a symbol.

The complexity of human communication is further indicated by the various levels of perception now thought to exist. We talk of subliminal or subthreshold perception, that is, a receiving below the level of conscious awareness. This is not to be confused with so-called extrasensory perception. Many experiments have been conducted in this field, most of them involving visual projections at speeds above our physiological level of perception, but below our awareness level, or, in some cases, at our awareness level, but below our recognition level. They are complicated by the fact that people vary in their perceptual abilities not only one from another, but also in their own individual range of acuity. The best-known of all subthreshold experiments involved the projection of nonsense syllables.[2] Meaningless combinations of letters were associated with electric shock. When these stimuli were later presented subthresholdly (at speeds too rapid to permit their conscious identification), the subjects' emotional reactions were more intense than their reactions to other nonsense syllables not previously associated with shock. The subjects had been able to identify the stimuli unconsciously before they could do so consciously.

A person's set, expectancy, or preparation to perceive has much

---

PROBE 6. Your perceptions may be a prime obstacle to effective communication.

to do with his level of perception as well as his individual acceptance of a stimulus.[3] The consciousness defends itself through an apparent refusal to accept certain messages. On the other hand, we may wish or desire so very much to hear something that, regardless of the actual code or words emitted, we attend, interpret, and attach meaning in terms of what we wish to hear. One of the great barriers to good communication is the tendency to hear what we wish to hear, see what we wish to see, and believe what we wish to believe. This kind of behavior is called *autistic thinking*. Piaget defines autism as "thought in which truth is confused with desire."[4] In its extreme form this kind of perception and thinking grows out of an abnormal emotional need for ego-satisfaction, and we actually have a mental disorder known as *paranoia*. The foregoing indicates that perception is a function of *internal* as well as external sources of stimulation. Signals which originate within us also enter into the perceptual act.

Another closely related perceptual and communication problem arises because of a normal tendency to completeness. In communications which appear to be only partially complete, we often read in the unsaid part or complete the pattern. If we do not arrive at a sense of completeness or closure we often feel upset, ill at ease, confused, and unhappy. This tendency can be an important factor in motivation. Perhaps you have had a teacher who communicates just enough knowledge in a stimulating way, motivating you to do further reading and research so that you can complete or close the pattern. The problem arises when we close incomplete communication patterns in ways not intended by the speaker. This tendency is illustrated by an incomplete triangle. We find it more reasonable, more comfortable to see figure 1 as a completed triangle.

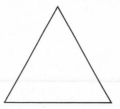

Fig. 1. *Pattern closing tendencies*

Sometimes our habits and previous experience cause us to leave things out. Read the next three messages quickly.

Many people see nothing unusual about these messages even after two or three readings. The good, rapid readers seem to have the most trouble. Why should this be so? A group of second and third graders had no trouble finding the double words in each message. We perceive to a certain extent what our habits, our emotions, and our knowledge and past experiences let us perceive. A good reader has learned to skim and to ignore nonessential words. The beginning reader sees literally one word at a time.

Test your perceptual ability on the next two stimuli. Do you see anything familiar or identifiable? Do you see a message?

You should see the words LEFT and FLY in white on a partial black field. Your experience is typically just the opposite—the area *between* the letters is in black instead of the letters themselves.[5] Even after you see the messages they may escape you momentarily as your longstanding habits and previous experience patterns fight to assert their influence.

Conventionalized Perception

The problem of stereotyped or stylized communication, particularly where gesture and bodily movement are concerned, is also an interesting aspect of perception. Experimental studies of the portrayal and recognition of emotion illustrate this point. Landis performed an experiment designed to discover whether reported emotions are accompanied by definite and easily recognized facial expressions. A series of photographs were taken of his subjects while they were actually undergoing various emotion-producing situations, not simply portraying emotions as an actor would. Landis had a regular torture-chamber experiment, and after many comparisons he writes: "There is no expression typically associated with any verbal report."[6]

A study similar to the one described above was conducted by Feleky, but with one vital difference: the photographs of emotions were artifically portrayed or acted. The experimenter found in this case a remarkable agreement on the description of the poses, indicating that we may interpret an individual's emotional state with reasonable accuracy from a posed photograph.[7]

A study with more specific conclusions was conducted by Knower and Dusenbury. The design of the study was almost identical to Feleky's. Knower and Dusenbury concluded:

1. Interpretation of the facial expression of emotional tendencies and attitudes may be made with a high degree of reliability.

2. There are significant individual and group differences in ability correctly to interpret facial expressions of the emotions.

3. Women are more accurate in the interpretation of facial expressions of the emotions than men.

4. Patterns of facial expression extended in time, as on a short, moving picture, are judged more accurately than are still photographs of the same emotional tendencies.

5. Accuracy in the interpretation of facial expressions of the emotions is influenced by the conditions under which such expressions are judged.[8]

As far as communication (recognition) is concerned in these experiments, we can say that simulated or stereotyped emotions can be perceived or identified with some reliability. With recognition of real emotions one might just as well leave the judgment to chance.

Good actors and capable speakers appear to communicate emotions with regularity. The actor has the play, the set, the other actors, and the stylized conceptions of the audience to help him. If the cause of whatever emotion the actor is portraying is also perceived (for example, a gun and fear), the communication pattern is easier to follow.

But though certain peripheral patterns or expressions have become stylized, we still have a po-tential barrier to communication, for these patterns may vary so much from person to person, sender and receiver, that excepting perhaps skilled acting, it remains difficult to communicate the precise emotion intended.

The conclusion of all this research is that the "meaning" is in the eyes, ears, and other senses of the beholder to some extent, but it is more in his previous experience, learning, knowledge, feelings, attitudes, and emotions.

1. L. Postman, "Toward a General Theory of Cognition," in J.H. Rohrer and M. Sherif, eds., *Social Psychology at the Crossroads* (New York: Harper & Row, Publishers, 1951), p. 251.
Also see J.S. Bruner, "Personality Dynamics and the Process of Perceiving," in R.R. Blake and G.V. Ramsey, eds., *Perception: An Approach to Personality* (New York: The Ronald Press Company, 1951).

2. R.S. Lazarus and R.A. McCleary, "Automatic Discrimination Without Awareness: A Study in Subception," *Psychological Review*, 58 (1951), 113–22.

3. Charles M. Solley and Gardner Murphy, *Development of the Perceptual World* (New York: Basic Books, Inc., 1960), p. 239.

4. J. Piaget, *The Child's Conception of Physical Causality* (London: Routledge & Kegan Paul, Ltd., 1930), p. 302.

5. This is referred to as a figure-ground transformation.

6. "Experimental Studies of the Emotions: The Work of Cannon and Others," in Henry E. Garrett, *Great Experiments in Psychology* (New York: Appleton-Century-Crofts, 1941), p. 331.

7. Garrett, *Great Experiments in Psychology*, p. 330.

8. D. Dusenbury and F.H. Knower, "Experimental Studies of the Symbolism of Action and Voice–I: A Study of the Specificity of Meaning in Facial Expression," *Quarterly Journal of Speech* XXIV, No. 3 (1938), 435.

Problems in Active Listening

Carl B. Rogers and Richard E. Farson

Active listening is not an easy skill to acquire. It demands practice. Perhaps more important, it may require changes in our own basic attitudes. These changes come slowly and sometimes with considerable difficulty. Let us look at some of the major problems in active listening and what can be done to overcome them.

The Personal Risk

To be effective at all in active listening, one must have a sincere interest in the speaker. We all live in glass houses as far as our attitudes are concerned. They always show through. And if we are only making a pretense of interest in the speaker, he will quickly pick this up, either consciously or unconsciously. And once he does, he will no longer express himself freely.

Active listening carries a strong element of personal risk. If we manage to accomplish what we are describing here—to sense deeply the feeling of another person, to understand the meaning his experiences have for him, to see the world as he sees it—we risk being changed ourselves. For example, if we permit ourselves to listen our way into the psychological life of a labor leader or agitator—to get the meaning which life has for him—we risk coming to see the world as he sees it. It is threatening to give up, even momentarily, what we believe and start thinking in someone else's terms. It takes a great deal of inner security and courage to be able to risk one's self in understanding another.

For the supervisor, the courage to take another's point of view generally means that he must see *himself* through another's eyes—he must be able to see himself as others see him. To do this may sometimes be unpleasant, but it is far more *difficult* than unpleasant. We are so accustomed to viewing ourselves in certain ways—to seeing and hearing only what we want to see and hear—that it is extremely difficult for a person to free himself from his needs to see things these ways.

Developing an attitude of sincere interest in the speaker is thus no easy task. It can be developed only by being willing to risk seeing the world from the speaker's point of view. If we have a number of such experiences, however, they will shape an attitude which will allow us to be truly genuine in our interest in the speaker.

Hostile Expressions

The listener will often hear negative, hostile expressions directed at himself. Such expressions are always hard to listen to. No one likes to hear hostile words. And it is not easy to get to the point

From "Active Listening" by Carl B. Rogers and Richard E. Farson. Reprinted by permission of publisher—Industrial Relations Center, The University of Chicago, Chicago, Illinois 60637.

Hi and Lois *by Mort Walker and Dik Browne*

where one is strong enough to permit these attacks without finding it necessary to defend oneself or retaliate.

Because we all fear that people will crumble under the attack of genuine negative feelings, we tend to perpetuate an attitude of pseudo peace. It is as if we cannot tolerate conflict at all for fear of the damage it could do to us, to the situation, to the others involved. But of course the real damage is done to all these by the denial and suppression of negative feelings.

Out-of-place Expressions

There is also the problem of out-of-place expressions — expressions dealing with behavior which is not usually acceptable in our society. In the extreme forms that present themselves before psychotherapists, expressions of sexual perversity or homicidal fantasies are often found blocking to the listener because of their obvious threatening quality. At less extreme levels, we all find unnatural or inappropriate behavior difficult to handle. That is, anything from an off-color story told in mixed company to a man weeping is likely to produce a problem situation.

In any face-to-face situation, we will find instances of this type which will momentarily, if not permanently, block any communication. In business and industry, any expressions of weakness or incompetency will generally be regarded as unacceptable and therefore will block good two-way communication. For example, it is difficult to listen to a supervisor tell of his feelings of failure in being able to "take charge" of a situation in his department, because *all* administrators are supposed to be able to "take charge."

11

Ric Masten

put me in your human eye
come taste
the bitter tears
that i cry
touch me
with your human hand
hear me with your ear
but notice me
damn you
notice me
i'm here

we can't be
bothered now
the distant voice said
when i'd come
to share
the butterfly i found
and i'd look
up
into the nostrils
of the faces
overhead
and i never caught
the giant
lookin' down

notice me
damn you
i'm here
yeah
i' the poor
misshapen figure
in the backroom
of your home
your little baby's
gone
and blown his mind
he's at the nursery
window
standing all alone
tryin' to catch the eye
of the blind

put me in your human eye
come taste
the bitter tears
that i cry
touch me
with your human hand
hear me with your ear
but notice me
damn you
notice me
i am

SO WHAT'S THE CRITICISM?

Songs

Words by CYNTHIA WEIL
Music by BARRY MANN

1. Peo - ple, I can't un-der-stand 'em; nev - er can and nev - er could.
2. Ev - 'ry - one seems to be mov - in', mov - in' up or mov - in' on;

The more I get to know 'em, the
just when you try to touch 'em, that's

less I think I should. They don't mean the
when you find they're gone. We pass through each

things they say or say the things they mean; You've
oth - er's lives and fade in - to the past; You

got to try and find the mes - sage some-where in be - tween.
just don't know who to be - lieve in, no one seems to last.

But songs are such good things,

(continued on page 33)

Accepting Positive Feelings

It is both interesting and perplexing to note that negative or hostile feelings or expressions are much easier to deal with in any face-to-face relationship than are truly and deeply positive feelings. This is especially true for the businessman, because the culture expects him to be independent, bold, clever, and aggressive and manifest no feelings of warmth, gentleness, and intimacy. He therefore comes to regard these feelings as soft and inappropriate. But no matter how they are regarded, they remain a human need. The denial of these feelings in himself and his associates does not get the executive out of the problem of dealing with them. They simply become veiled and confused. If recognized, they would work for the total effort; unrecognized, they work against it.

Emotional Danger Signals

The listener's own emotions are sometimes a barrier to active listening. When emotions are at their height, which is when listening is most necessary, it is most difficult to set aside one's own concerns and be understanding. Our emotions are often our own worst enemies when we try to become listeners. The more involved and invested we are in a particular situation or problem, the less we are likely to be willing or able to listen to the feelings and attitudes of others. That is, the more we find it necessary to respond to our own needs, the less we are able to respond to the needs of another. Let us look at some of the main danger signals that warn us that our emotions may be interfering with our listening.

Defensiveness

The points about which one is most vocal and dogmatic, the points which one is most anxious to impose on others—these are always the points one is trying to talk oneself into believing. So one danger signal becomes apparent when you find yourself stressing a point or trying to convince another. It is at these times that you are likely to be less secure and consequently less able to listen.

Resentment of Opposition

It is always easier to listen to an idea which is similar to one of your own than to an opposing view. Sometimes, in order to clear the air, it is helpful to pause for a moment when you feel your ideas and position being challenged, reflect on the situation, and express your concern to the speaker.

Clash of Personalities

Here again, our experience has consistently shown us that the genuine expression of feelings on the part of the listener will be more helpful in developing a sound relationship than the suppression of them. This is so whether the feelings be resentment, hostility, threat, or admiration. A basically honest relationship, whatever the nature of it, is the most productive of all. The other party becomes secure when he learns that the listener can express his feelings honestly and openly to him. We should keep this in mind when we begin to fear a clash of personalities in the listening relationship. Otherwise, fear of our own emotions will choke off full expression of feelings.

(continued from page 32)

(continued on page 34)

(continued from page 33)

blue___ songs,___ sweet songs,___ soul___ songs,___ good old rock___

___ and roll___ songs_____ make such ea-sy friends:___ all you do is sing___ a-long.___

___ and you can't stay___ a stran - ger to___ a song.___

Listening to Ourselves

To listen to oneself is a prerequisite for listening to others. And it is often an effective means of dealing with the problems we have outlined above. When we are most aroused, excited, and demanding, we are least able to understand our own feelings and attitudes. Yet, in dealing with the problems of others, it becomes most important to be sure of one's own position, values, and needs.

The ability to recognize and understand the meaning which a particular episode has for you, with all the feelings which it stimulates in you, and the ability to express this meaning when you find it getting in the way of active listening will clear the air and enable you once again to be free to listen. That is, if some person or situation touches off feelings within you which tend to block your attempts to listen with understanding, begin listening to yourself. It is much more helpful in developing effective relationships to avoid suppressing these feelings. Speak them out as clearly as you can, and try to enlist the other person as a listener to your feelings. A person's listening ability is limited by his ability to listen to himself.

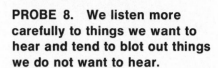

Are You Listening?

Manuel Escott

"Who me, not listen?" you protest. "I've been listening for years. To my parents, to my teachers, to my boss, sometimes to my kids. And my wife. Man, when she talks, you listen."

The chances are, however, that you don't listen properly. Studies by psychologists who specialize in human behavior show that listening is the least developed of our comprehension skills. Yet we spend 70 per cent of our day communicating with each other; and 45 per cent of that figure is spent in actually listening.

What is even more distressing, researchers have found that we remember only about one-third of what is said to us. And this information loss occurs within eight hours.

Everyone has experienced the situation where the new guy at the cocktail party is introduced as, say, Bill Goodbody. If your host or hostess has the average retention span, by the time old Goodbody has reached the end of the introductions, he's Charlie Goodenough or Joe Goodbye.

Ineffective listening can lead to critical and often frustrating situations. A salesman—it's as important for a salesman to listen properly as to talk well—could lose a big sale because he missed the critical content of what was being said to him. A secretary, if she's an average listener, will retain only one-third of what is said to her.

Take the case of the police officer interviewing witnesses to an accident or a crime. If he's a poor listener and doesn't take notes immediately, statements that are ultimately to become evidence in a court case might be inaccurate or have some vital fact omitted.

"We're all more fond of articulating than listening," says Brian Mitchell, national sales manager of Xerox of Canada Ltd. Six years ago, Xerox marketed in Canada a course in effective listening. Since that time, Mitchell estimates that some 10,000 people a month from industry, government and police forces, have taken the four-and-a-half hour taped course under the guidance of a moderator.

"Poor listening is the cause of more problems than people imagine," says Mitchell. "It's really incredible that we're taught to read and write properly yet never given instruction on listening when so much of our time is spent doing just that."

The experts tell us that we tend to listen more carefully to the things we want to hear. You'll be all ears if someone phones to tell you that you're a big winner in the Irish Sweepstakes. And you'll be able to pick up the sound of your own name—the sweetest sound of all—across a noisy, crowded room.

Conversely, we tend to blot out or listen poorly to things we don't

---

PROBE 8.   We listen more carefully to things we want to hear and tend to blot out things we do not want to hear.

want to hear. A classic example of this, according to Mitchell, is the confrontation situation in a bargaining session between management and union. Both sides have fixed ideas, fixed positions and a fixed verbal approach in most cases.

"When one speaks the other is not really listening, but waiting until he's finished to rebut the position and put his own views forward," Mitchell says. "Consequently key points are missed by both sides, points that could lead to a settlement. Effective listening avoids situations like this and brings people together more."

Mitchell claims this is one of the added benefits of being a good listener—in a culture where more emphasis is being placed on "togetherness," careful listening can affect a more meaningful association with your peers. "A person always senses when you're listening to him empathetically and sympathetically, and responds to you."

There are four rules of good listening:

Think ahead of the talker and try to anticipate what he's going to say; weigh the evidence used by the talker to support his points and ask yourself if it is valid; mentally review and summarize each point of the talk as it proceeds; watch nonverbal communication or "body language" used by the speaker—facial expressions, gestures—which can be as important as verbal messages.

Anyone who takes a listening course soon realizes that the skills he is learning can be used to make other people listen to him. Use of key words and visual images for certain points, analysis and review of material are useful aids to effective speaking. "Most good listeners can make the extrapolation that if this is

Professional 'Listener' Charges $5

KANSAS CITY, KAN. (AP)— When people talk, Kirk Martin listens—for a price.

Martin advertises that he "will listen to you talk for 30 minutes with no comment for $5."

Martin, 48, who earns his living mainly by driving trucks, says he started his listening business because he feels "the Lord gave me a capacity to work with people. I almost went into psychiatry, you know. And this is an inexpensive alternative to a psychiatrist."

Martin holds a bachelor's degree in business administration from the University of Missouri, Columbia. He said he gets about 10 to 20 calls a day.

what it takes to be a good listener, then one should learn to speak properly," Mitchell believes.

One behavioral psychologist blames the fantastic efficiency of the human brain for our low listening capacities.

Why are most of us low-grade listeners? Behavioral psychologist Dr. Ralph Nichols, of the University of Minnesota, blames the fantastic *efficiency* of the human brain.

Most of us talk at the rate of about 125 words a minute, but we think very much faster than we talk. Words play a major part in our thinking processes. When we listen we are asking our brains to receive words at a snail-slow pace compared to the brain's capabilities. It could be compared to driving a high-powered sports car at 15 miles an hour.

So, the spoken word arrives slowly and we're thinking at high speed. Hence the lapse in listener concentration. We listen, but have lots of time for idling, mentally dawdling down sidetracks.

Use or misuse of spare thinking time holds the key to effective listening, says Nichols. And he gives this example:

A product manager is telling a salesman about a new program the company is to launch. While the manager talks, the salesman's mind slips down a sidetrack. He already knows most of what the manager is going to say.

Unfortunately, he stays too long on the sidetrack. By the time he's back, the manager is ahead of him. Now our salesman finds it harder to understand what's being said. The private sidetracks

---

Nobody Listens Any More

Hal Boyle

NEW YORK—Are you looking for a profitable hobby or a way to earn post-retirement income? Well, why not become a paid listener? It's a new and wide open field. Hardly anybody in America listens any more. Employees don't listen to their employers. Children don't listen to their parents. Students don t listen to their teachers. Husbands don't listen to their wives. Waiters don't listen to their customers. There are even signs that Congress no longer hears everything that Lyndon B. Johnson says.

The art of listening is about as dead as scrimshaw, which is the art of carving on whalebone.

Won't Listen to Each Other

People will do almost anything for each other except listen to each other. The guy who will gladly give you the shirt off his back balks at merely lending you his ear. Today it's even hard for a minister to recite the marriage ritual without either the bride or the bridegroom interrupting him to ask, "How's that again? What did you say?"

About the only people who do listen are psychiatrists and those who are paid to bug your telephones. And there is considerable suspicion among patients that psychiatrists don't really listen all the time.

The odd thing about it all is: While no one is willing to listen, everybody is more than willing to talk. Everyone has something he wants to get off his chest.

This means there has to be a tremendous market for good listeners. Why not tap it? Why not turn your idle hours to financial advantage by becoming a paid listener? Why not rent your ear?

This is my goal. As soon as I get my pension, I'm going to start a new career as a listener.

(continued on page 38)

Hi and Lois by Mort Walker and Dik Browne

(continued from page 37)

Earn Living by Listening

Whenever anyone grabs me by the lapels and starts wagging his jawbone, I'll silently hand him a printed folder which says:

"You are speaking to a man who earns his living by listening. So, please button your mouth unless you are willing to pay my rates, which are as follows:

"Listening to comments on the weather, baseball and politics: 50 cents an hour.

"Listening to husbands complain about their wives: 75 cents an hour.

"Listening to wives complain about their husbands: Ditto.

"Listening to campaign speeches and periodically breaking into loud cheers: $1 an hour.

"Listening at cocktail parties: $2 an hour before midnight, $4 after midnight, plus two free drinks for the road.

"Listening to views on Vietnam and other international problems: $5 for 15 minutes.

"Listening to gossip: No charge—if it's about anyone I know. Otherwise, $1 an hour.

"Listening over the telephone: Double usual rates, payable in advance.

"Listening to your troubles: $15 a morning, money to be refunded if you spend all afternoon listening to my troubles.

"Standby rate for waiting while you make up your mind what you want to talk about: 10 cents a minute.

"Pay up or shut up!"

What do you think of the idea? What, you didn't hear a word I said? See what I mean?

Nobody listens.

once more invite him and he slips away again. Slowly, he misses more and more of the manager's plans.

When the manager is through talking, it's a fair assumption that the salesman will have received and understood less than half of what was said to him.

Nichols, who's been preaching the benefits of effective listening since the 1950s, knocked down several long-held assumptions about the skill: That intelligent people listen better than unintelligent ones and that reading will automatically teach you how to listen.

Psychologists who specialize in human behavior say that listening is the least developed of our comprehension skills.

Because of these widely accepted assumptions, little attention has been paid to aural communication in our schools and colleges. Reading ability has been upgraded and listening ability left on its own has degenerated, Nichols claims.

The objective of the Xerox course is to double listening effectiveness. Mitchell says that validation studies show that this is achieved along with long and high retention. Refresher courses are seldom necessary.

The value of effective listening in business need hardly be emphasized. Failure to pass on verbal messages accurately can mean costly mistakes. There's even some evidence to support the fact that better oral communication leads to fewer memos.

And any scheme that could cut down on the paper war is worth hearing about.

Behavioral psychologists like to talk about upward communication, which merely means getting the boss's ear. There are lots of avenues for downward communication. Bad listeners in middle management, whose job it is to pass information up the line, can cause all kinds of morale problems.

Says Mitchell: "A man who knows he is listened to properly and whose beefs or ideas are getting to the right place is likely to be happy where he works. And if his wife is listening to him too, this could be Utopia."

Prods

1. Personality varies from person to person. What causes us to have differing personalities? Do we always see our personalities as others see them?
2. As no two personalities are alike, no two sets of human values are identical. What effects can these differing values have on our success as communicators?
3. Self-esteem is developed through contact with others. As we communicate with other people, what approaches are effective in developing our self-esteem? What kinds of behavior must we exhibit to maintain our self-esteem?
4. How can creative imagination help us build and maintain positive self-concepts? How can creative imagination make us a success?
5. Self-disclosure can create a strong relationship between you and another person. When is self-disclosure appropriate?
6. The way we perceive each other can be a prime obstacle to effective communication. How can active listening change our perceptions of one another and help us communicate effectively?

2
COMPONENT

THE MESSAGE

PROBE 9 Appropriate verbal and nonverbal symbols are essential to effective communication.

PROBE 10 The words you use should adequately represent what you want to say.

PROBE 11 Our language influences, reflects, maintains, and interacts with sex roles.

PROBE 12 The tools of clear thinking can help you create accurate messages.

PROBE 13 Nonverbal cues can help you read messages.

Component 2: The Message

Messages may be understood as the meanings that people assign to things. These things are limitless but include what people say and do, events, pictures, and other kinds of language symbols. Thus, when you listen to another person talk, the meanings that you assign to what that person says constitute the messages you are creating. Thus, messages develop inside of us. We often say that meanings exist only *in* people; the same can be said of messages, since a message is actually a group of meanings assigned to some experience.

The creation of a message depends on a person's ability to use symbols or to symbolize. Symbolizing involves making words, behaviors, diagrams, and other things stand for something else. So, if I use a name, like Brent, to stand for or represent or refer to a person, I am symbolizing. If I use a sketch of an elephant to stand for or represent or refer to one of the national political parties in the United States, I am also symbolizing. The meaning of something consists of the relationship a person sees between the symbol and what the symbol refers to.

The two most common types of symbols are verbal and nonverbal. The term *verbal* refers to language symbols. Some people confuse *verbal* with *oral*. It is possible, however, to have a verbal symbol that is also oral. It is also possible to have a written verbal symbol. A statement that is spoken consists of verbal oral symbols; on the other hand, the same statement typed on a page consists of verbal written symbols. The study of how people use language is a study of verbal symbols.

Nonverbal symbols are those nonlanguage behaviors, appearances, emblems, sounds, silence, and time/space relationships that stand for, represent, or refer to something else. If an event occurs and meaning is not assigned to it, we simply refer to the event as a nonverbal experience rather than as nonverbal communication. When a person assigns meaning to the nonverbal activity, we can say that communication through nonverbal means is taking place.

Often, in spite of what has been said above, the term *message* is used in a popular sense to refer to the form in which the symbols are presented. For example, written verbal symbols may be displayed or presented for interpretation by means of a typewritten letter, a printed book, a handwritten memo, or a handlettered poster. Oral verbal symbols may be displayed or presented for interpretation through the forms of a public speech, a telephone call, a face-to-face dialogue, a tape recording, or an announcement over a public address system. Care should be taken to make clear how we are using the term *message*. As long as we understand that a message technically represents the meanings that people assign to things, the term can also be used in a nontechnical way to refer to the form in which the symbols are presented.

The materials presented in The Message Component seek to analyze and explain the ways persons assign meanings to things. The effects that verbal and nonverbal symbols have in this process will be presented. The importance of selecting symbols that represent your meanings accurately and that evoke the meanings you intend in the mind of the person to whom you are communicating is stressed throughout the component.

The Message Symbolized

Gordon Wiseman and Larry Barker

Symbolic formulation involves the selection of appropriate symbols and is vital to any communication situation. Symbols clothe ideas and make them understandable. In everyday communication, both verbal and nonverbal symbols are the means by which you express your ideas, endeavor to understand what others are trying to say, and attempt to understand what you mean. Symbols are the medium which enables you to conduct your business affairs, form friendships, worship, learn new ideas, develop new formuli, explore new areas, and express your likes and dislikes. Symbols also help you to respond correctly, establish the appropriate mood, and make interaction with others possible. In other words, symbols enable you to adapt to and change your environment.

Symbolization

The symbolic process is the means by which you, as a human being, are able to let symbols stand for ideas, events, places, and things. Although most of the time words are the primary concern in communication, the symbolic process includes nonverbal as well as verbal symbols. If a fellow squeezes his girlfriend's hand and she squeezes back, communication occurs through a nonverbal symbol, a symbol that has been given meaning by our

culture. Communication takes place even if he squeezes her hand and she does not return the squeeze. Most human reactions, both present and future, are controlled by symbols. Life often seems to be a process to obtain and accumulate symbols that provide feelings of accomplishment and success. Good clothes, ornaments, new homes are symbols of wealth. Rags and shacks seem to symbolize poverty. Since symbols are an integral part of your life orientation, they need to be studied and understood.

Symbols need to be controlled so that they do not control you and determine your daily life. A girl who assumes that a person with freckles is homely and then considers herself homely because she has freckles is letting herself be controlled by the symbol. The mature individual differentiates between *structural reality* and symbols and reacts to symbols as only representations of events in the real world. At the present time a military command in the form of a few symbols could cause the destruction of civilization. Perhaps even more important is the knowledge that a few poorly chosen symbols can disintegrate a human spirit. Many a G.I. felt his world give way not so much by the shelling and the dangers of combat as by the words "Dear John." Personal destruction is always more real to the individual. Even though reactions to the symbolic process are

PROBE 9. Appropriate verbal and nonverbal symbols are essential to effective communication.

Dennis the Menace by Hank Ketchum

DENNIS, DO YOU KNOW WHAT'S BLACK AND WHITE AND *READ* ALL OVER!

A *COW!*

© 1969, Publishers-Hall Syndicate, T.M. ®

often incorrect, the process is still basic to human communication. The first step involved in the control of symbols is to understand and to recognize the symbolic process. Once this has been achieved then you are ready to implement this knowledge into your communication patterns.

Keeping in touch with *structural reality* is basic to control over the symbolic process, and symbolic control is basic to effective communication. The relationship between symbols and reality should be the same as the relationship between a map and the territory it represents. Alfred Korzybski used this analogy and suggested that the relationship should be considered in three ways: (1) the map is not the territory (the symbol is not the thing symbolized); (2) the map does not represent all the territory (symbols cannot say all there is to be said about a thing); (3) the ideal map would have to include a map of itself (symbols are self-reflective).[1] Korzybski based many of his theories of general semantics on these ideas. These theories expanded semantics to include the behavioral aspects of language and meaning.

The Triangle of Meaning

Ogden and Richards in their book, *The Meaning of Meaning*, have helped to clarify meaning.[2] Of particular interest in the understanding of communication is their triangle of meaning, which illustrates the relationship between language and symbols. The triangle presented in Fig. 1 is an adaptation on theirs.

Meaning usually starts with a thought. A person thinks of an object with four legs, a wagging tail, and a moist nose. He thinks of this object in relationship to

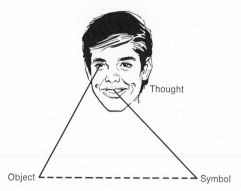

Fig. 1. *The triangle of meaning*

other objects and the mind sorts out the symbol *dog*. The thought, object, and symbol form the parts of the triangle. Each point of the triangle could be discussed at length, but in communication the important concepts to remember are these: There are definite relationships between thought and object, and between thought and symbol; however, the relationship between object and symbol is only inferred and the inference must be recognized. The symbol and the object symbolized are never exactly the same, just as a map and the territory it represents are independent of each other. The thought (perception) can even cause your concept of an object to be different from that of someone else.

The triangle of meaning aids in the understanding of other concepts about language. It illustrates the risk you often take in communicating when you assume that the other person thinks of the same object you have in mind when you use a symbol to represent that object. When you use the symbol *rose*, a variety of ideas immediately come to the minds of your responding communicators: petals, thorns, colors, scents, four, "mighty-lak-a," compass, war of the, long-stemmed, American Beauty, of Picardy,

climb up to her window, Billy, and the ring, dew on the, the yellow of Texas, or any of thousands of others. In word-association tests when the word *rose* is used, the word most commonly associated with it is red. Similarly many people think only of orange juice when the word *juice* is mentioned. They know there are other kinds of roses and juices, but the immediate response is one of red or orange.

Your life orientation determines your response to a certain symbol. This is best illustrated by the responses of two students in a class. When asked what came to their minds when the symbol *rose* was used, a girl replied, "I think of a beautiful little white cottage with a thatched roof on the hilltop surrounded by a beautiful blue sky with fleecy white clouds. All around the cottage are beautiful beds of flowers which are encircled by a white picket fence. Over the gateway of the picket fence is an archway that is covered by beautiful red roses." In the same class a fellow replied to the word *rose* by saying that he thought of dirt. Life orientations, philosophies, and other patterns are reflected in these two replies. As a communicator you cannot take for granted that your audience will have the same referent (ob-

ject) in their minds when you use a specific symbol, or that they will even associate the proper referent with your symbol. The learning of language is a complicated process. It is not sufficient to say that the symbol and the thing symbolized are not the same thing. A knowledge of the way you have learned symbols and the structure of language will give you insights into communication.

The Structure of Language

Learning Words and Symbols

Few stop to consider how they learned a word or the way in which they are learning new words and symbols now. Yet this process is so basic to understanding communication that you must be constantly aware of it. A word or symbol is usually learned in context rather than in isolation. This context is not always verbal, but may take the form of feelings, hopes, and aspirations. The meaning you attach to a word learned in this way is usually referred to as the connotative meaning. The connotative meaning of a word is the relationship between a word, an object, and a person. The connotative meaning is personalized; you attach personal meaning to the word as a result of past experiences. The denotative meaning of a word is the relationship between a word and an object and is concerned with structural reality. Sometimes this is called the historical or dictionary meaning of a word.

The establishment of connotative meanings for symbols may have lifelong effects. On the way home from school a boy learned a new word from his friends. The boy used this word at home. His parents, however, did not share

his enthusiasm and promptly suggested that if the word were used again, he would be punished by having his mouth washed out with soap. As the boy grew older that word carried many connotations with it that dated back to this incident. Although its effect is not always discernible, the setting in which a word is learned often colors the word. Therefore, the learning of words or symbols must be considered an individual matter. This is another example of the importance of understanding your life orientation in order to communicate effectively.

Word Meanings

A word is not a container like a glass. Words do not contain meaning within themselves, but are sounds in the air or marks on paper. One general semantics concept is that the meaning of words is not within the words, but within the individual. Since individuals have learned the same word in slightly different contexts, they have different meanings for the word. There are words which are frightful to some people and yet do not produce fear in others. To the individual who has had tuberculosis, the mention of "T.B." can bring reactions which would not be present in another individual who has not had the disease. The word *dead* might produce certain emotional responses within an individual who has just lost a loved one and yet not produce the same reaction two or three years later. Individuals are usually thought of as being different yet uniqueness in terms of reactions is not often comprehended. A communicator must be sensitive to feedback and constantly check the reactions of others as well as his own reactions, or as a student put it, "you need to put your antenna up."

Hidden Assumptions in Language

Communication is made more difficult, if not impossible at times, because of the silent or hidden assumptions that lie buried in language. In communicating, it is not enough to reason well; your reasoning must begin with correct premises. The connotative associations that are learned with a word, or a symbol, are disguised as premises or assumptions upon which you base your communication. The feeling that snakes are fearful, awful, and to be despised becomes attached to the symbol snake until you may react to the word *snake* as to a snake itself. These feelings are often generalized to an assumption that suggests all snakes are frightening and dangerous, while in reality many snakes are harmless.

Many times reactions are transformed into assumptions about racial and color characteristics. Some people's ideas about foreigners, Jews, Negroes, or Christians are based upon prejudices associated with the word, or symbol. One of the difficulties with these assumptions is that they are often below the threshold of consciousness and are not brought to the conscious level without a great effort. These hidden assumptions are ingrained in the nervous system and control the communication process, which in turn affects the nervous system. Language has conditioned your nervous system for the most part, which will control your reactions to the language of others. As you think, so you speak; as you speak, so you think.

Language and Your Nervous System

An analysis of language does not reveal all the characteristics of the nervous system, but it is dif-

ficult to discuss, shape, mold, change, or interpret your nervous system without language. Since language is the medium of interpretation, you should be constantly aware of the role it plays in your life. Also, understanding the way in which your nervous system operates will help you to understand your reactions to language. A bit of criticism given at one time will not have the same effect as a bit of criticism at another time. There are some areas within individuals in which a certain stimulus will generally evoke the same response. However, the connotative meaning in language will often alter the response when the time or circumstance changes.

A study of your life orientation should include the effect words, symbols, hidden assumptions, and language concepts have on you. An understanding of your life orientation will often give you a clue to the reason you react in a particular manner. More than half the battle is to recognize the reason for a reaction, even if the reaction cannot be altered. There are areas in which it is possible for a communicator to choose language that is appropriate to the responding communicator's nervous system. Listen to a boy who talks with his sister before he leaves the house and then listen to the same boy as he talks to his girlfriend on a date. He probably has altered his language to fit the nervous system of his date to produce the desired effect.

As you gain an understanding of language and its effect on your nervous system you will realize that words are only symbols and that to discover meaning you must properly interpret the symbol. This understanding will enable you to have symbol reactions to language and not signal reactions. If, in the course of a conversation, someone talks about "dirty labor leaders" and your father is a labor leader, you will not have a breakdown in your communication if you will realize that (1) the other individual is speaking from his nervous system, his background; (2) you are interpreting from your nervous system, your background; and (3) both of you may be correct to some extent. Communicators must recognize their sensitive areas and understand how they affect symbolization for them if they are to communicate successfully. They must also know and understand the sensitive areas of the responding communicator's life orientation if they are to move or change his nervous system.

You learn to interpret your world and yourself through language. This interpretation starts as you begin to learn words, their meanings and associations. Assumptions and concepts are soon built deeply into your nervous system. Communication is like the waters of a river; the flow of language controlled by past patterns forms new patterns for other language to flow over, as the river follows and enlarges its bed. Many rough places could be taken out of the flow of communication if you realized that it was your nervous system which created the rough place and not the language.

1. Alfred Korzybski, *Science and Sanity*, 4th ed. (Lakeville, Conn.: Institute of General Semantics, 1958), p. 58.

2. Charles K. Ogden and I. A. Richards, *The Meaning of Meaning* (New York: Harcourt, Brace and Company, 1946), p. 11.

Your Verbal Maps

Kenneth S. Keyes, Jr.

Clear thinking helps you to predict the future. It enables you to make plans that will get you what you want out of life.

Suppose you are starting out on a weekend trip to your favorite lake. You get one of the latest road maps and pick the best-looking route. But when you are a little beyond Plankerville, you find that road repairs make you detour through thirty miles of the dustiest dirt road you've ever breathed. You feel hot and grimy and the polish job on the car is shot.

Why did you get fouled up? *The map on which you relied did not represent the territory adequately.* Last week it may have represented the territory quite well, but that does not help get the dust out of your ears now. At the time you used it, your map lacked *predictability.*

Whenever you use maps that do not adequately represent the territory—maps that have poor predictability—you will not get what you want. Bad maps will lead you to anything from minor annoyance to sudden death, depending on the nature of the situation.

A verbal map is simply a map or a "picture" drawn with words. A reliable verbal map represents the territory adequately; a bad verbal map lies to you about the territory. For example, if I say, "Mosquitoes breed in standing water," I have made a verbal map that represents the territory.

If someone tells you, "Female canaries sing," he has given you an incorrect map that will mislead you if you rely upon it.

Every time you open your mouth to let out words, you are making a verbal map. If you tell Junior "George Washington was the first President of the United States," you are making a map of territory that existed over a century ago. If Henry Brown says, "Beginning next year, I will definitely cut out smoking," he is making a verbal map of future territory. If he stops smoking, as the map says, it represents the actual territory. Otherwise, no. When I say, "My big toe hurts," I am making a verbal map of some territory that I, alone, am able to survey. I am mapping territory within my own body. If I say, "I am very disappointed," I am again mapping territory within me—my feelings.

All the knowledge and memories we have filed away in our heads may be regarded as "mental maps." All the thousands of words we shoot at each other every day may be regarded as verbal maps representing past, present, or future territory.

Inadequate Maps Put Us in Hot Water

Tim McCarthy was hit by a truck, and the first report of the doctor was discouraging. "I'm afraid

---

Abridged from HOW TO DEVELOP YOUR THINKING ABILITY by Kenneth S. Keyes, Jr. Copyright 1950 By Kenneth S. Keyes, Jr. Used with permission of McGraw-Hill Book Co.

PROBE 10. The words you use should adequately represent what you want to say.

I am writing to the Welfare Department to say that my baby was born two years old. When can I get my money?

I am forwarding my marriage certificate and six children. I have seven but one died which was baptized on a half sheet of paper.

I cannot get sick pay. I have six children. Can you tell me why?

your husband hasn't long to live," he told Tim's wife. "I'll come again tomorrow."

The next day, the doctor's report was still gloomy. But when the doctor called a third time, the patient was rallying, and on the fourth day he was out of danger.

"Well, missus," the doctor said. "Tim is going to pull through all right."

"Puts me in a bit of a hole, though," said the woman. "I've gone and sold all his clothes for funeral expenses."

Whenever we act on maps that do not adequately represent the territory, it puts us in a "bit of a hole."

In everything we do, we need adequate verbal maps. If we make a mistake in our checking account and think the balance is $352 when it is only $241.50, some of our checks are going to bounce. The map in our checkbook must adequately represent the funds in our account if we are to avoid trouble. If the gas gauge in our car says half full when our tank is about empty, it does not map the territory very well. If we rely on it, our blood pressure is going up—especially if we want to get somewhere in a hurry.

Why Accurate Maps May Not Be Good Enough

You may have wondered why so much emphasis has been put upon "adequate" verbal maps. The word *adequate* has been carefully chosen. A verbal map may be considered strictly accurate and yet, *for our purposes*, be quite inadequate and misleading!

For example, Bob had fished all day without any luck. On his way home he went to Captain Tom's Fish Market and said:

"Tom, pick out five of your biggest fish and toss them to me."

"You mean throw them?"

"Yes, just throw them over to me one at a time so I can tell the family I caught them. I may be a poor fisherman, but I'm no liar."

Some people might say our fisherman was making an accurate verbal map if he said he caught the fish. But no one would insist it was an adequate verbal map. We see readily that however accurate that map is, it is thoroughly misleading and has nothing to do with the actual territory.

Manglish

Varda One

Since this is a sexist society it is only natural that our language should reflect this. However, language is not merely a reflection of reality; it also influences how we view it and thus it shapes that reality. The use of the term "girl Friday" to mean "all-around clerical worker" not only accurately reveals the fact that most people doing this work are young women but also determines who will apply for jobs advertised by using this description.

Power has been defined as the ability to define reality and to act according to that definition. Since women have been powerless they have not been able to define themselves, much less act on their definitions. They have been forced to see themselves through a male mirror which distorts and insults them. The process of the degradation of women in language I have termed Manglish. This paper will examine the mechanisms by which Manglish works to insure that women continue to see themselves as inferior beings.

1. The Myth of Lexicographic Objectivity

Both the Bible and dictionaries were written by men, men with special interests to forward. Both are contradictory, fallacious, and historically inaccurate. But the Bible has toppled from its eminence of God's word (always He with a capital "H") while the dictionary is still revered in classrooms as a final impartial authority. We are presently working on a Dictionary of Sexism to show how prejudiced an authority it really is. We hope this will act as a corrective as the Women's Bible by Elizabeth Cady Stanton did.

Some of the ways lexicographers commit Manglish are: (a) giving more space for male items; e.g., note entries for "man" and "woman"; (b) using sex-stereotyped examples in illustrative sentences; e.g., "world" – She bakes an apple pie that is out of this world. (*Random House Dictionary of the English Language*, 1966, p. 1645); (c) presenting the masculine in a sequence first. Deity is defined as "1. the state of being a god. 2. a god 3. a goddess" (*Webster's New World 20th Century Dictionary*, 1960, p. 479); (d) including more insulting terms for women than men. This practice is also followed in all thesauruses. There are unlimited terms, for example, for women who nag – shrew, termagant, scold, virago, vixen, fishwife, henpecker, she-devil, Biddy Moriarty, spitfire, Xantippe, porcupine, dragon, fury, fire-eater, Kate the Shrew, tigress, beldame, madcap, carper – but not *one* for a male nag; (e) including prejudiced comments of the author. Look up "girl" in Shipley's *Dictionary of Word Origins.* "You

---

PROBE 11.   Our language influences, reflects, maintains, and interacts with sex roles.

Sispeak: A Msguided Attempt to Change Herstory

Stefan Kanfer

"As the chairperson of Senator McGovern's task force on the environment," begins Robert N. Rickles' letter to constituents. Chairperson? The title is no partisan issue: the G.O.P. also had a chairperson in Miami Beach. Thus another label comes unglued. The man and his woman are Out; the neuter "person" is In—and only the chair is allowed to linger undisturbed. Chairperson is just the latest exchange in that great linquistic bazaar where new terms are traded for old. The elderly "Mrs." and the shy "Miss" now curtsy to the crisp, swinging "Ms." "Congressone" has been suggested in federal corridors to replace the Congressman-woman stigma.

Lexicographers Ms. Casey Miller and Ms. Kate Swift recently amplified the Women's Lib party line: men have traditionally used language to subjugate women. As they see it, William James' bitch-goddess Success and the National Weather Service's Hurricane Agnes are products of the same criminal mind, designed to foster the illusion of woman as Eve, forever volatile and treacherous. The authors therefore suggest the elimination of sexist terms. "Genkind," they think, would provide a great encompassing umbrella under which all humanity could huddle, regardless. Varda One, a radical philologist, asks for the obliteration of such repugnant pronouns as he and she, his and hers. In place she offers ve, vis and ver. "We don't go around addressing persons by their race, height or eye color," says One. "Why should we identify them by sex?" Unfortunately, such designations tend to remove rather than increase an individual's sense of self. "Personalized" Christmas cards are about as personal as a paper cup.

Through the echoes of the new verbalism, one can sense the distress of that crystal spirit, George Orwell. In *1984* he posited the principles of a new tongue. "In Newspeak," wrote Orwell, "words which had once borne a heretical meaning were sometimes retained for the sake of convenience, but only with the undesirable meanings purged out of them." "Goodsex" meant chastity; "crimethink" suggested equality. "The greatest difficulty facing the compilers of Newspeak," continued Orwell, "was not to invent new words, but, having invented them, to make sure what they meant: to make sure what ranges of words they canceled by their existence."

Certainly the compilers of the new Sispeak have no such totalitarian purposes. Big Sister is not yet watching, and from the beginning the feminist wordsmiths have had to endure mockery and ridicule. Cartoonists and satirists have suggested that the ladies were Libbing under a Msapprehension. Their inventions were Msanthropic and Msguided attempts to change herstory. *The Godmother* was to be Mario Puzo's new Mafia novel; Womandarin Critic Susan Daughtertag was the new bottle for the old whine. Shedonism, girlcotting and countessdowns were to be anticipated in the liberated '70s. As for the enemy, he could expect to be confronted by female belligerents inviting him to put up his duchesses. He would find, in short, that his gander was cooked. All flagrantly gendered words would be swiftly unsexed. The ottoman would become

(continued on page 51)

may guess freely here; Brewer lists several choices. There is *garrula*, a chatterbox (surely appropriate enough!) from L. *garrire*, to prattle. Then L. *gerula* is a nurse: AS. *coorl*, a churl? Brewer himself lists *girdle worn by maids and loosed by marriage*? also *gull* (impolitely!). The word is, we can at least say, a diminutive: perhaps of Gr. *koure*, lass; perhaps a corruption of darling from AS. *doorling*. A girl can keep any boy guessing." (An example of objective scholarship but also inaccurate. Originally *girl* meant a young person of either sex); (f) using drawings of mostly men and male animals. Since most artists are male, they find it easier to draw men but why male animals instead of female?; (g) reflecting the sexist character of general scholarship. For example, there is a listing for "penis envy" but none for womb envy.

2. The Appendage Complex

This assumes men are the only humans and women are an afterthought. This manifests itself in Manglish as: (a) using only a male form to mean both male and female as man/mankind or he; (b) considering the masculine form primary, the feminine secondary, e.g., poet, poetess, aviator, aviatrix, drum major, drum majorette, man, woman, male, female; (c) assuming a neuter form is male and adding a feminine qualifier, e.g., driver, woman driver, doctor, lady doctor.

3. Relating Function to Gender, Usually Reserving Low Prestige Jobs for Women

According to Dr. Sandra Bem, "There are only two jobs for which

all members of one sex or another would be disqualified—sperm donor or wet nurse." Here are some of the ways this works in Manglish: (a) incorporating a gender suffix in a word, e.g., policeman, policewoman; (b) assumption of one sex when no indicator is given. Which sex do you associate with these words? tycoon, prostitute, suitor, executive, secretary, virgin, maid, teamster, seamstress, warden. Is there any exorable physical reason for such typecasting?

4. Devolutionary Process of Words Involving Women

Since the reign of Charles II, a very misogynous period, many words have specialized and degenerated and some have done both. (Specialization means a word has narrowed its meaning. In Manglish this translates as sex-segregation. Degeneration means a word has acquired an invidious connotation.) Here are some examples of these processes:

WORD	FORMER MEANING
harlot	a fellow of either sex
hussy	a housewife (from OE. *huswif*)
whore	a lover of either sex
wench	a child of either sex, later a working girl or rustic woman
tomboy	a rude boisterous boy
beldame	grandmother (from ME. *beldame* "fair lady")
virgin	an independent female. The original meaning related to the dependence of married women; the distinction was not a sexual one based on an intact hymen since virgins often had children, but on eco-

(continued from page 50)

the ottoit, the highboy would metamorphose into the highthing, and ladyfingers· would be served under the somewhat less appealing name of person-fingers.

Yet beyond the hoots and herstrionics, the feminists seemed to have reason on their side. Tradition does play favorites with gender. Man, master, father are the commonplaces of theological and political leadership. Who, for example, could imagine the Four Horsepersons of the Apocalypse or George Washington, first in the hearts of his countrypeople? Even the literature of equality favors the male: Robert Burns sang "A man's a man for a' that!" *"Mann ist Mann,"* echoed Brecht. "Constant labor of one uniform kind," wrote Karl Marx, "destroys the intensity and flow of a man's animal spirits." The U.N. Charter speaks of the scourge of war, which "has brought untold sorrow to mankind." It is pathetically easy to spy in this vocabulary a latent slavery, a cloaked projudice aimed at further subjugating women in the name of language.

No wonder, then, that the movement has set out to change the dictionary. With a touching, almost mystical trust in words, it seems to believe that definition is a matter of will. And indeed sometimes it is. The change from Negro to black has helped to remake a people's view of itself. But it is a lone example. Far more often, words have been corrupted by change. The counterculture's overuse of "love" has not resulted in a lessening of hostilities; "heavy" has become a lightweight adjective. The abuse of the word *media* has resulted in a breakdown of intelligence; invitations have even been sent out to "Dear media person." For the most part, the new lexicographers behave like Humpty Dumpty in *Through the Looking Glass:* a word may mean whatever they want it to mean. Naturally, said Humpty, "when I make a word do a lot of work, I always pay it extra." One wonders what Women's Lib's new words will be paid. They are, after all, working overtime, and against immense cultural and sociological odds.

In the philosophy of semantics there is a standard rhetorical question: Is it progress if a cannibal eats with a knife and fork? Similarly, if society is sexist, is it altered when its language is revised? Or do its attitudes remain when its platitudes change? The prognosis is not good. Words, like all currency, need to be reinforced with values. Take away the Federal Reserve and its dollar bill is waste paper. Take away meaning and a word is only noise. Changing chairman to chairperson is mock doctrine and flaccid democracy, altering neither the audience nor, in fact, the office holder. Despite its suffix, chairman is no more sexist than the French designation of "boat" as masculine, or the English custom of referring to a ship with feminine pronouns. Chairman is a role, not a pejorative. Congressman is an office, not a chauvinist plot. Mankind is a term for all humanity, not some 49% of it. The feminist attack on social crimes may be as legitimate as it was inevitable. But the attack on words is only another social crime—one against the means and the hope of communication.

For *A Clockwork Orange,* Anthony Burgess created a wall-to-wall nightmare in which society dissolves into violence and repression. The condition is reflected in the breakdown of language into "nadsat," a jumble of portmanteau constructions ("He looked a malenky bit poogly when he viddied the four of us"). To Burgess, language is the breath of civilization. Cut it short and society suffocates. That is an insight worth pondering. For if the world is to resist the nadsat future, readers and writers of both sexes must resist onefully any meaningless neologisms. To do less is to encourage another manifestation of prejudice—against reason, meaning and eventually personkind itself.

	nomic and psychological grounds.
virago	a woman of great stature, strength, and courage; one possessing supposedly masculine qualities of body and mind. Men thought it a compliment at one time to call a woman manly.

A good indicator of this process is the study of parallel forms: master-mistress, courtier-courtesan, governor-governess, patrimony-matrimony, patron-matron. (Another word, patroness, is now the feminine equivalent of patron.)

5. The Subsuming of Identity

In a patriarchal society women are thought of as property. The word "family" comes from Latin *famulus*, meaning slave. All members of a Roman family, the wife, the children, the servants, belonged to the master as his slaves, and they took his last name to signify ownership. This is reflected in Manglish in the following ways:

(a) patronymics. The children take their father's name. This is based on the old belief that only men had the power to transmit life. The sex cell was believed to be contained in their sperm only, and women served merely as incubators. Thus the offspring were his children only. It wasn't until recently that the custody of children in divorce cases was given to mothers instead of fathers.

Many surnames themselves are masculine, e.g., Robertson, meaning son of Robert. At one time there were names like Marysdaughter, but they were dropped. The Irish affix "O" as in "O'Hara" meant grandson of. There was also a matronymic affix "ni"

meaning daughter of, as in Katherine ni Rose, but this also has been discarded. We now say Lucy Johnson and no longer think of it as odd.

(b) married names. The suitor asked the father for his daughter's hand. This expression has its roots in slave-buying days when the master designated the slaves he was purchasing by laying his hand on them (mancipation). They were under the rule of manus (hand). Slaves could be emancipated but women could only be handed from one male to another. The girl gave up her "maiden" name (the property was intact) and took the name of her new master, her husband.

The woman completely subsumed herself in her new name, Mrs. John Doe. The etiquette experts declare that even using her own first name is incorrect. When she divorces John Doe, her children still bear his name.

(c) first names. Puritan names such as Charity, Patience, Hope, Purity, and Innocence reflect the socialization parents expected of girls. Modern names such as Candy, Joy, Honey, Belle, Cookie reflect a different but also limited role expectation. Many feminine first names are based on appendage concepts of adding a suffix to the masculine form, e.g., Jean-Jeanette, Henry-Henriette. The suffix "ette" in French means "little" so the feminine is of less importance than the male. It is also used to ridicule as in "suffragette" and "liberationette".

(d) herstorical omissions. Although many women have been discoverers and inventors they have often not been given credit. Many of the words based on the names of people immortalize men, e.g., silhouette (Etienne De Silhouette), douglas fir (David Douglas), dahlia (Anders Dahl),

mason jar (John Mason), boycott (Charles Boycott), galvanic (Luigi Galvani), guppy (R. J. Guppy), nicotine (Jean Nicot). The few words commemmorating women are generally from mythology like echo and cereal (Echo and Ceres).

6. The Woman as "The Other"

Not only do men see themselves as the sole humans but they postulate the feminine aspect as a goal outside themselves to be mastered and conquered. Examples in Manglish: (a) anything everwhelming in nature is feminine. Mother Earth, Death, Hurricane Ida, the sea, a mountain. This occurs more often in languages which are more gender-conscious such as French; (b) anything difficult or big is a substitute for a woman. Ships ("steady as she goes"), mines, dams, oil wells ("thar she blows"). These are generally places where only men work. The university which once used to be all-male is an alma mater (soul mother).

7. The Double Standard of Titles

Because there is no differentiating title for married and unmarried men, women cannot tell the marital status of men as easily as men can determine theirs. Some people have adopted Ms. (pronounced "miz") to mean either Miss or Mrs. as an equivalent form to Mr. Newspapers commonly refer to men by only their last names—using a title for women is a continuation of the auxiliary complex. We are to assume that "Kennedy" means he and not she.

8. The Use of Compliments and Insults

These reveal the true feelings many men have toward women: (a) virtue and virile both come from the Latin root *vir* meaning man. At one time they both meant manly. Since courage and fortitude were good qualities, they were associated with men and became *vir*tues. Thus the expression "womanly virtue" is a contradiction in terms, etymologically speaking.

9. Sexist Maxims

Manglish is a cornucopia of ways women are insulated. "A woman's place is in the home; women hate to work for other women; a smart woman is one who doesn't let her husband know how smart she is." Any Martian coming to live as a woman on Earth would have no trouble finding what is expected just by referring to these transmitters of hate.

10. The Use of Double-Think

The same quality, good or bad, manifested in a man is seen differently when expressed by a girl. A woman who is aggressive is called pushy; a man is called a go-getter. If a woman outthinks a man she is called castrating. There is no equivalent in Manglish for a man who outthinks a woman since this is supposedly the norm.

11. Sexist Expressions

We talk of priceless paintings as old masters but gossip is old wives' tales; we exclaim "Man!" and "O, boy!" but never "Woman!" and "O, girl!"; we call the deadliest insect a black widow spider, the cruelest torture instrument an iron maiden; a carnivorous plant is a Venus's-flytrap, and the device for hauling prisoners is a black Maria. We say weak sisters but never weak brothers, brilliant people are "seminal" thinkers, and women who attend universities are "co-eds" while males are students.

PROBE 12. The tools of clear thinking can help you create accurate messages.

Tools of Clear Thinking

Kenneth S. Keyes, Jr.

If you are not a hermit or a little dictator surrounded by "yes men," you will find the tools for thinking useful in helping you get along with people as you find them in this scrambled world of ours.

Tool No. 1: So Far As I Know

No argument can be settled when one or both parties blow up emotionally. One of the best ways I have ever found to turn aside wrath is to add "so far as I know" to my verbal maps. Most people will not mind your expressing an opinion that is different from theirs as long as you use "so far as I know" to indicate that your opinion is based upon your experiences and your evidence, and that you are not pretending to be God's mouthpiece. You have not weakened your position at all by saying "so far as I know." After all, who has a right to say more? In a changing world about which our knowledge is incomplete, no one is able to say the final word.

Look at the results Benjamin Franklin achieved when he dropped the dogmatic attitude. In his *Autobiography*, he attributes much of his success to his adoption of the "so far as I know" attitude:

I made it a rule to forbear all direct contradiction to the sentiments of others, and all positive assertion of my own. I even forbid myself the use of every word or expression in the language that imported a fixed opinion, such as *certainly, undoubtedly*, etc., and I adopted, instead of them, *I conceive, I apprehend*, or *I imagine* a thing to be so or so, or *it so appears to me at present*.

When another asserted something that I thought an error, I denied myself the pleasure of contradicting him abruptly and of showing immediately some absurdity in his proposition; and in answering, I began by observing that in certain cases or circumstances his opinion would be right, but in the present case there *appeared* or *seemed* to me some difference, etc. I soon found the advantage of this change in my manner; the conversations I engaged in went on more pleasantly. The modest way in which I proposed my opinions procured them a readier reception and less contradiction; I had less mortification when I was found to be in the wrong, and I more easily prevailed with others to give up their mistakes and join with me when I happened to be in the right.

And this mode, which I at first put on with some violence to natural inclination, became at length so easy, and so habitual to me, that perhaps for these fifty years past no one has ever heard a dogmatical expression escape me. And to this habit (after my character of integrity) I think it principally owing that I had early so much weight with my fellow-citizens when I proposed new institutions, or alterations in the old, and so much influence in public councils when I became a member; for I was but a bad speaker, never eloquent, subject to much hesitation in my choice of words, hardly correct in language, and yet I generally carried my points.

Tool No. 2: Up to a Point

When we criticize people it is important to tell up to what point that criticism is appropriate. Suppose, for example, someone complains that doctors are mercenary and think more of the long green lining their pockets than of the Hippocratic ideal of helping suffering humanity. Such a one-sided verbal map will needlessly antagonize the very doctors he would like to change. He has not told up to what point his verbal map represents the territory. His map implies that all doctors, everywhere, are that way in every respect.

But if he tries to make his verbal maps represent the territory and indicate, for example, that *certain doctors in certain places* accept "kickbacks" or "bonuses" from medical laboratories and supply houses that sometimes amount to from 25 to 50 percent of the money their patients pay for eyeglasses, X rays, medical appliances, Wassermann and other tests, then he will find that open-minded members of the medical profession will agree with him. Overstating one's case only causes antagonism. One should be careful not to let his assertions outstrip his facts.

Tool No. 3: To Me

A Chinese delegate to the United Nations was just leaving the gangplank of his ship at a New York dock. He was immediately surrounded by reporters. One of the questions shot at him was, "What strikes you as the oddest thing about Americans?"

The delegate thought seriously for a moment, then smiled. "I think," he said, "it is the peculiar slant of their eyes."

Cutting Words

A man of true science uses but few hard words, and those only when none other will answer his purpose; whereas the smatterer in science . . . thinks that by mouthing hard words he proves that he understands hard things.
"Dr. Cuticle"
in Herman Melville's White Jacket

By Melville's criterion, suggests Dr. Lois DeBakey in the *New England Journal of Medicine*, medicine must be full of "smatterers in science." Hospital records, casual conversations and technical reports "are loaded with shoptalk, incomprehensible to nonphysicians and often confusing even to physicians from other regions." A member of a notable family of surgeons—one brother is Houston Surgeon Michael DeBakey (Time cover, May 28), another brother, Ernest, is also a surgeon—Dr. Lois, who has a Ph.D. in English and is an associate professor in scientific communication at Tulane University, is a surgeon of language. She advises medical writers to concentrate on cutting out the "learned" words and using the simple substitutes in the following list of choices:

Agrypnia	Insomnia
Cephalalgia	Headache
Cholelithiasis	Gallstones
Deglutition	Swallowing
Emesis	Vomiting
Hemorrhage	Bleeding
Obese	Fat
Pyrexia	Fever
Respire	Breathe

Carrying her criticism right to the end (not "termination") of life, Dr. DeBakey thinks *"in extremis* is a pretentious expression for dying."

From "Cutting Words" in TIME, March 4, 1966. Reprinted by permission from TIME, The Weekly Newsmagazine; Copyright Time Inc.

Gobbledygook Must Go

Webster's defines *gobbledygook* as "wordy and generally unintelligible jargon." Others have described it as a conglomeration of flossy, pompous, abstract, complex, jargonistic words which we too frequently try to pass off as communications. Gobbledygook is almost always loaded with jargon of the writer's own professional interest—words seldom used by persons outside the writer's little word-world. It seems to stem from an ingrown (perhaps subconscious) professional desire to impress rather than to communicate, to be "proper" rather than personal and direct.

To show how easy it is to get balled up in the jargon of our own trade or profession, let's look at a little game we recently heard about. You play it with three groups of buzzwords numbered from zero to nine:

Group 1	Group 2	Group 3
0. evaluate	0. educational	0. competencies
1. coordinate	1. diffusion	1. research
2. upgrade	2. program	2. implications
3. formalize	3. professional	3. planning
4. total	4. leadership	4. subject matter
5. balanced	5. clientele	5. role
6. finalize	6. differential	6. image
7. systematized	7. decision-making	7. focal point
8. ongoing	8. innovative	8. flexibility
9. responsive	9. policy	9. programming

Now think of any three-digit number, and then, from each of the above groups, select the numbered word corresponding to each digit in the number you picked. For example, take the number 220, and you come up with "upgrade program competencies," or use 359 and your phrase turns out to be "formalize clientele programming." Your resulting phrases may lack real meaning, but most of them will have a ring of familiarity.

Abridged from "Gobbledygook Must Go" in *Inside Information*, July 1966. © 1966 *Inside Information*. Used by permission of Information and Publications Dept., University of Maryland.

We live in a world made up of five major skin colors, thousands of religions and philosophies, and a range of customs and mores of amazing diversity. If we are to get along with any people except those in our own group, we learn to add "to me" to our verbal maps. We must recognize that what seems "right" to us may not seem "right" to other people.

When the British movie film *The Wicked Lady* was sent to the United States, the American censors objected to the necklines of some of the dresses—there was too much "cleavage." For Americans, the censors said, the necklines are immoral. J. Arthur Rank, England's leading film producer, was unable to understand the situation, "In England," he said, "bosoms aren't sexy!"

A little later Hollywood sent *Her Husband's Affairs* over to England. In this movie, twin beds were shown touching each other. The flabbergasted producers in Hollywood could hardly believe their ears when the English explained that they just couldn't show the picture with the twin beds right together. It was necessary to reshoot that scene with the beds placed one foot apart in order to make it in good moral taste for English audiences.

The only way we can get along with people who have a contrasting background is to add "to me" to our verbal maps. We must admit we are fallible humans trying to do the best we can. We must not act as if we alone have the key to the treasury of truth.

Our Judgments Are Self-Reflective

When we say, "Jane is an interesting girl," we're talking about ourselves just as much as we are talking about Jane. The way we react to things is partly determined by what is outside us and

Tom Tracy

Nick Pavloff

Tom Tracy

Component 1: **The Person**

Component 2: **The Message**

Component 3: **The Environment**

Tom Tracy

partly by what is inside us. When we say, "Jane is an interesting girl," we really mean that we find Jane interesting for one or more reasons. That statement gives other people very little information about Jane—it only expresses the way *we feel about her.*

If we hear someone say, "That building is hideous," we must remember that he is expressing his standards and his ideas of architecture just as much as he is talking about the building. That statement simply means he doesn't like the building.

The tool "to me" will help us become conscious of the way our own nervous system abstracts differently from other nervous systems. All we have the right to say is, "To me this is beautiful. To me this is bad. To me this is fun. To me this tastes wonderful. To me this is interesting. To me this is dull," and so on. We can speak only for ourselves.

Tool No. 4: The What Index

A retired judge once remarked to one of his friends that during his career on the bench, he had *on the average* done a pretty good job. "Of course," he admitted, "I have sent to the gallows a good many innocent people and have set free a good many guilty people, but I feel on the whole my errors of leniency have been pretty well offset by the times when I was too severe."

From a *statistical* point of view the judge may have averaged out all right—but from an *individual human* point of view there is no such thing as averaging out. It is small comfort to an innocent man about to be hanged to realize that his execution will be balanced out by the mistake of setting a murderer free!

What Is Prejudice?

Prejudice arises when people take a statistical approach to man_1 or $thing_1$. We are prejudiced when we react to labels instead of looking at man_1 or $thing_1$. We are prejudiced when we are content with "averaging out."

All of us carry around in our heads a pack of prejudices. We may be prejudiced against certain races and certain classes. We may be prejudiced against people with immigrant heritages. We have political prejudices, religious prejudices, prejudices against people in other parts of the world and in other parts of our own country, and we can even be prejudiced against people in the next town or in another part of our own town. We can have prejudices about newfangled contraptions, red automobiles, or modern art.

We get an unfavorable picture in our heads and then proceed blindly as though that picture were an adequate map to represent all people or things that are included under the label. Or we can get a favorable picture in our heads and then blind ourselves to all sorts of unfavorable aspects of man_1 or $thing_1$. We ask what a person or thing "is." Then we react to the label. Why bother getting acquainted with the territory—it's too much trouble.

Regardless of whether few, many, or most of the people are covered by a generalization, we will meet some who are not. We must observe man_1 who stands before us in order to act intelligently and fairly toward him.

The index numbers can remind us that we do not deal with people-in-general. We deal with individual people and an individual person may or may not fit the average map we have. We must remember that man_1 is not man_2,

$Democrat_1$ is not $Democrat_2$, $Republican_1$ is not $Republican_2$, $Southerner_1$ is not $Southerner_2$, New $Englander_1$ is not New $Englander_2$, $Catholic_1$ is not $Catholic_2$, etc. As Henry van Dyke said, "There is one point in which all men are exactly alike and that is that they are all different." By using index numbers we can avoid being misled by the stereotyped notions we carry around in our heads.

Tool No. 5: The When Index

In dealing with people, we must remember that although their names do not change, they may act differently with the passing of time. $Susie^{(1960)}$ may have had many habits that made people call her selfish. $Susie^{(today)}$ may not have those habits. You cannot simply meet $Susie^{(1960)}$ and decide she is selfish, then for the rest of your life assume that's the way she is because that's the way she was. Susie may have changed (and, of course, Susie may not have changed). The point is, again, to survey the Susie-territory before you hang a 1960 label on her today.

If we want to react to people as they *are* (rather than to people as they *were*), we must recognize the process factor in knowledge. We must remember with Whitehead that "Knowledge keeps no better than fish."

All of us make missteps. All of us have done mean, selfish, illegal, unworthy, and terrible things. If people make verbal maps of us at such unfortunate times, and then set them in concrete in their minds and refuse to reevaluate us at later times, then we're sunk. When that happens, a person may feel there is no need to try to act better or improve himself. He may feel that his reputation is

Intra-campus MEMORANDUM

State University

July 31, 1972

FROM: Acting Chairperson, Speech Communication
TO: Academic Deans and Department Chairpersons

Please be advised that effective September 1, 1972, official correspondence and material associated with the Department of Speech Communication will carry the terms "Acting Chairperson" or "Chairperson" instead of "Acting Chairman" or "Chairman."

This change is an attempt to reflect cultural change and avoid sex bias associated with the department and the university.

Intra-campus MEMORANDUM

State University

August 1, 1972

FROM: Dean, College of Arts and Sciences
TO: Acting Chairman, Speech Communication

I am against your intended change for the following reasons:

1. We have "chairmen"—not "chairpersons"— on the university records.
2. *Man* can be interpreted as "mankind" as well as "male."
3. We have no chairwomen.

established, and no matter how he changes, it will not help him because people are not openminded enough to revise their verbal maps when the territory changes. You can see what unhappiness poor thinking habits can cause. Clear thinking demands that we use the when index to attune ourselves to the possibilities of change.

Tool No. 6: The Where Index

According to words, Mary Williams is Mary Williams. But according to facts, Mary Williams *(married to Roger Brown in Boston, Mass.)* is not the same as Mary Williams *(married to Tom Smith in Miami, Fla.)*. We act differently in different environments and with different people. For example, with some people you usually feel lighthearted and gay, and you get known to them as a clever and witty person. With others, the serious aspect of your personality is brought out.

Suppose two friends of Mary Williams get together:

"Mary is certainly full of the devil. She doesn't have a serious thought in her head."

"We must not be talking about the same person. The Mary I know is quite serious. Her grasp of current affairs is amazing."

"Well, that's not the Mary I'm talking about."

"Mary Williams?"

"Yes, Mary Williams. Lives at the Wingate Apartments."

"I don't know what's the matter. You must not know her very well."

"Why, I've known her for years."

"Well, you certainly aren't much of a judge of character then."

"Well, I like that. I think you're the batty one." (At this point they stop talking about Mary Williams entirely, and inferences and judgments are exchanged that have no relation to the territory.)

To get along in this world, we need to develop a deep feeling for the way different situations, circumstances, or surroundings bring out different aspects of people and things. The where index can help us understand where we might otherwise misunderstand.

To Sum Up

The tools for thinking can do a great deal to help you get along with other people. When you say so far as I know, you can keep from antagonizing people by your dogmatic assertions. The tool "up to a point" can help you to avoid irritating people needlessly by keeping you from implying "all" when "some" is more in accordance with the facts. The tool "to me" tells you that your reactions are determined both by what is outside you and your own nervous system. When you use "to me" you admit you're a human being and are not pretending to see things from the cosmic aspect of eternity. By using index numbers, you will remember to discriminate *between* individuals and not *against* individuals. No matter how accurate your generalizations and averages are, they do not put the finger on any individual. You must survey the territory to find out if a generalization applies to the man_1 or $thing_1$ you are dealing with. The when index will remind you that two verbal maps may seem to contradict each other, but when the date is added both may be found adequate. The where index will remind you that people and things act differently in different places.

Intra-campus MEMORANDUM

State University

August 4, 1972

FROM: Chairman, Department of English
TO: Acting Chairman, Speech Communication
RE: Your July 31 memo addressed to Academic Deans and Department Chairpersons

Dick, please don't give in to this women's lib nonsense. I am all for the desirable aspects of the movement, but the linguistic gobbledygook is more than I can take. When I accepted the job of Chairman of the English Department, I accepted the job of *Chair*man—not Chair*person*. If we go this route, we may as well start talking about *flagperson, personkind, policeperson, personful, personhole, personhood, person-hour, personhunt, person-in-the-street, person of the street, every person jack, person-made, person of God, person of letters, person of straw, person of the world, person-of-war, person-of-war bird, personpower, personservant, person slayer.* We may even have to talk about *personing the ship, personing the capstan, personing the production lines.* And then we run into *personish, person of the house,* and finally *persons' room.* Now, surely we do want to be able to tell what is behind the door labeled "Persons' Room," don't we? So, we will have to start talking about *persons' room* in contrast to *wopersons' room.* Then we can distinguish *person of the house* from *woperson of the house.* Next we can go to *person* and *woperson kind,* to *flagperson* and *flagwoperson,* to *policeperson* and *policewoperson,* et cetera, et cetera. Surely, wopersons—or fepersons—would want to distinguish *woperson power* from *person power, woperson suffrage* from *person suffrage,* and most of all *wopersons' lib* from *persons' lib!*

Nonverbal Communication: Basic Perspectives

Mark Knapp

Those of us who keep our eyes open can read volumes into what we see going on around us. E. Hall

---

PROBE 13. Nonverbal cues can help you read messages.

Herr von Osten purchased a horse in Berlin, Germany in 1900. When von Osten began training his horse, Hans, to count by tapping his front hoof, he had no idea that Hans was soon to become one of the most celebrated horses in history. Hans was a rapid learner and soon progressed from counting to addition, multiplication, division, subtraction, and eventually the solution of problems involving factors and fractions. As if this were not enough, von Osten exhibited Hans to public audiences where he counted the number in the audience or simply the number of people wearing eye glasses. Still responding only with taps, Hans could tell time, use a calendar, display an ability to recall musical pitch, and perform numerous other seemingly fantastic feats. After von Osten taught Hans an alphabet which could be coded into hoofbeats, the horse could answer virtually any question—oral or written. It seemed that Hans, a common horse, had complete comprehension of the German language, the ability to produce the equivalent of words and numerals, and an intelligence beyond that of many human beings.

Even without the promotion of Madison Avenue, the word spread quickly and soon Hans was known throughout the world. He was soon dubbed "Clever Hans." Because of the obviously profound implications for several scientific fields and because some skeptics thought there was a "gimmick" involved, an investigating committee was established to decide, once and for all, whether there was any deceit involved in Hans' performances. Professors of psychology, physiology, the director of the Berlin Zoological Garden, a director of a circus, veterinarians, and cavalry officers were appointed to this commission of horse experts. An experiment with Hans from which von Osten was absent demonstrated no change in the apparent intelligence of Hans. This was sufficient proof for the commission to announce there was no trickery involved.

The appointment of a second commission was the beginning of the end for Clever Hans. Von Osten was asked to whisper a number into the horse's left ear while another experimenter whispered a number into the horse's right ear. Hans was told to add the two numbers—an answer none of the onlookers, von Osten, or the experimenter knew. Hans failed. And with further tests he continued to fail. The experiment-

---

er, Pfungst, discovered on further experimentation that Hans could only answer a question if someone in his visual field knew the answer.[1] When Hans was given the question, the onlookers assumed an expectant posture and increased their body tension. When Hans reached the correct number of taps, the onlookers would relax and make a slight movement of the head—which was Hans' cue to stop tapping.

The story of Clever Hans is frequently used in discussions concerning the capacity of an animal to learn verbal language. It also seems well suited to an introduction to the field of nonverbal communication. Hans' cleverness was not in his ability to verbalize or understand verbal commands, but in his ability to respond to almost imperceptible and unconscious movements on the part of those surrounding him. It is not unlike that perceptiveness or sensitivity to nonverbal cues exhibited by a Clever Carl, Charles, Frank, or Harold when picking up a girl, closing a business deal, giving an intelligent and industrious image to a professor, knowing when to leave a party, and in a multitude of other common situations.

Perspectives on Defining Nonverbal Communication

Conceptually, the term *nonverbal* is subject to a variety of interpretations—just like the term *communication*. The basic issue seems to be whether the events traditionally studied under the heading *nonverbal* are literally *non* verbal. Ray Birdwhistell, a pioneer in nonverbal research, is reported to have said that studying *nonverbal* communication is like studying *noncardiac* physiology. His point is well taken. It is

---

Every Human Being Is a Separate Language

Pat Hardman
IN Correspondent

Sometimes silence is best.

Words are curious things, at best approximations. And every human being is a separate language.

If the knowledge of that paralyzes you, withdraw for a little. Silence is best.

And even if you accept the awkwardness of language and try to work with it, you can have times when you agonize over your inability to make the phrase empathetic with the moment.

Maybe silence is best, for a little while.

Conflict over abstract ideas, the fact that man is a finite being and has no omniscient knowledge and no answers to metaphysical questions—that can paralyze, too. You start wondering: What is reality?

So hold your tongue, turn your back and be silent.

If there are no words, or no right words, choose quiet. Better to be silent than communicate on a mediocre level. Better to be quiet than uneasy over what you have said.

You can still smile or frown or laugh or cry, can't you? And in turning your back, you do not lose your eyes. You are always looking at something. You have simply changed your view for awhile. Restraint is not rejection.

Problems From People

The problem comes from the people around you. Who can ask for privacy and have others watching their aloneness? Demand time by yourself and people—know. They don't understand, they just know and that destroys all chance of being really alone and quiet.

A friend's knowledge of you is an increase and sharing. For a stranger to hold knowledge of you is an invasion and violation.

So don't tell anyone, don't ask for anything, just take what you need. Follow the demands of your confusion and find your place. Don't worry about consequences of opinion. If you do, you have forgotten who you want to listen to you.

Impulse to Silence

There are times when nothing is more important that your own impulses, the impulse to silence or isolation among them. The call of a friend: "Come here." The call of a moment: "Experience me." The call of yourself: "Go and find me."

High points and low points, too deep for words. Indecision and conflict that cannot be voiced. Doubt of your own tongue.

Very well, then, choose silence. If you cannot be great with words, be great in quiet.

Nick Pavloff

not easy to dissect human inter-action and make one diagnosis which concerns only verbal be-havior and another which con-cerns only nonverbal behavior. The verbal dimension is so inti-mately woven and so subtly rep-resented in so much of what we have previously labeled *non-verbal* that the term does not always adequately describe the behavior under study. Some of the most noteworthy scholars associated with nonverbal study refuse to segregate words from gestures and hence, work under the broader terms *communica-tion* or *face-to-face interaction.*

The theoretical position taken by Dance concerning the whole process of communication goes even further in order to call to our attention that perhaps not everything labeled nonverbal is literally nonverbal. Dance might even argue that there is no such thing as uniquely human commu-nication that is nonverbal. He takes the position that all symbols are verbal and that human com-munication is defined as the elic-iting of a response through verbal symbols. He does not deny the fact that we may engage in non-verbal behaviors, but the instant these behaviors are interpreted by another in terms of words, they become verbal phenomena.

While many researchers rec-ognize this theoretical and con-ceptual problem with the term *nonverbal,* their research pro-ceeds. Most of this research is based on the premise that if words are not spoken or written, they become nonverbal in nature. Also included in the term *non-verbal* under this definition are all those nuances which surround words—e.g., tone of voice or type of print. This is frequently called paralanguage. In their early clas-sic, *Nonverbal Communication: Notes on the Visual Perception*

of Human Relations, Ruesch and Kees took essentially this point of view. But, in addition, the authors outlined what they considered to be the primary elements in the study of nonverbal communica-tion. This classification system has been highly influential in providing a basis for most of the work done in this field to date.

In broad terms, nonverbal forms of codification fall into three distinct categories:

Sign Language includes all those forms of codification in which words, numbers, and punctuation signs have been supplanted by gestures; these vary from the "monosyllabic" gesture of the hitchhiker to such complete systems as the language of the deaf.

Action Language embraces all movements that are not used exclu-sively as signals. Such acts as walk-ing and drinking, for example, have a dual function: on one hand they serve personal needs, and on the other they constitute statements to those who may perceive them.

Object Language comprises all in-tentional and nonintentional display of material things, such as imple-ments, machines, art objects, archi-tectural structures, and—last but not least—the human body and whatever clothes or covers it. The embodiment of letters as they occur in books and on signs has a material substance, and this aspect of words also has to be considered as object language.[2]

Another way of defining a field of study is to examine the work that has been done to see if any common directions have been fol-lowed. As previously mentioned, one common trend is the assump-tion that nonverbal communica-tion encompasses those events in which words are not spoken or written. Other recurring trends are exemplified by the following classification system which repre-sents a definition of the field of nonverbal human communication as evidenced in the writing and research available.

Nonverbal Dimensions of Human Communication

Body Motion or Kinesic Behavior

Body motion, or kinesic behavior, typically includes gestures, movements of the body, limbs, hands, head, feet and legs, facial expressions (smiles), eye behavior (blinking, direction and length of gaze, and pupil dilation) and posture. The furrow of the brow, the slump of a shoulder and the tilt of a head—all are within the purview of kinesics. Obviously, there are different types of nonverbal behavior just as there are different types of verbal behavior. Some nonverbal cues are very specific, some more general; some intended to communicate, some expressive only; some provide information about emotions, others carry information about personality traits or attitudes. In an effort to sort through the relatively unknown world of nonverbal behavior, Ekman and Friesen developed a system for classifying nonverbal behavioral acts.[3] These categories include:

Emblems. These are nonverbal acts which have a direct verbal translation or dictionary definition—usually consisting of a word or two or a phrase. There is high agreement among members of a culture or subculture on the verbal definition. The gestures used to represent "A-OK" or "Peace" are examples of emblems for a large part of our culture. Toffler notes in his bestseller, *Future Shock*, that some emblems which were perceived as semi-obscene are now becoming more respectable with changing sexual values. He uses the example of the upraised finger—designating "up yours." Emblems are frequently used when verbal channels are blocked (or fail) and are usually used to communicate. The sign language of the deaf, nonverbal gestures used by television production personnel, signals used by two underwater swimmers, or motions made by two people who are too far apart to make audible signals practical—all these are emblems. Our own awareness of emblem usage is about the same as our awareness of word choice.

Nonverbal messages come from body motions, physical characteristics, touching behavior, vocal cues, social and personal space, objects, and environmental factors.

Illustrators. These are nonverbal acts which are directly tied to, or accompany, speech—serving to illustrate what is being said verbally. These may be movements which accent or emphasize a word or phrase; movements which sketch a path of thought; movements pointing to present objects; movements depicting a spatial relationship; or movements which depict a bodily action. Illustrators seem to be within our awareness, but not as explicitly as emblems. They are used intentionally to help communicate, but not as deliberately as emblems. They are probably learned by watching others.

Affect Displays. These are simply facial configurations which display affective states. They can repeat, augment, contradict, or be unrelated to, verbal affective statements. Once the display has occurred, there is usually a high degree of awareness, but it can occur without any awareness. Often, affect displays are not intended to communicate, but they can be intentional.

Regulators. These are nonverbal acts which maintain and regulate the back and forth nature of speaking and listening between two or more interactants. They tell the speaker to continue, repeat, elaborate, hurry up, become more interesting, give the other a chance to talk, etc. They consist mainly of head nods and eye movements, and there seem to be class and cultural differences in usage—improper usage connoting rudeness. These acts are not tied to specific spoken behavior. They seem to be on the periphery of our awareness and are generally difficult to inhibit. They are like overlearned habits and are almost involuntary, but we are very much aware of these signals sent by others. Probably the most familiar regulator is the head nod—the equivalent of the verbal mm-hmm.

Adaptors. These nonverbal behaviors are perhaps the most difficult to define and involve the most speculation. They are labeled adaptors because they are thought to develop in childhood as adaptive efforts to satisfy needs, perform actions, manage emotions, develop social contacts, or perform a host of other functions. They are not really coded; they are fragments of actual aggressive, sexual or intimate behavior and often reveal personal orientations or characteristics covered by verbal messages. Leg movements can often be adaptors, showing residues of kicking aggression, sexual invitation, or flight. Many of the restless movements of the hands and feet which have typically been considered indicators of anxiety may be residues of adaptors necessary for flight from the interaction. Adaptors are possibly triggered by verbal behavior in a given situation which is associated with condi-

What Your Tongue May Really Be Saying

On a conscious level, the human tongue is regularly put to a wide variety of useful purposes: it licks postage stamps, demolishes ice-cream cones and also performs a major function in the delivery of that staccato sputter of derision known as the Bronx cheer, or raspberry. In Tibet, when one hill tribesman encounters another, the two exchange greetings by protruding their tongues, much as two Westerners might wave or shake hands.

Now, however, a team of evolutionary biologists at the University of Pennsylvania has completed a five-year study of how people use their tongues at the unconscious level. Their major finding seems to be that the unconscious display of the tongue is a universal sign of aversion to social encounter—a sign that is used alike by all races, and also by such other primates as orangutans and gorillas.

Drs. W. John Smith and Julia Chase, assisted by graduate student Anna Katz Lieblich, first studied tongue displays at Philadelphia's Mulberry Tree Nursery School. There, they noted that toddlers tend to show their tongues when they are engrossed in difficult tasks, such as finger painting or climbing over obstacles, and also when they are involved in awkward social situations, such as receiving a scolding for misbehavior. This suggested to Smith that the action indicated a desire to be left alone, so he decided to test the hypothesis by trying to provoke tongue showing.

(continued on page 65)

Reprinted from "What Your Tongue May Really Be Saying" in *Newsweek*, April 2, 1973. Copyright Newsweek, Inc. 1973, reprinted by permission.

United Press International Photo

tions occurring when the adaptive habit was first learned. We are typically unaware of adaptors.

Physical Characteristics

Whereas the previous section was concerned with movement and motion, this category covers things which remain relatively unchanged during the period of interaction. They are influential nonverbal cues which are not movement-bound. Included are such things as: physique or body shape, general attractiveness, body or breath odors, height, weight, hair, and skin color or tone.

Touching Behavior

For some, kinesic study includes touch behavior; for others, however, actual physical contact constitutes a separate class of events. Some researchers are concerned with touching behavior as an important factor in the child's early development; some are concerned with adult touching behavior. Subcategories may include stroking, hitting, greetings and farewells, holding, guiding another's movements, and other, more specific instances.

Paralanguage

Simply put, paralanguage deals with how something is said and not what is said. It deals with the range of nonverbal vocal cues surrounding common speech behavior. Trager felt paralanguage had the following components:[4]

Voice Qualities. This includes such things as pitch range, pitch control, rhythm control, tempo, articulation control, resonance, glottis control, and vocal lip control.

Vocalizations. *Vocal characterizers* include such things as laughing, crying, sighing, yawning, belching, swallowing, heavily marked inhaling or exhaling, coughing, clearing of the throat, hiccupping, moaning, groaning, whining, yelling, whispering, sneezing, snoring, stretching, etc. *Vocal qualifiers* include intensity (overloud to oversoft), pitch height (overhigh to overlow), and extent (extreme drawl to extreme clipping). *Vocal segregates* are such things as "uh-huh," "um," "uh," "ah," and variants thereof.

Related work on such topics as silent pauses (beyond junctures), intruding sounds, speech errors, and latency would probably be included in this category.

Proxemics

Proxemics is generally considered to be the study of man's use and perception of his social and personal space. Under this heading, we find a body of work called small group ecology which concerns itself with how people use and respond to spatial relationships in formal and informal group settings. Such studies deal with seating arrangements, and spatial arrangements as related to leadership, communication flow, and the task at hand. The influence of architectural features on residential living units and even on communities is also of concern to those who study man's proxemic behavior. On an even broader level, some attention has been given to spatial relationships in crowds and densely populated situations. Man's personal space orientation is sometimes studied in the context of conversational distance—and how

(continued from page 64)

Adults: Smith stationed himself in the path of a 4-year-old girl who was running a repeated route from room to room, and caught her eye as she approached him. The girl averted her eyes and protruded her tongue. She repeated this behavior four times. But on the sixth circuit, now sure that Smith would not grab her, the girl showed no hint of her tongue.

The biologists then made unobtrusive observations of tongue-showing among the general public in Philadelphia and in Panama. They found that it occurred among adults in exactly the same settings as with children. Adults show their tongues during tasks requiring intense concentration—when making a tricky shot at pool, for example, or backing into a small parking space—and also in socially threatening situations, such as being interrupted in conversation. Extending the study further, Smith and his colleagues watched a number of gorillas and orangutans at close quarters, with identical results. For although the apes tended to show their tongues more prominently than did humans, the circumstances involved either complex tasks such as peeling bananas with their toes, or unpleasant situations in which the apes were scolded for fighting. On a conscious level, apes also use their tongues to eat ice-cream cones.

it varies according to sex, status, roles, cultural orientation, etc. The term "territoriality" is also frequently used in the study of proxemics to denote the human tendency to stake out personal territory—or untouchable space— much as wild animals and birds do.

Artifacts

Artifacts include the manipulation of objects in contact with the interacting persons which may act as nonverbal stimuli. These artifacts include perfume, clothes, lipstick, eyeglasses, wigs and other hairpieces, false eyelashes, eyeliners, and the whole repertoire of falsies and "beauty" aids.

Environmental Factors

Up to this point we have been concerned with the appearance and behavior of the persons involved in communicating. This category concerns those elements which impinge on the human relationship, but which are not directly a part of it. Environmental factors include the furniture, architectural style, interior decorating, lighting conditions, smells, colors, temperature, additional noises or music, etc. within which the interaction occurs. Variations in arrangements, materials, shapes, or surfaces of objects in the interacting environment can be extremely influential on the outcome of an interpersonal relationship. This category also includes what might be called traces of action. For instance, as you observe cigarette butts, orange peels, and waste paper left by the person you will soon interact with, you are forming an impression which will eventually influence your meeting.

Summary

The term *nonverbal* is commonly used to describe all human communication events which transcend spoken or written words. At the same time we should realize that many of these nonverbal events and behaviors are interpreted through verbal symbols. In this sense, then, they are not truly *non*verbal. The theoretical writings and research on nonverbal communication can be broken down into the following seven areas: (1) body motion or kinesics (emblems, illustrators, affect displays, regulators, and adaptors), (2) physical characteristics, (3) touching behavior, (4) paralanguage (vocal qualities and vocalizations), (5) proxemics, (6) artifacts, (7) environment. Nonverbal communication should not be studied as an isolated unit, but as an inseparable part of the total communication process. Nonverbal communication may serve to repeat, contradict, substitute, complement, accent, or regulate verbal communication. Nonverbal communication is important because of the role it plays in the total communication system, the tremendous quantity of informational cues it gives in any particular situation, and because of its use in fundamental areas of our daily life. Nonverbal behavior is partly taught, partly imitative, and partly instinctive. There is a growing body of evidence which suggests a pancultural (or universal) element in emotional facial behavior, but this does not suggest there are not cultural differences in such things as the circumstances which elicit an emotion, the display rules which govern the management of facial behavior in certain settings, and the action consequences of an emotion.

1. O. Pfungst, *Clever Hans, The Horse of Mr. Von Osten* (New York: Holt, Rinehart and Winston, 1911).

2. J. Ruesch and W. Kees, *Nonverbal Communication: Notes on the Visual Perception of Human Relations* (Berkeley and Los Angeles: University of California Press, 1956): 189. Originally published by the University of California Press; reprinted by permission of The Regents of the University of California.

3. P. Ekman and W. V. Friesen. "The Repertoire of Nonverbal Behavior: Categories, Origins, Usage, and Coding," *Semiotica* 1 (1969): 49–98.

4. G. L. Trager, "Paralanguage: A First Approximation," *Studies in Linguistics* 13 (1958): 1–12.

Every Little Movement Has a Meaning All Its Own...

Flora Davis

Did you ever walk into your own living room, hold an innocuous two-minute conversation with your husband, and come away feeling vaguely disturbed not by what he had said but by what he hadn't? Perhaps you began with a question about his plans for the afternoon; he outlined them briefly for you; you made some remark about the weather and what it might do to your begonias; he sympathized. A perfectly ordinary conversation but somehow—and you couldn't possibly say why—you went away convinced that he was secretly angry about something.

That is called intuition and it is not the elusive "sixth sense" it is made out to be, but a skill like any other: the ability to interpret nonverbal behavior. You *saw* your husband's anger in the tenseness of his body, and, if he gestured at all as he spoke, in something sharp and aggressive in his movements. Possibly there were hints of anger in his expression, since it's difficult for a man to lie convincingly with his face. He might keep his mouth carefully neutral, for example, but the tip-off could be faint scowl lines in his forehead, or something cold in the expression of his eyes.

Whenever two people meet face to face, they communicate both in words and in body movements. Professor Ray L. Birdwhistell of the University of Pennsylvania, inventor of the young science of

Nick Pavloff

kinesics (the study of communication through body motion) believes that less than 35 percent of the social meaning in any situation is carried by the words that are spoken. All the rest is nonverbal.

In childhood we learn to read nonverbal signals almost as if we were learning a code. A small boy learns to move like a boy, and like an American—because an American moves less gracefully than a Frenchman, for example, and without the verve of an Italian. A child also learns to interpret facial expressions and body movements; before he is distracted by words, he is more dependent upon body signals than he ever will be again.

Until a few years ago, only a few scientists realized that there *was* a nonverbal code. Today, however, there is a growing interest in face-to-face communication, and as studies of the subject progress, we are at last beginning to find out how the code works.

Body movements communicate in many different ways. Sometimes they emphasize or illustrate what is said ("He went *that* way"—with a jab of the finger or a nod of the head). They may act as conversational traffic signals, indicating when someone is finishing what he has to say. His eyes meet yours and hold; his ankle, which has been flexed, relaxes. Before his voice trails off you have realized that it is now your turn to talk.

It is, of course, the nonverbal clues to emotion that interest people the most because they are so enormously important to many relationships. We pick them up intuitively and they tell us when the other person is angry, sad, bored, whether he likes us or not—feelings often not put into words.

A friend of mine recently told me this story: "I was at a party the other night and was introduced to the most attractive man. We talked for quite a while—mostly about drainpipes, because he'd been having trouble with his —and suddenly I began to feel that he was attracted to me, just as I was to him. Yet there we were, standing talking about his drainpipes, and I couldn't imagine why I should feel so sure."

Folklore tells us that people in love tend to stand or sit close together and to look often and deeply into one another's eyes. If the clues to this man's emotions had been that obvious, undoubtedly my friend would have picked them up quite consciously. There are, however, other, subtler symptoms that have been analyzed in detail by Dr. Albert Scheflen of Bronx State Hospital, working with Professor Birdwhistell, at Eastern Pennsylvania Psychiatric Institute.

There may be small but visible changes in the way a person holds his body. Women in love (and men, too) really can become briefly more beautiful, for with that first rush of pleasure that is triggered by sexual attraction, muscles snap to attention. Lines in the face no longer sag and bags beneath the eyes tend to disappear. Jowls diminish, pot bellies recede and a woman's legs may take on the sleek, taut look of a cheesecake photograph. Her eyes shine, too, and her lower lip swells softly.

A courting woman is apt to play with her hair, stroking it or twining a strand about one finger. There is, in fact, a particular gesture of smoothing the hair with a twist of the hand so that the palm faces outward that women typically make in courtship situations with a man. Men go in for grooming and tidying when they are courting. Scientists, for example, speak of "tie-preening" and "sock-preening," meaning the gestures a man makes as he adjusts the knot on his tie or smooths his socks. These usually are not serious attempts to improve his appearance. A woman who is sexually attracted to a man often will hold her head to one side and stand with her pelvis tipped up and forward in that familiar model-on-the-runway pose, while a man is apt to stand with his pelvis rolled back.

Couples court not only with gestures and with their eyes, but in the way they arrange their bodies, too. Standing close together, they generally face each other squarely or touching, though in a nonsexual relationship at that distance each would be more apt to twist slightly to one side to avoid body contact. When sitting and talking to a third person, they may leave their upper bodies politely open, arms down or out but not folded across the chest, yet form a closed circle with their legs, knees crossed from the outer sides in so that the tips of the toes almost meet. People often dramatize a relationship with their bodies in this way, building a barricade with their arms or legs, shutting others out or including them in.

And sometimes a couple will go in for touching—though they don't quite touch each other. In a restaurant, a woman may run a fingertip slowly around the rim of a glass, or trace patterns in the tablecloth, indicating a silent conflict between the desire to touch the man and the feeling that, really, perhaps she ought not to.

Palming is the subtlest signal of all. An Anglo-Saxon woman usually holds her hands curled and rarely shows her palms. When she is attracted to a man, however, gestures she would normally make with her palm in, such as raising a cigarette to her lips or covering up a cough, she may make, awkwardly perhaps, with her palm facing out. We might say that whenever a woman shows a man a flash of palm, she is attracted to him, whether consciously or not—and often that would be true.

Palming is something people also do in greeting one another—sometimes when they like each other, sometimes when they are simply meeting for business reasons. This is an example of the problems inherent in trying to read nonverbal messages consciously rather than intuitively—a gesture may not signify the same thing in every situation. The message always is modified by whatever the person is doing with the rest of his body at the time, and even by what he is saying.

But if you will operate largely on intuition you can frequently pick up much that you otherwise might have missed. Posture-watching can be great fun. I remember one evening observing two men, close friends, earnestly discussing personal matters. They sat at opposite ends of a sofa, each with legs propped up and one knee bent in an unusual and identical posture. They were as alike as matching bookends, except that one—the one who had come to ask for advice—had an arm stretched across the back of the sofa, opening himself toward his friend, while the other sat with arms folded, expressing in this, as well as by what he said, certain basic reservations.

In almost any social gathering you will see people echoing one another's body positions. Two individuals may sit in precisely the same way, right leg crossed over left, for example, hands clasped behind head. Or they may do it in the mirror-image way, one reversing to left leg over right. Dr. Scheflen calls these congruent postures and believes that whenever people strongly share a point of view, they are very apt to share a posture.

At a party where four or more people get together, it is not uncommon for several distinct postural sets to develop. This is not merely coincidence, for if one person rearranges his body the other members of his set often will follow suit until *all* are congruent again. and if you listen to the conversations, you usually will find that those who think alike on the subject being discussed sit alike as well.

There are people who deliberately assume postures to convey a message. A psychiatrist may strike the posture of his patient as a way of getting a clue to his feelings, or sometimes to establish rapport. A lawyer I know says that occasionally he attempts to read a jury by assuming a particular posture – hand cradling chin, for example, one arm crossing his chest. He believes that the jurors who imitate him are the ones sympathetic to his case.

Posture-matching usually is done unconsciously. There is a research film in which a young girl from time to time companionably adopts her mother's posture – only to have the mother shift immediately to a different position. When this sequence is repeated several times, it becomes clear that this is a way the mother shuts the girl out. Though she does not do it deliberately, apparently the message registers on some unconscious level, because the girl's reaction is to turn her head aside and withdraw from the conversation.

People relate to each other not only by their postures but by body orientation. In a group of three what you will notice is each person pointing the upper part of his body at one of his companions and the lower part at the other. If, on the other hand, two of the three are relating only to each other, the third will feel inexplicably left out, no matter how carefully he is included in the conversation.

For you and me what is most interesting about all of this is the discovery that people are so physically sensitive to one another. If you observe, you will see a husband and wife mirror each other's facial expressions in the same way they share certain words and phrases. Or you may see friends or family members who have certain gestures in common. A son pulls thoughtfully on his earlobe in a way poignantly reminiscent of his father. Two women, close friends, adjust their skirts as they sit down with the same graceful scooping motion. The scientists say this is visible evidence of the way people identify with each other. In these small but revealing ways we are related to one another; we share more than we know.

It is also true, of course, that sometimes what we pick up intuitively is not a feeling of closeness but a sense of distance. A woman I know recently returned from a routine medical checkup feeling rather annoyed with her doctor. She had a number of minor complaints and the doctor did not really listen to her, she said. He seemed, in fact, almost bored. Her husband said it was all in her imagination, but I don't think so. I suspect she was reacting at least in part to the doctor's eye behavior – where he looked and when and for how long. This is one way a person signals the fact that he is paying attention.

Eye movements are a subtle but enormously important element in body language. In childhood we learn instinctively what to do with our eyes in different situations and what to expect of others. The pattern common to ordinary, fairly formal conversation has been described by Dr. Adam Kendon, a British psychologist. It might have applied to my friend's conversation with her doctor. It works like this:

As she began to speak, she looked away from the doctor. But as she talked on she glanced back at him from time to time, usually as she paused at the end of a phrase or sentence. When she did, he nodded or perhaps murmured something and she looked away again. Her glances at him lasted about as long as her glances always did, but she didn't look at him when she hesitated or tripped over a word. As she came to the end of her talk, she gave him a significantly longer glance. If she had not, he probably would not have realized it was his turn to talk – and an awkward pause might have followed.

When the doctor in turn took up the conversation, she spent much more time looking at him than she had while she was speaking. Now when their eyes met, it was her turn to make a reassuring sign. It is not difficult to see the logic behind this. She looked away at the start of her talk and during pauses to avoid being distracted while she organized her thoughts. She glanced at the doctor from time to time to make sure that he was listening and to see how he was reacting. While he talked she looked at him steadily to show that she was paying attention.

Now let's examine what could have been conveyed by only slight exaggerations of the normal pattern:

When the doctor was talking, if he looked away from her more than she expected him to, she would get the impression that he was uncertain about what he was saying. If he looked at her steadily, however, she would feel that he was both confident and interested in her reactions.

If he looked at her quite steadily while she talked, she would feel that he agreed with her, or at least that he was paying close attention. But if he glanced away very often she might simply feel that he was either bored or not listening—which is exactly how she did feel.

The more time a person spends looking at you, assuming there is a warm, interested expression on his face, the more you will feel that he is interested in *you* rather than only in what you are saying. Looking is one say of saying "I like you."

"I always know within the first five minutes after I meet a person whether we're going to hit it off or not," said a young mother. "I know what *I* feel—whether I like, dislike, or am indifferent—and somehow or other it's almost always mutual and I can tell that it is."

There are all kinds of bodily ways of expressing liking, and they are important because it's something we often are too embarrassed or reserved to put into words. A person may do it by standing closer to you than she otherwise might, by facing you squarely, by leaning slightly toward you, by smiling often, by sharing your posture, by picking up the very rhythm of your gestures. Of course, if all these things were done at once, you would feel distinctly uncomfortable. Except in passionate love affairs these body messages are seldom sent simultaneously. Taken together, they constitute intimacy. If you vary one element, you must make compensating changes in the others or the intimacy level will shoot up. (This illustrates again that the nonverbal message comes from the whole body, not from an isolated gesture.) For example, if you're suddenly forced to stand very close to someone with whom you are not intimate, you will find that he avoids your eyes and probably avoids smiling, too. If he is really uncomfortable about it, he may even barricade himself behind folded arms and tightly crossed legs.

Just as body signals reveal when someone likes you, they may warn you that a person is evasive or lying. Have you ever wondered why you believe your child's most outrageous stories at some times, and at other times disbelieve more plausible ones? When I was a child, I used to think my mother was a mind reader, because I was never really able to fool her; now it seems clear to me that she was simply a shrewd observer—and not afraid to trust her intuition.

It is difficult but not impossible to lie nonverbally. Dr. Paul Ekman, a San Francisco psychologist, has found that some people do it so well that it is impossible to find them out. Most people, however, reveal that they are lying in many small ways. They may fail to meet your eyes, or you may notice that they keep picking at themselves, or that a foot taps nervously. And their facial expressions betray insincerity. They may smile but somehow the smile spreads across the face at the wrong speed—it disappears either too slowly or too fast.

The wrong kind of smile in the wrong situation is a distinct tip-off to emotions a person is trying to conceal. Scientists in Britain have now classified several varieties of smiles. Friends greet each other, for example, with smiles that show only the upper teeth. Formal introductions, on the other hand, call for upturned lips with no teeth showing. If you meet a close friend on the street and she gives you that polite and formal smile, you may wonder what is wrong. If, however, she gives you a broad grin that bares both upper and lower teeth, you probably will feel that she is overdoing it, since this is the smile usually reserved for moments of particular pleasure. When a person bites her lower lip as she smiles, it is often because she feels subordinate to another person.

We all recognize the cold smile, the one that touches the mouth only, quite easily. Changes in the expression of the eyes bring the warmth to a smile—even a broad one is phony if the eyes are unaffected.

Scientists speak of body language as a complicated code—one that is difficult to interpret. To the layman it is literally an eye-opening experience to learn about, though I believe ultimately what you become *most* aware of are the signals you send yourself. Midway in a conversation you may realize that you are sharing postures comfortably with a friend, or that you have just smoothed your hair in that provocative grooming gesture, palming all the way. Or it may strike you that you have been avoiding someone else's eyes.

If, instead of becoming self-conscious about it, you can accept the fact that people always have known intuitively more than you told them in words about what you feel, about who you are, then you may profit and achieve a new openness—possibly even an increased ability to make use of your intuition.

Of course, it is taking a chance to leap to conclusions on the basis of a single gesture or posture. Sometimes however, when your intuition is whispering that "he's lying" or "she's angry," you may catch a small, revealing gesture that makes you absolutely sure—that is the fascination of the study. Eventually, you may find that your intuition, once buried deep in the unconscious, is operating at least partly on a conscious level and that you are picking up feelings that you never dreamed were there.

What you do with insights such as these is up to you. Some, perhaps, are best ignored. But in many cases, within the family or with your friends, it is helpful to talk about them. It can be, you will find, completely liberating to get the unspoken emotions out in the open where they always have belonged.

Prods

1. Verbal maps are maps or pictures drawn with words. Why is it important that our verbal maps represent the territory they describe?
2. Appropriate verbal and nonverbal symbols are essential to effective communication. How can we develop the skill to send and interpret symbols properly?
3. What are some of the tools of clear thinking? How can they help us communicate more effectively?
4. What are nonverbal messages? What are their special characteristics?
5. Look up ten nouns in a dictionary. Count the number of examples following the definition that list a male illustration first and a female illustration second, if at all. For example, MESS—a dirty or untidy condition: *His* room is a mess. Are there any differences?

3
COMPONENT

THE ENVIRONMENT

PROBE 14 Communication environments are affected by space-age technology.

PROBE 15 Social trends and technological advancements influence your life.

PROBE 16 Communications may shape our future environments.

PROBE 17 Mass communication is more effective among people who are predisposed toward the message.

Component 3: The Environment

The environmental component of human communication concerns the conditions in which communication occurs. Part of the environment is the social context, or cultural milieu, which consists of the physical surroundings, setting, and location. For three people in a room, their immediate environment might be the room (its shape, size, and furnishings), the air (its circulation, temperature, and humidity), the sounds (their tone, frequency, and quality).

Part of the environment is cultural, determined by community, state, national, and international affairs. Our community may decide to authorize a cable television option for TV owners, immediately prompting message campaigns in support of or opposed to such action. Our state may increase its sales tax, igniting mass demonstrations, protests, and picketing of the legislature by irate consumers. Our nation may allow supersonic jets to land at our airports, creating listening and noise pollution problems for nearby residents. Or an international terrorist organization may hijack an airplane forcing several nations' police and military personnel to cooperate in seeking the release of the passengers.

In all of these cases, people are interacting with others within the context of both immediate and broader cultural environments. Most of us live in an environment molded by institutions and mass media. It is an environment of unrest and change. In this component we examine specific variables within our environment and show how they affect our dyadic, small-group, serial, and speaker-audience communication relationships.

Space-Age Communication

L. S. Harms

We are probably the first humans to see our planet through the eye of a spaceship camera; and, as a curious consequence, we have come to call the blue planet our spaceship earth. We now talk of life support systems and interstellar communication systems as casually as we talk about hamburgers and recorded music. We expect that before the year 2000, the first human child will be born on the moon. We begin to develop a space-age attitude. Space-age technology changes the way we communicate about our earth spaceship and our earthman culture.

Our space-age attitude is best described as cybernetic. We employ cybernetic methods. Cybernetics is defined as the processes of control and communication in man and machine; cybernetics includes both communication facilities and messages. The term *cybernetics* most often appears along with terms such as *technology, communication,* and *culture.*

From our cybernetic view of human communication, we find that technology and communication and culture are so closely related that it often is difficult to deal with them separately. But we must separate technology and culture from communication just enough to help us discover how communication does what it does. That separation or analysis provides a starting point for the study of human communication in the space age.

Technology

Technology may be viewed as those inventions of man that became widely useful through the process of manufacturing. Communication satellites and telephones are good examples; so are spaceships and jet planes. Technology is inanimate and nonliving.

Technological devices, taken one by one, amount to rather little. A disconnected telephone mechanism in a new home is only a fair paperweight. But wire that same telephone mechanism into the telephone network of the community, and it suddenly has a thousand known and potential uses. The home community network can also be connected to a satellite; and three properly positioned satellites provide a world network. Each home community can be connected to any other community; any telephone can be connected to any other telephone in the world; any person can talk to any other person. How many digits would be required for worldwide direct dialing?

A car parked in a garage is a big toy for a small child. But decide to go—rather than telephone—to a destination anywhere in the world. Drive your car to a nearby airport. From that airport board an airplane and fly to any other airport in the world, rent a car, and drive to your destination. All road networks lead to a nearby airport. Each airport is a ground station in a worldwide air

---

PROBE 14. Communication environments are affected by space-age technology.

Automation and Communication: A Legend

Florence B. Freedman

Not once upon a time, but now; not make-believe, but real: In a clearing of a remote forest, in a country which shall be nameless, stands a completely automated atomic power plant.

So cleverly designed is this plant that the only human needed to tend it is an old watchman whose sole duty is to see that no human enters to interfere with the superbly functioning machinery.

Since even the most cleverly designed machine made by men might conceivably develop a fault, this plant has a device for self-diagnosis and control. If the machinery overheats, it quickly turns itself off; then it dials the phone number of the chief engineer, whose office is in the metropolis. To him it delivers a pre-recorded message: "The machinery has overheated and turned itself off. Please send a repair crew." (If you wonder at the "please," be assured that just because the machine is inhuman, there's no reason for it to be impolite.)

In the life of the atomic power plant it dialed the chief engineer's number three times. Twice the message was received and men were sent to make the necessary repairs. But before the third incident occurred the telephone company, ever alert to improve its system, had made some changes in automatic dialing. This time, instead of reaching the engineer, the message met with this response: "This is a recording. The number you have reached is not a working number. This is a recording. The number you have reached is not . . ."

Soon after, a soothsayer who lived in the neighborhood forest learned of this in the manner in which soothsayers are wont to acquire information. And he made a notation in his diary:

This is the way the world will end: There will be neither a bang nor a whimper. The only sound or semblance of prayer will be a tape intoning, "The world is ending. The world is ending. Please send a repair crew."

To which the sole reply will be, "This is a recorded message. The number you have reached is not a working number."

Reprinted from "Automation and Communication: A Legend" by Florence B. Freedman in *ETC., A Review of General Semantics*, Vol. XXIII, No. 4, December 1966, pp. 484–85. Used by permission of the publisher, the American Association of Colleges for Teacher Education.

transportation network. How many airline passenger seats are needed? Where? When?

Our use of communication technology often creates both problems and possibilities on a world scale. Fifteen digits are required for worldwide direct dialing. But when each person learns to want his own mobile telephone, the problem changes again. How many airline passenger seats are needed? All of us know we sometimes can't reserve a seat at the exact time we wish to travel; other times, we are one of but 20 passengers on a 200-seat airliner for a 2,000-mile flight. We have problems to solve.

Telecommunication technology and transportation technology encircle the globe. The telecommunication technology— satellites, telephones, radio, television—makes possible a worldwide telecommunication network; the transportation technology— airplanes, automobiles, trains, ships—make possible a transportation communication network. Taken together, the two world networks create new choices and open new opportunities for man.

Both the telecommunication and transportation networks are *demand limited*. Their present size is limited by present demand. We can now manufacture more satellites and airplanes, for instance, than our world can use. The supply can exceed the known demand. But how can we predict the demand for major worldwide services when such services have not been abailable before? The use of technology is strongly influenced by culture.

We turn now to the matter of human culture.

Culture

Culture can be considered to be everything man learns from and creates through experience that he values enough to pass on from one generation to the next. Speech communication patterns and dramatic literature are convenient examples; so are human institutions such as local political parties and the United Nations. Cultural heritage contrasts with biological inheritance. Culture is not inherited; it is relearned by each man.

Technological change in the world leads to a change in culture; it may promote cultural variety or cultural similarity. Machines make time for more human leisure. Greater leisure time may provide the opportunities for development of new patterns of human experience that move through the stages from fad to cult to subculture. Worldwide television news broadcasts and other informational programs can lead on to cultural similarity. The question before us is this: In any culture, to what extent should it promote similarity? What mix of variety and similarity is best for us as we live in our world?

Today a man may become monocultural, bi-cultural, or multi-cultural. Culture can be viewed as something that can be ordered on a line from one to several. A man may consider himself to be a member of one, two, or several cultural groups. Culture may also be viewed as something more fluid. A man may consider himself at one time to be a member of a single cultural group; at another time, of several groups; or he may not wish to look at the matter of cultural identity that way at all. There are choices today, and increasingly persons feel strongly about those choices they have.

The possible viewpoints about culture are as varied as the cultures that develop them. McLuhan, for instance, insists that the technologies of telecommuni-

Which American Lit Course Should You Choose?
Compare Professor Murray Mangrove's
"THE AMERICAN NOVEL"
With All The Others

	Prof. Mangrove	Prof. "B"	Prof. "C"	Prof. "D"	Prof. "E"
Special "Breeze-Through" Mid-Terms	YES	NO	NO	NO	NO
Six "No-Penalty" Class-Cuts	YES	NO	YES	NO	NO
Less Than 5% Failures Guaranteed	YES	NO	NO	NO	NO
"Second Chance" Final Exams	YES	NO	NO	NO	YES
Toleration Of Stoned Students	YES	NO	NO	NO	YES
Avoidance Of Dull Authors Like Henry James	YES	NO	NO	NO	NO
Selection Of Groovy Authors Like Kurt Vonnegut	YES	NO	NO	YES	NO
Elimination Of Surprise "Quickie" Quizzes	YES	NO	NO	YES	NO
Valuable Door Prizes	YES	NO	NO	NO	NO

Select The American Lit Course That Offers You MORE!
THE AMERICAN NOVEL   2 p.m. M-W-F   Brindle Hall

Don't Miss Doctor Hans Jungfrau's
THE LITERATURE OF YODELING
11 a.m.   Tues.—Thurs.   Brindle Hall

cation and transportation make all of us members of the same global village; we are each of us members of a family and live in a small community with others of similar ethnic origins and cultures; and that culture must be maintained and passed on to the next generation. These feelings of "global village" and "ethnic enclave" represent diverse views of culture. Agreement there is not.

From the human viewpoint, the linkages provided by the technologies of transportation and telecommunication shrink the size of the world. A man walks to a nearby community. He associates with members of that community and exchanges information with them. Later, he may engage in drum talk with them. Or, the events may occur in reverse order. The drum network may carry the message, "Come to the meeting." Either way, humans are linked by their networks of communication.

So far as we know, from 500,000 B.C. up to about 1750 A.D., change was rather slow. A few of the traditional villages had become cities. Paris, London, New York, and Tokyo are among the early cities that are "world cities" today. They were then and are now *communication centers* for their regions. In and around these cities, communication facilities were invented and developed. The period from 1750 to about 1900 saw transoceanic steamboats and telephone, trains and telegraph, automobiles and wireless radio come into use. By 1900, the transportation and telecommunication technologies had gathered force to the point of becoming a communication revolution.

The transportation and telecommunication revolution unfolds in a seventy-year period from about 1900 to about 1970. By 1900, national rail and telegraph networks

exist. The nation-state is created by the telegraph and the train. International Telecommunication Union works out the agreements necessary for the later emergence of world communication networks.

At the beginning of the space age in 1970, the separate national linkage of the transportation and telecommunication technologies were taking shape as full-service world communication networks. The jet plane and the communication satellite forge these networks and make a world community possible and, perhaps, inevitable.

Space-Age Communication

In a word, the space-age revolution in communication is *cybernetic*. More precisely, the space age is cybernetic in method. The space age is sometimes also called the communication era. Thus, the usual definition of cybernetics as the art and science of communication and control in man and machine seems doubly appropriate. Space-age developments in communication are intertwined with cybernetic theory, or method, or approach, or viewpoint.

In the space age, the central question is: What does human communication do? What communication does, and what happens as a consequence of human communication are the basic matters. Notice the different directions in which the basic question leads the asker:

What *is* communication?
What *does* communication do?

The "is" question leads on to classification; for example, "There are twenty-two types of public speeches." The "does" question leads on to the study of purpose, network, system, and messages. Communication systems operate to achieve a purpose—that is what they *do*.

In the space age, there are three milestones of importance to us. The Telstar communication satellite demonstrated international television capabilities; Apollo II demonstrated that man could travel to another "planet;" and Pioneer 10 demonstrates our interest in engaging in communication with "intelligent life" on other planets. The "message" of Pioneer 10, in some ways, is the most profound of all. Pioneer 10 documents the emergence of a space-age attitude. It is this attitude that leads us to extend our communication skills and to pose the searching new questions required by our changing situation.

The major change brought about by the space-age revolution in communication is deceptively simple. At first glance some persons even assume it is just another word game. But the larger message is that cybernetic concepts enable men to "hook their brains" together in new ways and thereby achieve mutually shared purposes beyond those that could be achieved by a single individual.

Future Revolutions

Even before the space-age cybernetic revolution in communication runs its course, several more revolutions may occur. We shall mention only three such "changes" here.

Micro Communication Technology

Communication technology grows smaller, faster, cheaper, and smarter. The first radio receivers were packaged in boxes that took

two men to carry. Bigger was better. Year by year the radio has been reduced in size and increased in portability. Some radios now are hearing-aid size. Next ones may be implanted, as the heart pacemakers now are, under the human skin. But instead of a receive-only radio, such a device could be a transceiver—both transmit and receive—for both audio and visual signals. The visual device could be in the eye, the audio in the ear. Connected directly to satellite, such a device would augment human intelligence in difficult-to-predict ways; it would also open the possibilities of control. What consequences would you expect from such a transceiver?

Man-Machine Communication

In the immediate future, we humans will spend more time talking with intelligent machines. We have grown accustomed to receive "prerecorded" time-of day, weather, airflight arrival, and stock report messages. We also respond when we are "asked by a machine" to leave a message. At some medical centers, basic medical information is obtained from a patient by a computer. More than half of the persons so interviewed refuse to believe that they were not in contact with a real human being. In time, might we humans come to prefer to communicate with a friendly machine rather than another human? If so, what might the consequences be?

Earthman-ETI Communication

A third possibility for a next communication revolution arises from the possibility of earth contact

with intelligences from a distant galaxy, an extraterrestrial intelligence or ETI. Planets other than earth appear suitable for life. Such being the case, at least some of that life might well be more intelligent than earthman. We are more likely to contact, or be contacted by, the more rather than the less intelligent of those beings. When such contact is made, it seems certain communication on earth will change. The question is, in what ways?

Acceleration of Change

The human, it is said, is the only animal who knows that a day will come when he no longer lives. He is told of the day he was born; he celebrates that day each year as family and friends honor him on his birthday. He knows in a general way how many birthdays he will celebrate. He knows he has a lifespan, but he has no sure way at this time of knowing how great that span will be.

Human communication develops, and from time to time, redevelops during the full lifespan of everyone. For an individual, looking at his own communication activity, it is helpful to consider that communication in a lifespan framework. To appreciate the tides of change that affect human communication, a look two generations into the past and two generations into the future will be helpful.

The birth of your grandparents and the death of your grandchildren provides a family-span of nearly a hundred years into the past and a hundred years into the future — the better part of the two great centuries in the story of human communication.

Man is the animal who communicates. Quite clearly, if by some misfortune, he does not develop the skill necessary to communicate with his fellow man, he lives as a stranger in his home community, and he does not fully develop as a human. If you grant this much, does it not also follow that the better communicator a man is, the more human a man he is?

The acceleration of change can be observed in many areas. Means of transportation are a case in point. For most of human history, a man could travel no further in a day than he could walk. A man can walk ten to twenty miles a day. If he extends himself he can cover as much as fifty miles a day. Now even the slower forms of surface transportation — cars, trains, and ships — exceed that distance per hour. Traffic jams are, of course, a different and instructive matter.

A similar acceleration in change is obvious throughout the field of communication. For thousands of years after man learned to communicate through speech, no major new developments are evident. Handwriting comes about 3000 B.C. Printing follows at about 1400 A.D. Telecommunication and transportation can be dated at about 1900 A.D. Space-age communication begins at about 1969. It seems likely the next communication revolution(s) will be underway well before the year 2000. We live at a time made distinctive and, sometimes, uncomfortable by its rate of change.

Communication Shock

Alvin Toffler

Time and Change

How do we *know* that change is accelerating? There is, after all, no absolute way to measure change. In the awesome complexity of the universe, even within any given society, a virtually infinite number of streams of change occur simultaneously. All "things"—from the tiniest virus to the greatest galaxy—are, in reality, not things at all, but processes. There is no static point, no nirvana-like un-change, against which to measure change. Change is, therefore, necessarily relative.

It is also uneven. If all processes occurred at the same speed, or even if they accelerated or decelerated in unison, it would be impossible to observe change. The future, however, invades the present at differing speeds. Thus it becomes possible to compare the speed of different processes as they unfold. We know, for example, that compared with the biological evolution of the species, cultural and social evolution is extremely rapid. We know that some societies transform themselves technologically or economically more rapidly than others. We also know that different sectors within the same society exhibit different rates of change— the disparity that William Ogburn labeled "cultural lag." It is precisely the unevenness of change that makes it measurable.

We need, however, a yardstick that makes it possible to compare highly diverse processes, and this yardstick is time. Without time, change has no meaning. And without change, time would stop. Time can be conceived as the intervals during which events occur. Just as money permits us to place a value on both apples and oranges, time permits us to compare unlike processes. When we say that it takes three years to build a dam, we are really saying it takes three times as long as it takes the earth to circle the sun or 31,000,000 times as long as it takes to sharpen a pencil. Time is the currency of exchange that makes it possible to compare the rates at which very different processes play themselves out.

Given the unevenness of change and armed with this yardstick, we still face exhausting difficulties in measuring change. When we speak of the rate of change, we refer to the number of events crowded into an arbitrarily fixed interval of time. Thus we need to define the "events." We need to select our intervals with precision. We need to be careful about the conclusions we draw from the differences we observe. Moreover, in the measurement of change, we are today far more advanced with respect to physical processes than social processes. We know far better, for example, how to measure the rate at which blood flows through the

PROBE 15. Social trends and technological advancements influence your life.

BE FREE

Words and Music by
JIM MESSINA

Moderately
Tacet

I can see the world a-chang-ing,
You can hear the cit - ies call-ing,
I can hear the school bell ring - ing,

I can see it re - ar - rang-ing, hap - pen-ing__ be - fore my ver - y
climb- in' high you feel you're fall - ing, beck - on-ing__ for all of us to
from the yard the chil - dren sing - ing, "...mer - ri - ly,____ life is but a

eyes.
see.
dream."

Ev -'ry-where there's ce - ment grow-ing,
See the thief in the ce - ment hol - low,
In the street their old - er broth-ers

(continued on page 83)

body than the rate at which a rumor flows through society.

Even with all these qualifications, however, there is widespread agreement, reaching from historians and archaeologists all across the spectrum to scientists, sociologists, economists and psychologists, that many social processes are speeding up—strikingly, even spectacularly.

Psychophysiologists studying the impact of change on various organisms have shown that successful adaptation can occur only when the level of stimulation—the amount of change and novelty in the environment—is neither too low nor too high. "The central nervous system of a higher animal," says Professor D. E. Berlyne of the University of Toronto, "is designed to cope with environments that produce a certain rate of . . . stimulation . . . It will naturally not perform at its best in an environment that overstresses or overloads it." He makes the same point about environments that understimulate it. Indeed, experiments with deer, dogs, mice and men all point unequivocally to the existence of what might be called an "adaptive range" below which and above which the individual's ability to cope simply falls apart.

Future shock is the response to overstimulation. It occurs when the individual is forced to operate above his adaptive range. Considerable research has been devoted to studying the impact of inadequate change and novelty on human performance. Studies of men in isolated Antarctic outposts, experiments in sensory deprivation, investigations into on-the-job performance in factories, all show a falling off of mental and physical abilities in response to understimulation. We have less direct data on the impact of overstimulation, but such evidence as does exist is dramatic and unsettling.

Bombardment of the Senses

We still know too little about this phenomenon to explain authoritatively why overstimulation seems to produce maladaptive behavior. Yet we pick up important clues if we recognize that overstimulation can occur on at least three different levels: the sensory, the cognitive and the decisional.[1]

The easiest to understand is the sensory level. Experiments in sensory deprivation, during which volunteers are cut off from normal stimulation of their senses, have shown that the absence of novel sensory stimuli can lead to bewilderment and impaired mental functioning. By the same token, the input of too much disorganized, patternless or chaotic sensory stimuli can have similar effects. It is for this reason that practitioners of political or religious brainwashing make use not only of sensory deprivation (solitary confinement, for example) but of sensory bombardment involving flashing lights, rapidly shifting patterns of color, chaotic sound effects—the whole arsenal of psychedelic kaleidoscopy.

The religious fervor and bizarre behavior of certain hippie cultists may arise not merely from drug abuse, but from group experimentation with both sensory deprivation and bombardment. The chanting of monotonous mantras, the attempt to focus the individual's attention on interior, bodily sensation to the exclusion of outside stimuli, are efforts to induce the weird and sometimes hallucinatory effects of understimulation.

At the other end of the scale, we note the glazed stares and numb, expressionless faces of

(continued from page 82)

(continued on page 84)

(continued from page 83)

(continued on page 85)

youthful dancers at the great rock music auditoriums where light shows, split-screen movies, high decibel screams, shouts and moans, grotesque costumes and writhing, painted bodies create a sensory environment character-ized by high input and extreme unpredictability and novelty.

An organism's ability to cope with sensory input is dependent upon its physiological structure. The nature of its sense organs and the speed with which impul-ses flow through its neural sys-tem set biological bounds on the quantity of sensory data it can accept. If we examine the speed of signal transmission within various organisms, we find that the lower the evolutionary level, the slower the movement. Thus, for example, in a sea urchin egg, lacking a nervous system as such, a signal moves along a mem-brane at a rate of about a centi-meter an hour. Clearly, at such a rate, the organism can respond to only a very limited part of its en-vironment. By the time we move up the ladder to a jellyfish, which already has a primitive nervous system, the signal travels 36,000 times faster: ten centimeters per second. In a worm, the rate leaps to 100 cps. Among insects and crustaceans, neural pulses race along at 1000 cps. Among anthro-poids the rate reaches 10,000 cps. Crude as these figures no doubt are, they help explain why man is unquestionably among the most adaptable of creatures.

Yet even in man, with a neural transmission rate of about 30,000 cps, the boundaries of the system are imposing. (Electrical signals in a computer, by contrast, travel billions of times faster.) The limi-tations of the sense organs and nervous system mean that many environmental events occur at rates too fast for us to follow, and we are reduced to sampling experience at best. When the signals reaching us are regular and repetitive, this sampling process can yield a fairly good mental representation of reality. But when it is highly disorganized, when it is novel and unpredictable, the accuracy of our imagery is necessarily reduced. Our image of reality is distorted. This may explain why, when we experience sensory overstimulation, we suffer confusion, a blurring of the line between illusion and reality.

Information Overload

If overstimulation at the sensory level increases the distortion with which we perceive reality, cognitive overstimulation interferes with our ability to "think." While some human responses to novelty are involuntary, others are preceded by conscious thought, and this depends upon our ability to absorb, manipulate, evaluate and retain information.

Rational behavior, in particular, depends upon a ceaseless flow of data from the environment. It depends upon the power of the individual to predict, with at least fair success, the outcome of his own actions. To do this, he must be able to predict how the environment will respond to his acts. Sanity, itself, thus hinges on man's ability to predict his immediate, personal future on the basis of information fed him by the environment.

When the individual is plunged into a fast and irregularly changing situation, or a novelty-loaded context, however, his predictive accuracy plummets. He can no longer make the reasonably correct assessments on which rational behavior is dependent.

To compensate for this, to bring his accuracy up to the normal level again, he must scoop up and

(continued from page 84)

Nick Pavloff

process far more information than before. And he must do this at extremely high rates of speed. In short, the more rapidly changing and novel the environment, the more information the individual needs to process in order to make effective, rational decisions.

Yet just as there are limits on how much sensory input we can accept, there are in-built constraints on our ability to process information. In the words of psychologist George A. Miller of Rockefeller University, there are "severe limitations on the amount of information that we are able to receive, process, and remember." By classifying information, by abstracting and "coding" it in various ways, we manage to stretch these limits, yet ample evidence demonstrates that our capabilities are finite.

The acceleration of change, overstimulation from the environment, and information overload result in communication shock.

To discover these outer limits, psychologists and communications theorists have set about testing what they call the "channel capacity" of the human organism. For the purpose of these experiments, they regard man as a "channel." Information enters from the outside. It is processed. It exits in the form of actions based on decisions. The speed and accuracy of human information processing can be measured by comparing the speed of information input with the speed and accuracy of output.

Information has been defined technically and measured in terms of units called "bits."[2] By

now, experiments have established rates for the processing involved in a wide variety of tasks from reading, typing, and playing the piano to manipulating dials or doing mental arithmetic. And while researchers differ as to the exact figures, they strongly agree on two basic principles: first, that man has limited capacity; and second, that overloading the system leads to serious breakdown of performance. . . .

Managers plagued by demands for rapid, incessant and complex decisions; pupils deluged with facts and hit with repeated tests; housewives confronted with squalling children, jangling telephones, broken washing machines, the wail of rock and roll from the teenager's living room and the whine of the television set in the parlor—may well find their ability to think and act clearly impaired by the waves of information crashing into their senses. It is more than possible that some of the symptoms noted among battle-stressed soldiers, disaster victims, and culture shocked travelers are related to this kind of information overload.

One of the men who has pioneered in information studies, Dr. James G. Miller, director of the Mental Health Research Institute at the University of Michigan, states flatly that "Glutting a person with more information than he can process may . . . lead to disturbance." He suggests, in fact, that information overload may be related to various forms of mental illness.

One of the striking features of schizophrenia, for example, is "incorrect associative response." Ideas and words that ought to be linked in the subject's mind are not, and vice versa. The schizophrenic tends to think in arbitrary or highly personalized categories. Confronted with a set of blocks of various kinds – triangles, cubes, cones, etc. – the normal person is likely to categorize them in terms of geometric shape. The schizophrenic asked to classify them is just as likely to say "They are all soldiers," or "They all make me feel sad."

In the volume *Disorders of Communication*, Miller describes experiments using word association tests to compare normals and schizophrenics. Normal subjects were divided into two groups, and asked to associate various words with other words or concepts. One group worked at its own pace. The other worked under time pressure – i.e., under conditions of rapid information input. The time-pressed subjects came up with responses more like those of schizophrenics than of self-paced normals.

Similar experiments conducted by psychologists G. Usdansky and L. J. Chapman made possible a more refined analysis of the types of errors made by subjects working under forced-pace, high information-input rates. They, too, concluded that increasing the speed of response brought out a pattern of errors among normals that is peculiarly characteristic of schizophrenics.

"One might speculate," Miller suggests, ". . . that schizophrenia (by some as-yet-unknown process,

perhaps a metabolic fault which increases neural 'noise') lowers the capacities of channels involved in cognitive information processing. Schizophrenics consequently . . . have difficulties in coping with information inputs at standard rates like the difficulties experienced by normals at rapid rates. As a result, schizophrenics make errors at standard rates like those made by normals under fast, forced-input rates."

In short, Miller argues, the breakdown of human performance under heavy information loads may be related to psychopathology in ways we have not yet begun to explore. Yet, even without understanding its potential impact, we are accelerating the generalized rate of change in society. We are forcing people to adapt to a new life pace, to confront novel situations and master them in ever shorter intervals. We are forcing them to choose among fast-multiplying options. We are, in other words, forcing them to process information at a far more rapid pace than was necessary in slowly evolving societies. There can be little doubt that we are subjecting at least some of them to cognitive overstimulation. What consequences this may have for mental health in the technosocieties has yet to be determined.

Dale E. Boyer

---

1. The line between each of these is not completely clear, even to psychologists, but if we simply, in commonsense fashion, equate the sensory level with perceiving, the cognitive with thinking, and the decisional with deciding, we will not go too far astray.

2. A bit is the amount of information needed to make a decision between two equally likely alternatives. The number of bits needed increases by one as the number of such alternatives doubles.

THE CHICKEN SEES

Excerpted from *Remember: Be Here Now* by Richard Alpert. © Lama Foundation, 1971, Year of the Earth Monkey, Box 444, San Cristobal, New Mexico. Distributed by Crown Publishing, 419 Park Ave. S., New York, N.Y. 10016. Used by permission of the Lama Foundation.

WHEN I MET MY GURU WHO KNEW

EVERYTHING

IN MY HEAD,

I REALIZED

THAT HE KNEW

EVERYTHING

IN MY HEAD

WHETHER "I" LIKED IT OR NOT.

HE KNEW IT.

AND THERE WOULD BE TIMES AFTER A PARTICULARLY BEAUTIFUL DARSHAN WITH HIM WHEN HE'D SAY TO ME: "OH! YOU GAVE MUCH MONEY TO A LAMA," AND I'D SAY YES AND HE'D SAY:"YOU'RE VERY GOOD. YOU'RE COMING ALONG WITH YOUR SADHANA," AND I FELT SO GOOD AND THEN I'D GO BACK TO THE TEMPLE AND THINK "BOY! I'M GOING TO BE A GREAT YOGI. I'LL HAVE GREAT POWERS. WHAT AM I GOING TO DO WITH THEM?"... AND I'D START TO HAVE THESE HORRIBLE THOUGHTS AND ALL MY IMPURITIES WOULD RISE TO THE SURFACE AND THEY WOULD REALLY BE... AND THEN I'D GO TO BED AND HAVE ALL KINDS OF SEXUAL FANTASIES AND I'D THINK "LOOK YOU'RE BEING A YOGI AND YOU SEE THE ABSURDITY OF THAT SITUATION YOU'RE IN..." BUT I'D STILL HAVE THE THOUGHT. AND THEN, IN THE COURSE OF IT, I'D HAVE A THOUGHT (I'D BE GOING THROUGH MY SHOULDER BAG AND COME ACROSS A NOTE I'D WRITTEN TO MYSELF: "REMEMBER TO VISIT LAMA GOVINDA") AND I'D THINK, "I MUST VISIT LAMA GOVINDA WHILE I'M IN INDIA."

AND THE NEXT MORNING AT 8 O'CLOCK THERE IS THE MES-SENGER WITH INSTRUCTIONS: "THE GURU SAID YOU'RE TO GO VISIT LAMA GOVINDA."

NOW! THERE ISN'T A MESSAGE SAYING:"CUT OUT THOSE SEXUAL THOUGHTS," BUT HE MUST OBVIOUSLY KNOW THEM. DO YOU THINK HE JUST PICKED UP ON THE LAMA GOVINDA THING?

CAN I ASSUME THE PROBABILITIES ARE HE ONLY TUNES IN EVERY TIME I HAVE A POSITIVE THOUGHT?

AND THEN I COME BEFORE HIM AND NOW I'M FREAKED BECAUSE I KNOW HE KNOWS IT ALL; AND I WALK IN, AND HE

LOOKS AT ME WITH TOTAL
LOVE

AND I THINK: HOW CAN HE DO IT?
THIS GUY MUST BE NUTS! HE'S LOVING
THIS CORRUPT... WHY ISN'T HE...?
YOU SEE THE PREDICAMENT I WAS IN?
AND THEN! WHAT I UNDERSTOOD WAS:
HE WAS LOVING THAT IN ME WHICH WAS
BEHIND MY PERSONALITY AND BEHIND
MY BODY.
NOT: "I REALLY LOVE RAM DASS"
IT WASN'T INTERPERSONAL LOVE
IT WASN'T POSSESSIVE LOVE
IT WASN'T NEEDFUL LOVE
IT WAS THE FACT THAT

HE IS  LOVE

How Communications May Shape Our Future Environment

Ben H. Bagdikian

In thinking about communications and the future, there are some truths that are obvious but often ignored, as obvious things frequently are.

The first is that new communications are agents of change, whether intentional or not. The telegraph and printing techniques in the early nineteenth century for the first time permitted human knowledge to travel faster than a running horse; at the time this seemed mechanically fascinating and full of promise for convenience and profit. But if the early users had been told that their new gadgets would change the form of human government all over the world, they would have considered the idea ridiculous. Yet this is what happened.

In the 1950s and 1960s the transistor radio accelerated the world view among the uneducated populations in less developed countries by permitting cosmopolitan information to reach areas without good roads, vehicles or literacy. During this same period television in the developed countries has had revolutionary impacts we are just now appreciating. Novel channels of information carry messages to previously inert audiences and this produces profound change. We should stop being surprised.

Since such changes are inexorable, we need to ask how new techniques can best serve the individual and society. Mechanical efficiency and profit will always be important factors, but they cannot be the only ones. The real power in new technology does not lie in particular gadgets, but in the conceptions men have of their uses. The quality of life must be a part of this conception.

The second obvious truth is that we can use our techniques to meet large-scale social problems not ordinarily thought of as formal communication.

We can look back on our first 20 years of television and envision a more imaginative use of this new instrument. One of the great demographic upheavals of our time has occurred in this period. About 18 million rural people, most of them poorly educated to the point of semi-illiteracy, moved to urban centers. They now constitute an accumulation of despair and alienation that raises doubts whether our cities can survive and whether a democratic consensus is still possible.

A peculiar characteristic of this migration is that most of the adults involved probably would prefer to remain in farming if they did not face starvation and hopelessness.

We might have taken what amounts to about three years of city welfare for a family and loaned it to the same family while it was still in the countryside to buy enough arable land and equipment to become self-supporting. We might have augmented the limited county agent system with televised instruction for the farm family, not in spherical trigonometry or the history of the Hanseatic League, but in land use techniques, maintenance of farm equipment, repair of the home, farm management, literacy, how to fill out tax forms and other elementary arts of coping with the environment.

And what if we had taken the same view of those who migrated to the city, moving into an environment more strange to them than the cities of the nineteenth century were to the foreign immigrants?

What if we offered television instruction in solving their immediate personal problems, like how to read an installment loan contract, job information, how the local bus system works, how to shop in the city, how to maintain a city tenement, what the new and strange city laws were?

And what if we had provided televised instruction for the preschool children of these migrants, so that they would not enter first grade to find the standard curriculum a total mystery?

It is easier to see these possibilities in retrospect, but at least it tells us that we have not been very imaginative in using our communications to solve practical problems.

The third truth is more difficult and involves the less precise dimension of individual and social needs in aesthetic, intellectual and emotional activity. We need to know more about this because in a short time we must make decisions affecting these needs.

For example, it seems likely that in the future our channels of communication may become an almost limitless resource. Where we now have a maximum of seven VHF television channels in our largest cities, in the future we

Reprinted from the Neuman University Cartoon Ads in *Mad Magazine*, January, 1976. © 1975 by E. C. Publications, Inc. Reprinted by permission of the publisher.

At the Flip Point of Time — The Point of More Return?

Marshall McLuhan
Director of the Centre for Culture and Technology, University of Toronto

Andrew Marvell wrote, in his celebrated poem "To His Coy Mistress":

> *But at my back I always hear*
> *Time's winged Chariot hurrying near:*
> *And yonder all before us lye*
> *Deserts of vast Eternity.*

It is interesting that time is presented under the auditory or acoustic figure, and space and the future is presented visually—for the acoustic is simultaneous, and the visual is sequential. The acoustic is all-involving, and the visual offers detachment and alienation. The simultaneous has created the mass media and mass publics, for the mass has less to do with numbers than with speed. At electric speed it is the *sender* who is *sent*. This instantaneous factor may well have changed the mass audience from passive receivers to active participants and producers.

Any process has a reversal point. Early mass-media programs may have been created as capsules of packages for a consumer public, but we seem to have reached the flip point of chiasmus, or reversal, where the mass public produces, rather than consumes, the show. At this point might we not for the first time be able to appeal directly to the mass audience to participate in problem-solving at the highest level? Is there not always one in a million who can see through the matter that baffles the experts?

That "one man in a million" for whom any problem is easy because it does not present a problem exists in the mass audience. Organized knowledge inevitably blocks the approach to many problems; it is the person innocent of such "expert" knowledge. Robert Oppenheimer used to say: "There are kids playing in the street who could solve some of my toughest problems because they have sensory modes which I lost long ago."

One of the greatest of all human discoveries was made by an eight-year-old child whose job was to pull a string on a steam-cock of an early model steam engine. Wishing to leave the job and play marbles, the child tied the string to the fly-wheel, creating the first cybernetic mechanism in history. Might not this same type of awareness be available now for use from the mass audience? When we look back on the answers to past problems, we are not blinded by expert knowledge; we simply look at the problem and the answer, as in an

(continued on page 95)

Excerpted from "At the Flip Point of Time—The Point of More Return?" by Marshall McLuhan in *Journal of Communication* (vol. 25, no. 4), Autumn 1975. © Marshall McLuhan. Used by permission of the author and the publisher.

may have any number of multiples of 20 to 24,000 TV channels in each community.

But the capacity of man to absorb information is not limitless, either intellectually or emotionally. We ought to consider what man needs and society requires. But we must do this without the illusion of looking for the universally perfect single program, since there is none, although our present mass media are largely based on the assumption that there is.

This introduces the philosophical dilemma we will never solve completely, but which we have to cope with: How do we use a social instrument for good as we see it without imposing uniformity and cultural dictatorship?

The need for variety and renewable decisions is not always recognized. Increasingly we hear during troubled times that what we need for survival is uniformity, regularity and order. But the human condition has infinite variety and in relations among millions of individuals, there are unpredictable combinations of emotions, ideas and values. This human scene is forever creating new situations, and in order for society to survive, it must produce an unending supply of ideas in order to increase the odds that among them will be some that will fit the peculiar circumstances of each moment in history.

The New England Town Meeting that became obsolete when every citizen in the community could no longer fit in the same hall could come back, given large numbers of channels at very low cost, with a capacity for the citizen to respond.

It would make sense to reserve some of the many TV channels in every community as soapbox channels, for announcements, gripes or recitations of "Hiawatha." If this is done in neighborhoods, it is feasible that people will be able to respond from their homes in meaningful ways. They might signal applause or tell the performer that his lawn needs cutting.

This sounds strange to us because we know only the present conception of a small number of one-way communications channels serving very large areas. If your neighborhood had 50 channels of its own, it would not be so strange.

Similarly, we are not yet used to the combination of computer and communications channel, but this is already having an impact.

It is quite conceivable, for example, that in the not-too-distant future, the average home will have something like a teletypewriter connected with a computer that is connected with something like a television set that will be connected with every major library, newspaper, town hall, community center and mass access computer in the country.

By typing on the teletypewriter the individual in his home can send messages to particular people all over the world, without using the mails or his telephone. Or he can ask a computerized library for available materials on any given subject. Or his wife can ask for a visual display on the television screen of all children's raincoats in a certain size and price range, and when she sees the one she wants, she can signal and the store will send it to her. And at the moment that she orders it, the computer will instantly deduct the price from her bank account.

Men doing business will communicate this way with secretarial services, with other businessmen and with sources of information now considered so sophisticated that today only the

(continued from page 94)

equation. When we look ahead, however, we assume the vast body of relevant data that have nothing to do with the problem in hand. When the mass audience looks at the current problem, it need not be blinded by great quantities of irrelevant data.

Instant electric information creates the "mass man" by involving everybody in everybody. It is the same instant information which enables the mass man to participate in solving tough technical problems. Typically, big problems result from asking the wrong questions, and they can appear simple to those who have never asked those questions. The flip point is like playing a giant lottery in reverse: Instead of holding the winning ticket, there is always an ignoramus who, in all simplicity, is holding the winning answer to a problem.

Granted, however, that the problem presented to the mass audience may have been instantly solved by the "one in a million" in that audience, the question remains: how does the answer reach those who are searching for it? Here again, the new electric technology seems to offer the solution. The video cassette is even now awaiting programs and themes to bring to the mass audience. The makers of video cassettes have been baffled by the question of programming. The natural impulse is to repeat, in this new form, the existing shows from older media. That is called "the law of implementation": we use the new to do the old, even if it doesn't need doing at all. New unsolved problems from widely selected areas of the community of knowledge, having first been shown to the mass audience, could reach much smaller publics by video cassettes. From smaller groups, the solutions to problems could move back to the searchers.

Prof. Vernon Farkis' HISTORY COURSES for the Now Student!

10 a.m. M—W
The Hundred Years War and It's Effect on Patty Hearst.

2 p.m. T—Th
The Decline of the Ottoman Empire As Seen Through the Life of Cat Stevens.

9 a.m. W—F
The Industrial Revolution and The Weathermen —A Comparison.

11 a.m. W—F
Timothy Leary and His Influence on the Balkan Congress of 1813.

Room 1809 Grunion Hall

CLIP THIS COUPON!

It's Worth
15 BONUS POINTS

On Your Mid-Term
In Prof. Asa Troon's
American History I

9 a.m. Mon.-Wed. Grunion Hall

Was General Custer "Gay"?

Who Was Martha Washington's "House Guest" While George Was Away At Valley Forge?

What Was The Embarrassing Disease Millard Fillmore Tried To Hush Up?

American History I

Told Like You've Never Heard It Before!

Prof. Morris McCool   1 p.m. M-W   Grunion Hall

THE FEMALE KOREAN STRIPED TERMITE LAYS FOUR THOUSAND EGGS...THEN GETS DEPRESSED AND REFUSES TO COMMUNICATE!

Learn This and Thousands of Other Unusual Insect Facts in Dr. Humbert Hubbard's
INSECTS OF EAST ASIA 2

1 p.m. Tuesdays & Thursdays
Science Hall

---

largest corporations and research groups have them available.

The student can get programmed learning, being told what is correct and incorrect, and, more important, pursuing ideas and questions at his own pace and direction, going as deeply and as broadly as he wishes.

Because all this could replace transportation and face-to-face contact for largely impersonal transactions, there would be less need for dense population concentrations in cities. Home would be a more important place, with the need for communication drawing the individual into his home instead of its present tendency to pull him out of it.

If we are wise, we shall make this kind of facility plentiful, so that every neighborhood, every community, every school district will have many channels, often vacant, so that it becomes easy and inexpensive to circulate information, ask questions and get a response on the items of social and political need at the grass roots—communications that are now impossible in systems that have relatively few one-way channels addressing everyone in thousands of square miles.

The Social Effects of Mass Communication

Joseph T. Klapper

The first point I wish to make is rather obvious, but its implications are often overlooked. I would like to point out that the audience for mass communication consists of people, and that these people live among other people and amid social institutions. Each of these people has been subject and continues to be subject to numerous influences besides mass communication. All but the infants have attended schools and churches and have listened to and conversed with teachers and preachers and with friends and colleagues. They have read books or magazines. All of them, including the infants, have been members of a family group. As a result of these influences, they have developed opinions on a great variety of topics, a set of values, and a set of behavioral tendencies. These predispositions are part of the person, and he carries them with him when he serves as a member of the audience for mass communication. The person who hears a radio address urging him to vote for a particular political candidate probably had some political opinion of his own before he turned on the set. The housewife who casually switches on the radio and hears the announcer state that a classical music program is to follow is probably already aware that she does or does not like classical music. The man who sees a crime play on television almost surely felt, before

seeing the play, that a life of crime was or was not his dish.

It is obvious that a single movie or radio or television program is not very likely to change the existing attitudes of audience members, particularly if these attitudes are relatively deep-seated. What is not so obvious is that these attitudes, these predispositions, are at work before and during exposure to mass communications, and that they in fact largely determine the communications to which the individual is exposed, what he remembers of such communications, how he interprets their contents, and the effect which mass communications have upon him.

Communications research has consistently revealed, for example, that people tend in the main to read, watch, or listen to communications which present points of view with which they are themselves in sympathy and tend to avoid communications of a different hue. During pre-election campaigns in the United States, for example, Republicans have been found to listen to more Republican-sponsored speeches than Democratic-sponsored programs, while Democrats do precisely the opposite. Persons who smoke have been found to be less likely to read newspaper articles about smoking and cancer than those who do not smoke. Dozens of other research findings show that people expose themselves to mass communication selectively. They

PROBE 17. Mass communication is more effective among people who are predisposed toward the message.

Quotes from pages 66–70 from THE SCIENCE OF HUMAN COMMUNICATION, edited by Wilbur Schramm, © 1963 by Basic Books, Inc., Publishers, New York.

select material which is in accord with their existing views and interests, and they largely avoid material which is not in accord with those views and interests.

Research has also shown that people *remember* material which supports their own point of view much better than they remember material which attacks that point of view. Put another way, retention, as well as exposure, is largely selective.

Finally, and in some senses most importantly, perception, or interpretation, is also selective. By this I mean that people who are exposed to communications with which they are unsympathetic not uncommonly distort the contents so that they end up perceiving the message as though it supported their own point of view. Communications condemning racial discrimination, for example, have been interpreted by prejudiced persons as favoring such discrimination. Persons who smoke cigarettes, to take another example, were found to be not

only less likely than non-smokers to read articles about smoking and cancer, but also to be much less likely to become convinced that smoking actually causes cancer.

Now it is obvious that if people tend to expose themselves mainly to mass communications in accord with their existing views and interests and to avoid other material, and if, in addition, they tend to forget such other material as they see, and if, finally, they tend to distort such other material as they remember, then clearly mass communication is not very likely to change their views. It is far, far more likely to support and reinforce their existing views.

Now this does not mean that mass communication can *never* produce changes in the ideas or the tastes or the values or the behavior of its audience. In the first place, as I have already mentioned, the factors which promote reinforcive effects do not function with 100 per cent efficiency. In the second place, and more importantly, the very same factors

sometimes maximize the likelihood of mass communications serving in the interest of change. This process occurs when the audience member is *predisposed* toward change. For example, a person may, for one reason or another, find his previous beliefs, his previous attitudes, and his accustomed mode of behavior to be no longer psychologically satisfying. He might, for example, become disillusioned with his political party, or his church, or—on another level—he might become bored with the kind of music to which he ordinarily listens. Such a person is likely to seek new faiths, or to experiment with new kinds of music. He has become, as it were, *predisposed to change*. And just as his previous loyalties protected him from mass communications which were out of accord with those loyalties, so his new predispositions will make him susceptible to the influence of those same communications from which he was previously effectively guarded.

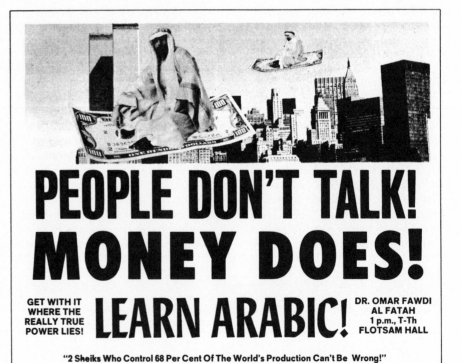

The Slogan Society

In politics, it seems, bad times make good slogans. Herbert Hoover's promise of "a chicken in every pot" did not get him re-elected in 1932, but it was a far more ingenious catch phrase than the Republicans' 1944 theme, "Time for a change," or "I like Ike" in 1952. And for all John F. Kennedy's eloquence, no Democratic orator since the Depression has matched Franklin D. Roosevelt's phrasemaking prowess on behalf of "the forgotten man." Lyndon Johnson's vision of "the Great Society" is not only vague, but *vieille vague* as well; the term was the title of a 1914 book by British Political Psychologist Graham Wallas, and the idea is as old as Plato's *Republic*. Equally lackluster is Barry Goldwater's "In your heart you know he is right" – which L.B.J. could not resist parodying in his speech before the Steelworkers Union last month ("You know in your heart that I am telling you the truth").

"Word Magic"

To many scholars, all slogans are bad slogans. George Mowry, dean of social sciences at U.C.L.A., argues that they "compress a lot of truth into what is basically an untruth." Indeed, for the majority of voters not inclined to analyze issues for themselves, slogans are a welcome substitute for logical argument. "Most people would rather die than think," says Bertrand Russell. "In fact, some

do." Russell's own ban-the-bomb marchers, mindlessly chanting "Better Red than dead," prove his point.

Phrases such as "Peace in our time" and "Prosperity is just around the corner" invoke "word magic," as linguists call verbal formulas that promise to make dreams come true through sheer repetition. On the other hand, observes San Francisco State College's S. I. Hayakawa, a pioneering U.S. semanticist, "You don't move a mass society with a volume by Galbraith." Particularly in the U.S., as Cambridge Historian Denis Brogan has pointed out, "the evocative power of verbal symbols must not be despised, for these are and have been one of the chief means of uniting the United States and keeping it united."

The most effective political slogans are timely, yet live long beyond their time. Passing into the language, they help crystallize great issues of the past for future generations: "Give me liberty or give me death"; *"Lebenstraum"*; "The world must be made safe for democracy"; "There'll always be an England"; "unconditional surrender"; "the Great Leap Forward"; "We shall overcome." In an increasingly complex society, as Hayakawa points out, such coinages are essential "short cuts to a consensus."

Seven Is Tops

The word "slogan," from the Gaelic *sluagh* (army) and *gairm*

(continued on page 100)

It's a matter of life and BREATH.

Visit San Clemente, ***You*** *paid for it.*

Peace with honor

BETTER RED THAN DEAD

A woman's place is in the home.

EQUAL PAY FOR EQUAL WORK

I'm not a Lincoln, I'm a Ford.

Impeachment with honor

The right to life

(a call), originally meant a call to arms—and some of history's most stirring slogans, from "Erin go bragh" to "Remember Pearl Harbor" have been just that. In peacetime, argues Hayakawa, electorates respond more readily to slogans that promise change, since people are rarely satisfied with things as they are. One notable exception was the catch phrase that helped return Britain's Tory Party to power in 1959: "You never had it so good." In general, though, Democrats, like detergent manufactures, favor slogans that offer a new and better product ("New deal," "New Frontier"). The Grand Old Party, like whisky distillers, prefers to emphasize aged-in-the-wood reliability, from Abraham Lincoln's "Don't swap horses in the middle of the stream" to 1924's "Keep cool with Coolidge."

To be fully effective, say psychologists, a slogan should express a single idea in seven words or less. "It is a psychological fact," says Harvard's Gordon Allport, "that seven is the normal limit of rote memory." (Example: telephone numbers.) Whether plugging cat food or a candidate,

sloganeers lean heavily on such verbal devices as alliteration ("Korea, Communism, Corruption"), rhyme ("All the way with L.B.J."), or a combination of both ("Tippecanoe and Tyler Too").* Other familiar standbys are paradox ("We have nothing to fear but fear itself"), metaphor ("Just the kiss of the hops"), metonymy ("The full dinner pail"), parody (a Norwegian travel folder promises "a Fjord in Your Future"), and punning ("Every litter bit helps"). By using what semanticists call "affective" language, many slogans deliberately exploit chauvinism ("Made in Texas by Texans"), xenophobia ("Yankee go home"), insecurity ("Even your best friends won't tell you"), narcissism ("Next to myself I like B.V.D. best"), escapism ("I dreamed I barged down the Nile in my Maidenform bra").

Long before Poet T. S. Eliot expounded his theory of the "auditory imagination," Pioneer Ad-

man Earnest Elmo Calkins used pocket poetry to make "Phoebe Snow" glamorize passenger service on the coal-burning Delaware, Lackawanna & Western Railroad. Slogans nearly always overload the language and often debase it ("coffee-er coffee"). English teachers curse Madison Avenue for institutionalizing bad grammar with such calculated lapses as "us Tareyton smokers" and "like a cigarette should." By contrast, some of history's most enduring slogans were plucked from literature. Winston Churchill's call to "blood, sweat and tears"—boiled down from his first statement as Prime Minister in 1940, "I have nothing to offer but blood, toil, tears and sweat"—was adapted from a passage in a 1931 book by Churchill; but strikingly similar words were used in previous centuries by the British poets John Donne, Byron and Lord Alfred Douglas.

---

*Tyler was the Whig vice-presidential candidate in 1840. "Tippecanoe" was used to glamorize Gentleman Farmer William Henry Harrison, who had scored a dubious victory over the Indians in a skirmish at Tippecanoe Creek twenty-nine years earlier, but routed Martin Van Buren in the election. A more forgettable Whig slogan affirmed: "With Tip and Tyler we'll bust Van's biler."

Prods

1. What effect do social trends such as popular interest in Eastern religions have on our lives?
2. In what ways have electronic media changed our lives in the last ten years?
3. List several of your desires that are thwarted by your environment.
4. How does communication shock develop? How can we maintain free and responsible communication in an environment of constant change and massive individual stress?

Summary

The first three units of *Communication Probes II* have dealt with the Person, the Message, and the Environment components of communication. The next four units will deal with the communication relationships in which people interact: The Dyad, in which one person communicates with one other; the Serial chain, in which one person reproduces a message for another person who reproduces the message for another person, through a series of dyadic interactions; the Small Group, in which a few persons interact face-to-face to achieve a desired outcome; and the Speaker-Audience, in which one person speaks to a large number of people.

Each of these relationships may be visualized by portraying them in simple diagrams. See if you can identify the relationships displayed in the following diagrams.

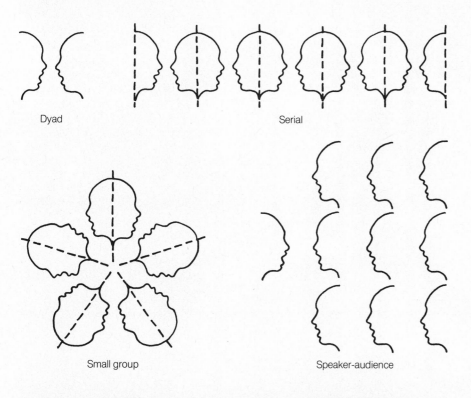

Dyad   Serial

Small group   Speaker-audience

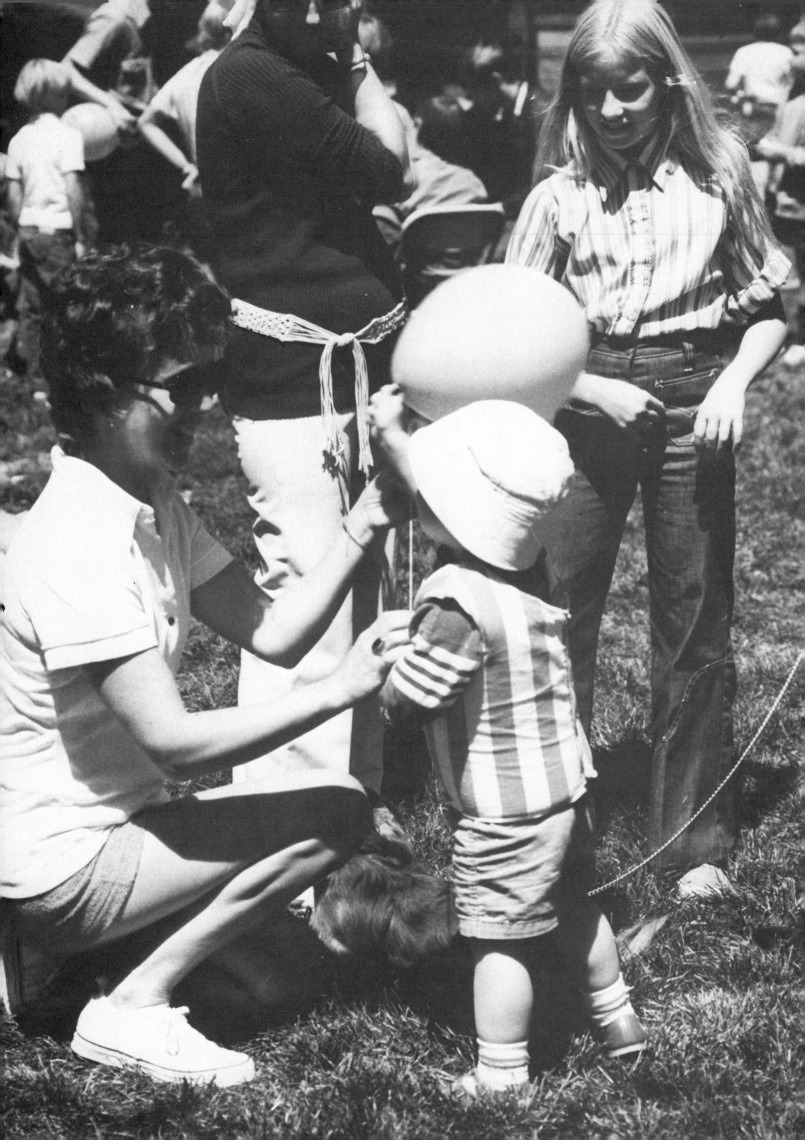

DYADIC

PROBE 18 Meaningful dialogue requires a depth of understanding of others and maximum involvement.

PROBE 19 A person may become a more effective communicator by applying principles of assertiveness.

PROBE 20 Intimate communication requires that the partners make explicit what they expect of each other.

PROBE 21 You can use transactional analysis to understand yourself better and improve your intimate communication.

PROBE 22 The interview is a form of dialogue in which at least one party has a preconceived and serious purpose and both parties speak and listen.

Relationship 1: Dyadic

The distinguishing characteristic of dyadic communication is that it involves two individuals. When you interact with another person, you are engaged in a dyadic encounter. Having a personal dialogue with your girl or boy friend, discussing a grade with a teacher, encouraging a member of your family to lend you the car, giving advice to a close friend about his or her dating problems, and telling your mom or dad how much you love them are examples of common dyadic relationships. Each of us devotes a large portion of our time interacting in dyadic relationships. The dyad—and dialogue—are intensely important in maintaining our sanity; having another person with whom we can talk is fundamental to development.

What kinds of results or outcomes tend to be associated with effective dyadic communication? As you reflect on this question, you might come up with some of these ideas:

A person should be able to maintain close relationships without having feelings of uncertainty or rejection develop.

A person should be able to understand himself or herself in relation to others.

A person should be able to help others understand themselves and achieve a degree of personal growth.

A person should be able to interpret and pass on information to another person with minimal distortion and misunderstanding.

A person should be able to listen so as to create a supportive atmosphere in which another person can talk without being defensive.

A person should be able to enjoy the pleasures of social conversation without resorting to tricks and negative games.

People engaged in managing, supervising, selling, and providing services depend on good dyadic communication to accomplish their objectives. Each of us can learn much about the skills of dyadic communication through an understanding of transactional analysis, assertiveness, the language of intimate loving relationships, and techniques of interviewing. Because the theory and skills of dyadic communication relate to success in other types of relationships, an exploration into what constitutes an effective dyadic relationship provides a foundation for developing skills in other areas. Check yourselves carefully on progress made in forming and continuing dyadic encounters. Dialogue is the framework of love. Learn all you can about building and maintaining that framework.

From Monologue to Dialogue

Charles T. Brown and Paul W. Keller

If you and I were to change places, I could talk like you . . .   The Book of Job

A girl amused the other students in one of our classes by telling about meeting a "guy" at a folk festival who was the best conversationalist she had ever known. It turned out that she couldn't remember anything in particular that he had said or that in fact he had even talked very much. She had been the one who talked and she really didn't remember what she had talked about. But she yearned to meet this person again and feared that she would not as it was one of those events where people came from long distances. "I have never been as free and as exhilarated in my talk with anyone. And you are wrong, I only had one drink all night. I ranged free and easy. I was so fluent and said things that were meaningful. My life seemed just right that night. There was no show-off— and that's not me. I knew he understood and that we understood much together. There was a strange intimacy—and yet there was no intimacy at all. This is one of the most beautiful and most precious memories of my life."

It turns out that occasionally complete strangers quickly develop openness and intense relationships, largely perhaps because they know that they will not meet again and thus entanglements and commitments are not endan-

gered. This may be what happened here. But it is well that the girl remembers the incident cited for she will know that moment when she is met, confirmed, and listened to in depth only a few times, even if she lives to be an ancient lady. Many many times she will talk to impress and her auditor will indulge her, especially if he is male. (She is an extremely attractive female.) Many times she will argue and be caustic. (She is an aggressive female too.) How much of her verbal demand is the consequence of hungering for a person who understands her, one can only speculate. How many people never know what it is to be listened to at all and spend their lives talking to themselves in the presence of other people?

The levels of interpersonal communication exist on a continuum between self-talk, at the one end, and a depth of understanding of others—real dialogue—at the other. . . .

Monologue

Communication marked by indifference for the other person results in a speech in which the intended receiver is the self. The other person serves almost exclusively as a stimulant. Just as an amputated leg or arm can be

---

PROBE 18. Meaningful dialogue requires a depth of understanding of others and maximum involvement.

feiffer by Jules Feiffer

NOBODY KNOWS ME.

WHO?

NOBODY SEES ME.

WHERE?

experienced as a phantom limb, so another person can be experienced as a part of one's own communication system—a kind of phantom.[1] And this is what happens in monologue, a kind of communication we learn early in life.

The Russian psychologist A. R. Luria found that children talk six times as much in the presence of others as when alone. Apparently, internal speech is excited by the presence of another child. Internal speech, or *verbal thought*, if you like, develops as the child internalizes the partner who is not present, a feat which depends upon, as a first stage, imagining he is talking to another person—best done when he has somebody present. In this way a child turns himself into the recipient of his own message. Recently we asked a four-year-old girl to repeat a comment that was unclear. She looked startled for a moment and then replied, "Oh, I was talking to myself."

But children are not the only ones who do this. Professors, the better ones, who are essentially our more mature children, behave similarly quite often in their lectures. Their faces may go vacant, eyes lose focus, perhaps the head will tilt back while they explore some thought just at the edge of awareness. All creative people have this self-orientation. While monologue, by definition, means a minimum of involvement with the other, the self-listening is at a maximum and it is extremely valuable as above suggested.

Narcissistic Monologue

However, the listening of monologue may be for the purpose of self-adoration, rather than for the exploration of one's thoughts. When this happens a self-reflective smile (the dead giveaway)

dominates the speech, especially at the end of sentences. The articulation of such speech, almost always unduly precise, expresses language to match, likely ornate. This behavior is all highly infuriating to others, often arousing caustic response.

However, we all do this "face work," and when it is half hidden it is socially acceptable.[2] Indeed one's feelings about himself, his position with his conversants, and his status at large, are always involved in his communication. One may lapse into silence, over-respond, joke, mimic, argue, ignore, belittle, bitch, praise, blame, or laugh in order to draw attention to himself. It is inevitable, for we are all self-conscious, one of the chief accomplishments of language. The laws of human interaction do not rule out "face work"; they can and do order it into the background.

Yet some people insist upon talking openly for their own amusement and amazement, and it is this that is infuriating. If one does this in most of his interaction he gradually evolves into a socialized isolate, that is, he spends much of his time with people, actually alone. Any honest emotional exchange initiated by another causes him to grow silent or flippant, in some way to evade the relationship suggested by conversation.

Narcissistic monologue is largely self-destructive, but exploratory monologue has its important value for both the individual and society, as noted above. . . .

Dialogue

In a day when we lean so heavily on attack and denunciation in social interaction, let us make clear at the onset of an examina-

tion of dialogue that dialogue is not some ideal that belongs to a nonexistent peaceful world. Even the gentle Martin Buber said that he often struggled with his partner in order to alter his view.[3] Dialogue goes directly and honestly to the difference between "me and thee," and this requires an immense toughness of self—for it does combat without going on the defensive. And so there is considerable difference between the struggle of dialogue and that of confrontation. In confrontation the purpose is the humiliation of the other person. When, however, conflict develops between people in dialogue the other person is confirmed. He is looked upon as responsible and competent though he may not be persuaded.[4] Even downright rejection of a view can still stay within the framework of dialogue. To reject ideas or behavior in another while confirming him as a person is, of course, difficult, requiring a deep faith in self. And yet this is the true test of one's ability to carry on dialogue. It is one thing to feel in such a way as to say, "I don't like you" and quite another thing to say, "I am getting angry with you." The former judges you and excludes you and initiates the termination of dialogue—the work of anxiety. To say, "I am getting angry," however, makes an authentic statement about one's feelings, recognizes the status of the relationship, and musters the courage to continue in dialogue. It does not cover up as in the distortion "I like you" (when actually I don't), nor does it polarize the feelings of the two conversants, as is likely, when one openly attacks the other. The upshot is this, that the deepest level of human interaction has a profound faith in the intentions, and the ideal self-concept of the other person—attained when

things and events are seen as he sees them.

Why is this empathy difficult to achieve in the face of conflict?

Above all else the need of every person is to be confirmed as he is. How else can we hope to be more? Without a future what is hope? And what is life without hope? But no person is capable of doing his own confirming. Indeed his confirmation rests in his impact upon others; again, a human self is a social satellite, not an independent planet. In our search for confirmation, however, we deceive ourselves if we dare not differ with others, for we are different. Only as we are confirmed in our uniqueness are we confirmed at all. Thus our greatest assurance depends upon support for what we are when we dissent from the other's opinion. But as Buber points out this is probably the Achilles' heel of the human race.[5] Almost all humans are stingy with support except when they are agreed with—when they themselves are confirmed. So the great moments in dialogue are not those nice exchanges between people when they agree with each other. We are talking about the nature of talk where the listening senses the deep differences with the other and yet trusts the other implicitly. Let it be clear we are not saying that people have to be in conflict with each other in order to have dialogue. Good exchange can take place when there is no conflict to threaten the listening. What we are saying is this: (1) we really have no test of the ability to carry on dialogue if the talk has no threat in it, and (2) that actually one does not know the deepest level of dialogue except when he is comfortably related to a person from whom he differs greatly.

The first point should be obvious. The test of anything is its ability to endure under stress. The second point is not so obvious. Let us approach it with a comment on the command of the ages, "To love thine enemy." This command is not basically a moral injunction but an invitation to know the deepest experiences in relationship—drawing heavily on one's courage. The ultimate in *self-confirmation*, thus, takes place when one trusts his enemy—an "untrustworthy" person. The Western movie has much of its appeal in the fact that it melodramatically explores this relationship when it pictures the hero talking calmly to an enraged man who has him covered with a cocked pistol. We, the audience, are entranced because we know the hero is saying to himself, "Circumstances call for me to calm this man. If I panic he will fire. If I put my trust in his stability and this I can do so long as I do not threaten him I have a good chance of surviving this encounter. I could be wrong. He may fire without provocation. That's the chance I take. Everything considered I choose to take the chance." If one can command himself to do this he learns several remarkable things at once:

1. That he has the capacity to face death calmly—and death is a reality each person must one day experience.

2. That, as a consequence he can probably face any experience calmly.

3. That he has attained a maximum command of himself.

4. That he has also attained the maximum in human freedom—for freedom is that internal state which permits choice among the choices made available by conditions.

5. That he has achieved the ultimate in self-confidence for he has achieved the minimum in self-hate, therefore the minimum in self-doubt.

In the end there is not hate except hate of the self; no anger, except anger with the self. All *our responses* toward other people are proofs of our potentials which others have but stimulated. All feelings are self-reflexive. Whether one panics or remains calm in the face of danger, the stimuli are the same. It is the self that is different.

Thus most talk and listening between nations in conflict—to illustrate the view—is not dialogue because the parties do not have the courage to experience dialogue. By definition the defensive posture is the acceptance of self-doubt. The political leader who insists "we shall bargain only from a position of strength" reflects his fears, not his strength. The perception of the self as strong when one is weak is a deception that comes because one blames the other for his feelings. He conceives of the enemy as wholly distrustful, thus freeing himself from responsibility for his own feelings. If he really wants to talk openly and defenselessly with his enemy he must develop sufficient trust in himself to stir responsible behavior in the other—which means he faces possible treachery, having dropped his guard. Conversely, by maintaining his guard, he excites the defensiveness of his enemy and thus insures the failure of dialogue—unless the enemy is actually the stronger person of the two, and creates the conditions for dialogue.

Perhaps the hardest of all lessons to learn is that defensive listening (which, as we all know, establishes pseudo dialogue) is irresponsible behavior. Defensive behavior insists that the responsi-

bility for one's feelings is in the other person. Let it be clear. The lowering of our defense, especially once mutual defense has developed, may be a miscalculation. But then the escalating of our defenses may be, too. There is no guaranteed safe path for people in conflict. The question is, shall we depend upon our capacity to survive in dialogue or in defense? Defense and dialogue are mutually exclusive behaviors, and there is danger in either course because no person has complete control over the other person.

In dialogue you risk more than in monologue.

We have cast this discussion, by our example, in the frame of the international conflict in order to highlight the mutually exclusive differences between dialogue and defense. But we should not limit ourselves to that frame of reference. The basic character trait of the effective psychotherapist, for instance, is his ability to trust his own health while listening to his sick patient. And this he can do only if he believes the relationship will stir the potential health of his patient. Two swim as one only as each gives up one swimming arm to embrace the other. Yes, the therapist confirms the sick man and thus initiates the healing, but this is not achieved without risk. And so the great test of the professional listener is his capacity to maintain the relationship when his partner is sinking.

In similar fashion, the great test of a marriage is the ability of partners to listen to each other when in conflict. Can the one

embrace the other when differences arise? Each is tested. "Do I have enough tolerance for myself to embrace a person whose very being I learn stimulates my awareness of those qualities I dislike in myself?"

The capacity of a person to carry on a dialogue with a politician, a policeman, a teacher, a teenager, a foreigner, a whore, a homosexual, a thief, a murderer, or an insane man is the capacity to tolerate the feelings about the self aroused when we identify with that other person—to understand life from his point of view. After all, life can be lived in his way. It is the fear aroused by contemplating that prospect that cuts off the dialogue.

Abraham Maslow asserts that safety holds priority over growth, which means that in the presence of threat defense is inevitable. One can hardly argue with him in the face of the evidence. But this is the reason that few humans experience much dialogue in the course of a lifetime.

Dialogue, then, above all else, is based (a) on faith in the self (b) entrusted to the other person in the exchange of communication. It does not necessitate full acceptance of the other person as he is. It does necessitate sufficient confirmation of the other as he is to entrust, to make oneself vulnerable to him.

Second, it means the one has a deep concern for the other person.[6] If dialogue exists between two people, each maintains an I-thou relationship with the other, that is, each holds the other as an inviolate entity, a person to be concerned about. Neither will use the other for his own personal gain. The relationship is prized above any control or advantage. It is the break in such a relationship, when romantic, that is the source of all sad love songs, ex-

pressing the sickening emptiness when a deep faith in a relationship with another has withered. The relationship of dialogue is one where each assumes responsibility for the relationship, and indeed, for the other.

Third, in dialogue *we walk at the edge* of our knowledge and our security, for to trust an unstable relationship is to let a phrase flow freely, to invent, to question, to challenge, to explore—to test an idea in the saying.

Fourth, in dialogue one reveals himself as he is, and as he is affected by the other. If he does this he is open; to be open is to listen.

The purpose of our dialogue is to try our values in social practice, to nurture our value scheme, to put our ideals to the test, to translate between language level six (where we order our values) and language level one (where we feel the experience of living them.) In dialogue we make our life complete, give ourselves our sense of meaning. A common consequence of real dialogue is the response, "I didn't know you were like this. I never really knew how your felt." Then perhaps to the self, "He is changing, and so am I." Hasidic wisdom adds this:

Faith should not rest in the heart; it should also be expressed by word of mouth. The utterance of faith strengthens a man's faith.[7]

Dialogue strengthens faith and faith is the source of dialogue.

The Language of Dialogue

In this description of dialogue we have used scattered examples of the language of dialogue. To fix the concepts and to initiate the attitudes of dialogue it may be helpful to speak further of the role and quality of the language. In so doing we should be careful

to recognize that there are no gimmicks that work; the language that works is that guided by appropriate intent.

Yet the language that works is a guide to us in those moments when dialogue is threatened. We had a call from a man this morning whose first response to a proposed meeting was "Well, it is a little premature. You and I have not yet discussed———." In our urge to maintain the best of relations we responded. "Perhaps I have forgotten something that should be taken care of first. What do you think we ought to do before the meeting?" This response was guided by the need to preserve the dignity of our conversant. Thus the language was, we hope, appropriate. We have noted that the language of people who are able to talk to many people at deep levels is replete with phrases such as: "I may be wrong, but here is the way I see it . . . It could be . . . What would you think . . . I think what I am trying to say . . . Isn't there something missing here . . . What you say might just be so . . . I don't think I know if . . . " The statement is tentative, open to alteration. For some people these phrases seem unsure and in direct opposition to the description of the courage of dialogue. But the peculiar thing about the language of confidence is that on the surface it sounds weak. It is tentative in order to insure accommodation for the other person. Conversely, language that says "This is the way it is. There are no ands, ifs or buts . . ." on the surface sounds like it comes from the mouth of a strong man. Such sure language allows if possible only one interpretation. But, again, it is the flexible man, seeing the possibility for several or many interpretations, who is strong, strong enough to accom-

Walk A Mile in My Shoes

Joe South

If I could be you and you could be me
* for just one hour,*
If we could find a way to get inside each
* other's mind,*
If you could see me through your eyes
* instead of your ego,*
I believe you'd be surprised to see that
* you'd been blind.*

Now your whole world you see around you
* is just a reflection,*
And the law of karma says you reap
* just what you sow.*
So unless you've lived a life of total per-
* fection,*
You'd better be careful of every stone that
* you throw.*

And yet we spend the day throwing stones
* at one another,*
Cause I don't think or wear my hair the
* same way you do.*
Well I may be common people, but I'm
* your brother,*
And when you strike out and try to hurt
* me, it's a hurtin' you.*

There are people on reservations and out
* in the ghettos;*
And, brother, there but for the grace of
* God, go you and I.*
If I only had the wings of a little angel,
Don't you know I'd fly to the top of the
* mountain.*
And then I'd cry.

Walk a mile in my shoes, walk a mile
* in my shoes.*
And before you abuse, criticize and accuse,
Walk a mile in my shoes.

modate, perhaps, his less flexible conversant.

Yet we hasten to add, strength is not wishy-washy accommodation to anything. It is not fearful confusion. And this should be added: the fearful conformist may use the language phrases of the strong man as a camouflage. "I really don't know what to think" may mean the speaker cannot tolerate the responsibility for taking a position—in which the nonverbal cues give us our best clues—but it is also the language of the man who truly has an open mind willing to listen and to find a position necessary to preserve a healthy relationship. When we are too sure of our words we are not listening to them or the words of others. We are listening to the fears which are demanding firm and legal definitions. Legal language is abstract, logical, and technically correct. But the language of dialogue is spontaneous, free, noncritical, tentative, reflective, searching—based on faith and tolerance. When people meet in dialogue, their language is not an analysis of the rights and privileges of each other, but a mutual participation of the lives involved.

1. Ludwig von Bertlanffy, "The Mind-Body Problem: A New View," in Floyd W. Matson and Ashley Montagu, eds., *The Human Dialogue* (New York: The Free Press, 1967), p. 233.

2. Erving Goffman, Interaction Ritual (New York: Doubleday & Company, Inc., 1967), pp. 5–45.

3. Martin Buber, *The Knowledge of Man* (New York: Harper & Row, 1965), p. 179.

4. Sidney M. Jourard, *Disclosing Man to Himself* (Princeton, N.J.: D. Van Nostrand Company, Inc., 1968), p. 123.

5. Martin Buber, "Distance and Relation," *Psychiatry*, 20 (1957), 97–104.

6. Milton Mayeroff, *On Caring* (New York: Harper & Row, Publishers, 1971).

7. Louis I. Newman, *Hasidic Anthology* (New York: Schocken Books, 1963), p. 104.

"Talk to me. I'm your mother."

Empathy Graphics, New York City

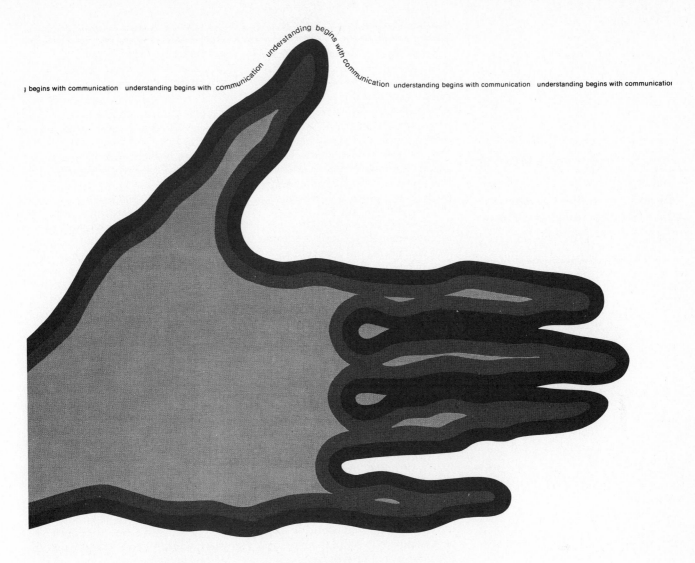

understanding begins with communication understanding begins with communication begins with communication understanding begins with communication understanding begins with communication understanding begins with communicatior

The old paper-between-the-hands-communication game

Number of players: It takes two.
Materials: Yourself, a stranger, hand cut-out.
How to play: Place your right hand on picture of hand. Have opposite
player place (his-her) right hand on opposite side. When both players
are in position, pull the paper out sharply with your left hand. Both
players then quickly close hands.
The *game* is over (or does it just begin?) when both players find they are
in the position to begin a friendship.
Who wins: Both players.

Courtesy of "Genesis," *Mountain Bell Magazine* (fall 1970).

PROBE 19. A person may become a more effective communicator by applying principles of assertiveness.

The Development of Assertive Behavior

Robert E. Alberti and Michael L. Emmons

A man who trims himself to suit everybody will soon whittle himself away. Charles M. Schwab

Perhaps you have heard it said that "when two engineers (lawyers, housewives, plumbers, nurses) are talking together and a psychologist walks up and joins the conversation, there are now two engineers and a psychologist, but when two psychologists are talking and an engineer (substitute your own favorite) walks up and joins them, there are now three psychologists!" Everyone believes he is a psychologist in some sense. Indeed, we all have some practical, firsthand knowledge of human behavior, beginning with ourselves.

Changing Behavior and Attitudes

Unfortunately there are occasional shortcomings in popular views of how people behave. One popular view which has been found by psychologists to be inaccurate is the notion that one must change his attitude before he can change the way he acts. In our experience with hundreds of clients in clinical assertive training, and in the feedback from some of the thousands of readers of this book, as well as from countless reports from our colleagues in psychological practice and research, it is now clear that *behavior can be changed first*, and it is easier and

more effective to do so in most cases.

As you begin the process of becoming more assertive, we won't ask you to wake up some morning and say, "Today I am a new, assertive person!" You will find here instead a guide to systematic, step-by-step changes in behavior. The key to developing assertiveness is *practice of new behavior patterns*.

We have observed a cycle of non-assertive or aggressive behavior which tends to perpetuate itself, until a decisive intervention occurs. A person who has acted non-assertively or aggressively in his relationships for a long period of time usually thinks poorly of himself. His behavior toward others—whether self-denying or abusive—is responded to with scorn, disdain, avoidance. He observes the response and says to himself, "See, I knew I was no damn good." Confirmed in his low self-evaluation, he continues his inadequate behavior patterns. Thus the cycle is repeated: inadequate behavior; negative feedback; attitude of self-depreciation; inadequte behavior.

The most readily observable component of this pattern is the *behavior* itself. We can easily see overt behavior in contrast with attitudes and feelings which may be hidden behind a practiced facade. In addition, *behavior* is the component most amenable to change. Our efforts to facilitate improved interpersonal functioning and a greater valuing of yourself as a person will focus on changing your *behavior* patterns.

We find the cycle can be reversed, becoming a positive sequence: more adequately assertive (self-enhancing) behavior gains more positive responses from others; this positive feedback leads to an enhanced evaluation of self-worth ("Wow, people are treating me like a worthwhile person!"); and improved feelings about oneself result in further assertiveness.

Harold had for years been convinced that he was truly worthless. He was totally dependent upon his wife for emotional support, and despite a rather handsome appearance and ability to express himself well, had literally no friends. Imagine his utter despair when his wife left him! Fortunately, Harold was already in therapy at the time, and was willing to try to make contact with other people. When his first attempts at assertiveness with eligible young women were successful beyond his wildest hopes, the reinforcing value of such responses to his assertions was very high! Harold's entire outlook toward himself changed rapidly, and he became much more assertive in a variety of situations.

Not everyone, to be sure, will experience such an immediate "payoff" for his/her assertions, and not all assertions are fully successful. Success often requires a great deal of patience, and a gradual process of handling more and more difficult situations. Nevertheless this example emphasizes a general rule we have found in facilitating assertive behavior: *assertiveness tends to be self-rewarding.* It feels good to

Blocks to Acting Assertively

Lynn Bloom, Karen Coburn, and Joan Pearlman

The following questionnaire covers six areas that are often blocks to assertive behavior. There are two questions for each area. The first allows you to assess your attitude and the second gives you a chance to examine your behavior.

Check one or more answers, as they apply.

Dealing with My Own Anger

1. When I am angry with someone I usually
   - (a) am afraid to say anything directly, because I don't want to hurt their feelings.
   - (b) am afraid that if I do say something, it will sound aggressive and they won't like me.
   - (c) feel okay about expressing what is on my mind.
   - (d) feel anxious and confused about what I want to say.

2. When I am angry with someone I usually
   - (a) drop hints about my feelings, hoping he or she will get the message.
   - (b) tell the person in a direct way what I want, and feel okay about it.
   - (c) avoid the person for a while until I calm down and the anger wears off.
   - (d) blow up and tell him or her off.
   - (e) express my anger sarcastically—getting my point across with some humor or a dig.

Dealing with Others' Anger

3. When someone gets angry with me I usually
   - (a) think he or she doesn't like me.
   - (b) feel too scared to ask why and to try to work things out.
   - (c) feel confused and want to cry.
   - (d) think I have a right to understand why he or she is angry and to respond to it.
   - (e) immediately feel wronged.
   - (f) feel angry in return.
   - (g) feel guilty.

(continued on page 114)

(continued from page 113)

4. When someone gets angry with me I usually
   (a) end up crying.
   (b) back off.
   (c) ask him or her to explain the anger further, or else I respond to it in some other straightforward manner.
   (d) get angry in return.
   (e) apologize, even if I don't understand why he or she is angry.
   (f) try to smooth it over.
   (g) make a joke out of it and try to get him to forget the flare-up.

Authoritarian Behavior

5. When I need time and information from a busy professional, I usually think he or she will
   (a) resent my taking up valuable time.
   (b) consider my request as legitimate and be pleased that I'm interested.
   (c) act as though he or she doesn't mind but secretly feel the person resents me.
   (d) make me feel inferior.

6. When I need time and information from a busy professional I usually
   (a) put off calling until I absolutely have to.
   (b) apologize for taking up his or her time when I call.
   (c) state directly what I need and ask for what I want.
   (d) let him or her know that I expect immediate attention. After all, I'm important too.

Refusing Requests

7. If someone asks me to do a favor for him or her and I refuse, I think he or she probably will
   (a) hate me.
   (b) be angry with me.
   (c) understand and not mind.
   (d) act as though he or she doesn't mind, but will secretly resent me.
   (e) think I don't like her.
   (f) hesitate to ask me again.

8. If someone asks me to do them a favor and I don't want to do it, I usually
   (a) do it anyway.
   (b) let him or her know that I resent the request, but do it grudgingly.
   (c) make up an excuse as to why I can't do it.
   (d) tell him or her I'd rather not do it.
   (e) tell him or her I'd rather not do it, and apologize profusely.

(continued on page 115)

have others begin to respond more attentively, to achieve one's goals in relationships, to find situations going one's way more often. *And you can make these changes happen!*

Remember to begin with assertions where you are somewhat certain of success before proceeding to more difficult ones requiring greater confidence and skill. It is often quite helpful and reassuring to obtain support and guidance from another person, perhaps a friend, teacher, or professional therapist.

Keep in mind that changed behavior leads to changed attitudes about one's self and one's impact upon people and situations. The balance of this chapter presents the steps involved in bringing about that changed behavior. Read *all* the material here carefully *before* you begin. Then return to this point and begin to follow the steps in your own life. You'll like the difference in you!

The Step-by-Step Process

Step 1: Observe your own behavior. Are you asserting yourself adequately? Are you satisfied with your effectiveness in interpersonal relationships?

Step 2. Keep track of your assertiveness. Make a log or diary for a week. Record each day those situations in which you found yourself responding assertively, those in which you "blew it," and those you avoided altogether so that you would not have to face the need to act assertively. Be honest with yourself, and systematic!

Step 3. Concentrate on a particular situation. Spend a few moments with your eyes closed, imagining how you handle a specific incident (being short-changed at the supermarket, having a friend "talk your ear off" on the telephone when you had too much to do, letting the boss make you "feel like 2¢" over a small mistake). Imagine vividly the actual details, including your specific feelings at the time and afterward.

Step 4: Review your responses. Write down your behavior in Step 3 (eye contact, body posture, gestures, facial expression, voice, message content). Look carefully at the components of your behavior in the recalled incident. Note your strengths. Be aware of those components which represent nonassertive or aggressive behavior.

Step 5: Observe an effective model. At this point it would be very helpful to watch someone who handles the same situation very well. If the model is a friend, discuss his/her approach, and its consequences.

Step 6: Consider alternative responses. What are other possible ways the incident could be handled? Could you deal with it more to your own advantage? Less offensively?

Step 7: Imagine yourself handling the situation. Close your eyes and visualize yourself dealing effectively with the situation. You may act similarly to the "model" in Step 5, or in a very different way. Be assertive, but be as much your "natural self" as you can. Repeat this step as often as necessary until you can imagine a comfortable style for yourself which succeeds in handling the situation well.

Step 8: Try it out. Having examined your own behavior, considered alternatives, and observed a model of more adaptive action, you are now prepared to begin trying out for yourself new ways of dealing with the problem situation. A repeat of Steps 5, 6 and 7

(continued from page 114)

Making Requests

9. When I need something from someone else, I usually feel
   (a) as though I shouldn't bother him or her by asking.
   (b) as though people don't really want to do things for me.
   (c) as though I don't want to put him on the spot by asking.
   (d) that it's okay to go ahead and ask.
   (e) afraid to ask, because he or she might say no.
   (f) as though he or she should do what I want.

10. When I need something from someone else, I usually
    (a) don't ask unless I'm absolutely desperate.
    (b) ask and apologetically explain why I need help.
    (c) do nice things for him or her, hoping she'll return the favor.
    (d) become demanding and insist on getting my way.
    (e) ask directly for what I want, knowing that he or she can refuse my request if he or she wants to.

Initiating Communication

11. When I walk into a party where I don't know anyone, I usually think
    (a) that no one there will talk to me.
    (b) that everyone else is relaxed except me.
    (c) that I'm out of place, and everyone knows it.
    (d) that I won't be able to say the right thing if someone does talk to me.
    (e) that it will be fun to meet some new people.
    (f) of ways to get attention.

12. When I walk into a party where I don't know anyone, I usually
    (a) wait for someone to come and talk to me.
    (b) introduce myself to someone who looks interesting.
    (c) stay on the sidelines and keep to myself.
    (d) put a lampshade on my head or otherwise behave in a bizarre manner, hoping someone will notice.
    (e) rush for food or drink or a cigarette to make it look as if I'm busy and having a good time.

The following answers on the questionnaire indicate assertive beliefs and behaviors:

1. c	4. c	7. c	10. e
2. b	5. b	8. d	11. e
3. d	6. c	9. d	12. b

But don't worry, nobody's perfect. Look over your answers. On questions where yours were the same as those above, you probably have no trouble in asserting yourself. For those where your answers differ, figure out which of the areas are the most difficult. Then think of specific situations in your life that fit those problem categories. Look at the questionnaire again and try to figure out just what may be blocking your assertiveness.

may be appropriate until you are ready to proceed. It is important to select an alternative, more effective way of behaving in the problem situation. You may wish to follow your model and enact the same approach taken by him or her in Step 5. Such a choice is appropriate, but should reflect an awareness that you are a unique person, and you may not find the model's approach one which you could feel good about adopting for yourself. After selecting a more effective alternative behavior, you now should role-play the situation with a friend, teacher, or therapist, attempting to act in accord with the new response pattern you have selected. As in Steps 2, 3, and 4, make careful observation of your behavior, using available mechanical recording aids whenever possible.

Step 9: Get feedback. This step essentially repeats Step 4 with emphasis on the positive aspects of your behavior. Note particularly the strengths of your performance, and work positively to develop weaker areas.

Step 10: Behavior shaping. Steps 7, 8, and 9 should be repeated as often as necessary to "shape" your behavior—by this process of successive approximations of your goal—to a point wherein you feel comfortable dealing in a self-enhancing manner with the previously threatening situation.

Step 11: The real test. You are now ready to test your new response pattern in the actual situation. Up to this point your preparation has taken place in a relatively secure environment. Nevertheless, careful training and repeated practice have prepared you to react almost "automatically" to the situation. You should thus be encouraged to proceed with an *in vivo* trial. If you are unwilling to do so, further rehearsals may be needed. (Persons who are chronically anxious and insecure, or who seriously doubt their own self-worth may need professional therapy. You are strongly urged to seek professional assistance if you believe it is indicated.) Again, remember that *doing*, honestly, spontaneously, is the most important step of all.

Step 12: Further training. You are encouraged to repeat such procedures as may be appropriate in the development of the behavior pattern you desire. You may wish to undertake a similar program relative to other specific situations in which you wish to develop a more adaptive repertoire of responses.

Step 13: Social reinforcement. As a final step in establishing an independent behavior pattern, it is very important that you understand the need for on-going self-reinforcement. In order to maintain your newly-developed assertive behavior, you should achieve a system of reinforcements in your own social environment. For example, you now know the good feeling which accompanies a successful assertion and you can rest assured that this good response will continue. Admiration received from others will be another continuing positive response to your growth. You may wish to develop a check list of specific such reinforcements which are unique to your own environment.

In conclusion, although we emphasize the importance of this systematic learning process, it should be understood that what is recommended is not a lock-step forced pattern without consideration for the needs and objectives of each individual. You are encouraged to provide a learning environment which will help you to grow in assertiveness. No one system is "right" for everyone. We encourage you to be systematic, but to follow a program which will meet your own unique individual needs. There is, of course, no substitute for the *active practice* of assertive behavior in your own life, when *you* choose to, as a means of developing greater assertiveness and enjoying its accompanying rewards.

A Gentle Shove

Now that you know what is involved in the process of developing assertive behavior, don't allow yourself to remain a passive observer. If you are interested enough to read this far, you are either thinking seriously about improving your own assertiveness or considering how you can help others to become more assertive. In either case, *do something about it!*

"But I Never Know What To Say!"

Robert E. Alberti and Michael L. Emmons

George B. Fry III

It almost doesn't matter *what* you say! Of the several components of an assertive message, we have discovered that *what* you say is a good deal less important than *how* you say it. Consider this example: You purchased a sweater ten days ago in a relatively expensive clothing store. After wearing it only twice, you notice that a sleeve has begun to unravel. Picture yourself returning the sweater to the store and saying, "I bought this sweater here ten days ago, and now it's unraveling. I'd like a new sweater or my money back."

Nonverbal cues reveal assertive communication.

How did you present yourself? *Using the same words* in each case, consider the relative impact of your message if:

(1) You walk up to the counter hesitatingly, look down at the floor frequently while speaking, talk almost in a whisper, maintain a fearful expression, put your hands in your pockets or grip the package tightly, and stoop over slightly while turned sideways to the clerk;

(2) You stride up to the counter, glare at the clerk, speak in loud tones and shake your fist, face the clerk squarely and draw up to your full height;

(3) You walk briskly up to the counter, smile pleasantly while looking directly at the clerk, speak in a conversational tone, maintain a calm, firm expression, gesture to point out the flaw or add emphasis, and face the clerk squarely while standing naturally and comfortably.

The difference in the three approaches is obvious. The first, representative of our "non-assertive" style, is a self-demeaning posture, sure to reveal you to the clerk as a pushover, destined to be an "easy mark." In the second (aggressive) case, you probably will get what you're after (the refund), but almost certainly the clerk will detest you and make the process as prolonged and unpleasant as possible. Approach (3) will in all likelihood achieve your goal, and the clerk (and whomever you may be with) will respect you for it.

The message here is that in many instances the non-verbal aspects of your behavior say more than do the words themselves. Although we don't really believe the words are *unimportant*, they are most certainly less important than many people believe. The fact that you assert yourself is primary, the way you handle it is next, and finally, what you say is of less importance.

In the past decade considerable research has been done in the area of non-verbal dimensions of communication. We now have evidence to demonstrate the man-

---

Photograph by *The New York Times*, Times Square, New York

ner in which we utilize these components of behavior to establish territoriality, dominance, relationship, emphasis, interest, caring, control, approval, recognition.

Watch some people expressing themselves. One effective way to do this is to watch a dramatic production on television with the sound turned down so you can't hear what is being said. Almost invariably you can detect the mood and some of the message of the speakers by noting their eye contact, facial expression, gestures, posture, etc.

Let's consider each of these components in greater detail.

Eye Contact

Looking directly at another person to whom you are speaking is an effective way of declaring that you are sincere about what you are saying, and that it is directed to that person. Looking away or looking down suggests a lack of confidence in oneself or deference to the other person. An aggressive stare may be an attempt to "overpower" the other. Continuous eye contact can be uncomfortable, inappropriate, or even a "game;" but a relaxed, steady gaze into the other's eyes, punctuated by occasional looking away, personalizes communication and

emphasizes your interest in that person.

The conscious use of eye contact is relatively simple to develop. Pay attention to your eye communication as you converse with others. Try to increase your eye attention. Don't overdo it, but let the other person know you are interested by looking at him/her, not at the floor, walls, or out the window as you are talking and listening.

Body Posture

The "weight" of your messages to others will be increased if you face the person, stand or sit appropriately close, lean toward him/her, and hold your head erect. We are continually amazed to observe the number of persons who maintain conversations — usually briefly! — while their entire bodies are aimed away from each other! For example, as two people sit beside each other, on an airplane, on a couch, in a classroom, at dinner, it is almost typical that each will face straight ahead for nearly all of the time, turning only the head slightly toward the other. A simple turn of the shoulders, say 30°, toward the other makes the conversation so much more personal! Interest in the other person is clearly demonstrated by this simple change of posture.

In a "stand up for yourself" assertive encounter, leaning toward the other presents a stronger case than leaning away. Also, an active, erect posture lends assertion to your communication, in contrast to a passive, slumping stance. Observing your own posture and your distance from others in conversation will help you to identify the effect of your own "physical presence."

Gestures

A message accented with appropriate gestures takes on added emphasis. Dr. Alberti is fond of referring to the importance of gestures in his Italian heritage. Latins typically utilize extensive gesturing to *describe* a scene or object visually as well as verbally, and to *emphasize* specific points in communication. While over-enthusiastic gesturing can be a distraction, a relaxed use of hands and arms while talking adds depth to the message and avoids the awkward stiffness of arms folded or straight at your

sides. Particularly powerful gestures include the angry fist shaken at your adversary, a soft hand on the arm or shoulder, an open hand extended in front of you ("Stop!").

Another important aspect of gesturing is its message that the speaker is relatively uninhibited, and therefore apparently self-confident. Freedom of arm and hand movements usually accompanies a willingness to express oneself freely, a lack of inhibition, a sense of personal power. Certain nervous gestures, of course, can have precisely the opposite effect, so it is important to develop expressive purposeful gestures which are congruent with your feelings and your verbal message. Such physical expression can be very helpful in increasing the spontaneity of your communication as well.

Facial Expression

Have you ever seen someone trying to express anger while smiling or laughing? Often persons who are very nervous about expressing anger will show their anxiety in a smile. Result: the anger just doesn't come across! Effective assertions require an expression that agrees with the message.

Right now, try looking at yourself in the mirror. Now smile as broadly as you can. Hold the pose. Pay attention to the feeling of tightness in your cheeks and around your eyes. Now relax your face. Release the tightness in the smile muscles. Let go of the tightness, and let your jaw relax. Keep on letting go until your jaw goes slack and your mouth opens slightly. Pay attention to the difference in the feeling in your face and the difference in your expression in the mirror.

© 1975 by NEA, Inc.

"Ask me how I'm doing in my assertiveness training program!"

Putting It All Together

Lynn Bloom, Karen Coburn, and Joan Pearlman

This checklist provides a thorough guide to all the steps to assertion. You can refer to it and go through the whole process, or select the parts that will be helpful to you at the time. Of course, there are times when we can't refer to the checklist but must assert ourselves spontaneously or lose the opportunity.

As we work with the process more and more, we begin to integrate the steps, so that after a while we can quickly focus on the questions that have to do with the specific situations we're in. As we become comfortable with the assertive skills, we can then begin to use them efficiently in situations requiring quick responses.

Steps to Assertion

1. Clarify the situation and focus on the issue. What is my goal? What exactly do I want to accomplish?
2. How will assertive behavior on my part help me to accomplish my goal?
3. What would I usually do to avoid asserting myself in this situation?
4. Why would I want to give that up and assert myself instead?
5. What might be stopping me from asserting myself?
   (a) Have I as a woman been taught to behave in ways that make it difficult for me to act assertively in the present situation? What ways? How can I overcome this?
   (b) What are my rights in this situation? State them clearly.
   (c) Do these rights justify turning my back on my conditioning?
6. Can I:
   (a) Let the other person know I hear and understand him?
   (b) Let the other person know how I feel?
   (c) Tell him what I want?

Exercises in Assertive Responses

Imagine yourself in the following situations, and practice asserting yourself, using the checklist to help clarify your goals and overcome your blocks to assertion.

(continued on page 121)

"Steps to Assertion: A Check List" excerpted from the book THE NEW ASSERTIVE WOMAN by Lynn Z. Bloom, Karen Coburn, and Joan Pearlman. Copyright © 1975 by Lynn Z. Bloom, Karen Levin Coburn, and Joan Crystal Pearlman. Reprinted by permission of DELACORTE PRESS. Originally published in FAMILY CIRCLE.

As you become more aware of the feelings in your face, you can better control your expression. When you want to appear firm, and/or angry, you won't smile, but will adopt a stern expression consistent with your feelings. Your smile can become more natural, and less the automatic, plastic face it may have been.

Voice Tone, Inflection, Volume

A whispered monotone will seldom convince another person that you mean business, while a shouted epithet will bring his defenses into the path of communication. A level, well-modulated conversational statement is convincing without intimidating.

It is relatively simple to get direct feedback about how your voice sounds to others. Most people have access to some sort of tape recorder, and you can try out your voice in several different styles. A regular conversational tone—perhaps reading some prose—will give you a "base line." Then try an angry blast at a make-believe enemy. Then a supportive, caring message. Try persuading someone to accept your point of view.

Each of these samples of your own voice will help you to see how you use your voice to express your feelings. Voice is one of our most valuable resources for communication. When you listen to yourself, pay attention to the *tone* of your voice. Does it have a raspy sharpness when you're angry? Does that change to a soft smoothness to express caring? How about the conversational quality?

Second, notice the inflection. Do you speak in a monotone? Or perhaps with a "sing-song" modulation? Does your inflection really emphasize what you want it to? Finally, how about volume? Do you ordinarily speak so softly that others can barely hear? That can be a subtle means of controlling people, by forcing them to listen carefully. Can you bring out a shout when you *want* to? Or is your conversational volume so loud that people think you're *always* angry?

Get control of your voice, and you'll have harnessed a powerful element of your developing assertiveness!

Fluency

Hesitation in speech is a signal to others that you are unsure of yourself. You need not be a polished speaker in order to get your point across, but you are encouraged to work at making your speech flow smoothly. Comments spoken clearly and slowly are more powerful than rapid, erratic speech filled with stammering and hesitation.

You can practice fluency with a tape recorder. First think of a subject about which you have some knowledge. Then speak into the recorder's microphone on that subject for thirty seconds. Your own words, please—no reading here! Now listen to the recording. Notice particularly the pauses— three seconds or more of silence— and "space fillers"—"uhh . . ." and "you know." Now try the same commentary again—speak more slowly if necessary—this time try to do the entire thirty seconds with no significant pauses, and without resorting to fillers. Keep on practicing this until you can easily handle the thirty seconds on a topic you know well. Then begin on a more difficult topic. Then on to an assertion, and so on until you are satisfied that your fluency is a genuine as-

(continued from page 120)

1. A close friend has taken you out to dinner, for a "special evening." You order your steak rare, and when you cut into it it is medium. You don't want to put a damper on the evening, but you definitely prefer your steak rare. The waiter is heading toward your table. *Rehearse what you would say now.*
2. You bump into a friend who tells you that she's furious with you. She goes on and on about how angry she is but never explains exactly why. She says: "Oh, come on, you know what I'm talking about. I've been upset all day just from thinking about it. I'm so mad I don't even know if I can discuss it with you." *Rehearse your response.*
3. You are in the midst of preparing dinner. The telephone rings; it's a friend who starts the conversation with, "I know this is a bad time to call you, but I have an important decision to make soon and I just have to talk it over with someone." *Rehearse your response.*
4. You have settled in for a quiet Sunday at home—the first in a long time. Your parents call and invite you over for the day. You don't want to go. *Rehearse your assertion.*
5. You go to pick up your car at the service station, where you had left it for a lubrication and one new tire. When you arrive, the mechanic hands you the bill, which is twice as much as you had anticipated. When you question him he says: "Look, lady, the guy who worked on your car left. What can I tell you? He found something wrong with your carburetor, and you needed a tune-up. Look, we're just trying to take care of your car. So let's settle up the bill now." *Rehearse your assertion.*
6. A man in your office always greets you with a leering comment. He thinks he's complimenting you. You want him to stop. *Rehearse your assertion.*

Evaluate Your Assertions

1. Did you say what you wanted to say?
2. Were you direct and unapologetic?
3. Did you stand up for your own rights without infringing on the rights of the other person?
4. Were you sitting or standing in an assertive posture?
5. Did your voice sound strong and calm? Were your gestures relaxed?
6. Did you feel good about yourself after you finished speaking?

We hope you have YES answers to most of these questions. Keep practicing your assertive responses until they feel comfortable to you.

Use the above list to help you evaluate your real-life assertions too!

set in your efforts at self-expression.

Timing

Spontaneous expression will generally be your goal, since hesitation may diminish the effect of an assertion. Judgment is necessary, however, to *select* an appropriate occasion — such as speaking to your boss in the privacy of his office, rather than in front of a group of his subordinates where he may need to respond defensively.

Indeed, although spontaneity is generally best, it is also true that to confront someone before a group will usually bring his/her defenses up. No one enjoys "looking bad" or being wrong in front of others. Creating an opportunity to talk with the person alone is advised in such an event. Your assertion. Judgment is necessary, however, to *select* an appropriate occasion — such as speaking to your boss in the privacy of his

Don't worry about being "too late" to express yourself. Even if your assertion cannot change anything now, go ahead. If you harbor resentment over something past, it will eat away at you, and diminish the relationship.

Content

We save this obvious dimension of assertiveness for last to em-

phasize that, although *what* you say is clearly important, it is often *less* important than most of us generally believe. We encourage a fundamental honesty in interpersonal communication, and spontaneity of expression. In our view, that means saying forcefully, "I'm damn mad about what you just did!" rather than "You're an S.O.B.!" People who have for years hesitated because they "didn't know *what* to say" have found the practice of saying *something*, to express their feelings *at the time*, to be a valuable step toward greater spontaneous assertiveness. A big vocabulary is *not* necessary — say what *you feel!*

One further word about content. We do encourage you to express your own feelings — and to *accept responsibility for them*. Note the difference in the above example between "I'm mad" and "You're an S.O.B." It is not necessary to put the other person down (aggressive) in order to express *your* feeling (assertive).

Your imagination can carry you to a wide variety of situations which demonstrate the importance of the *manner* in which you *express* your assertions. Let it suffice to say here that the time you may be spending *thinking about* "just the right words" will be better spent *making* those assertions! The ultimate goal is expressing *yourself*, honestly and spontaneously, in a manner "right" for you.

The Language of Love: Communications Fights

George R. Bach and Peter Wyden

It is fashionable nowadays for intimates to complain about their "communications." The very word has acquired a certain cachet as if it were something ultramodern. Husbands and wives accuse each other: "You never talk to me" or "You never listen to me." More honest couples take pride in confiding to each other, "We just can't communicate." Whatever the wording, these grievances are likely to be aired in a tone of acute frustration or resignation, much as if the partners were innocent victims of two electronic circuits that went haywire.

Executives know that communications are the life line of business; when the line becomes clogged or breaks down, two things occur: either (1) whatever shouldn't or (2) nothing. Intimates, on the other hand, usually just blame themselves or their mates for communications failures or wallow in lamentations of the "ain't-it-awful" variety. They rarely realize that intimate communication is an art that requires considerable imagination and creativity. They are almost never aware that only a conscious, resolute decision on the part of both partners to work at the problem— continually and for the rest of their lives—can produce good communications. And even if partners are ready to go to work to make their language of love

serve them better, they don't know how to go about it.

The job is big because intimate communication involves a lot more than transmitting and receiving signals. Its purpose is to make explicit everything that partners expect of each other— what is most agreeable and least agreeable, what is relevant and irrelevant; to monitor continually what they experience as bonding or alienating; to synchronize interests, habits, and "hangups"; and to effect the fusion that achieves the *we* without demolishing the *you* or the *me.*

Intimates usually fail to understand that the language of love does not confine itself to matters of loving and other intimate concerns. It permeates *all* communications between lovers. For example, if one business acquaintance says to another, "I'm hungry," this message almost certainly needn't be weighed for emotional implications. It can be taken at face value and acted upon accordingly. However, if an intimate sends the same message to another intimate, he may be engaging in several activities:

1. expressing a private sentiment, perhaps "feeling out loud" just to gauge whether the partner's reaction is sympathetic or indifferent;

2. appealing emotionally to the partner in order to persuade

PROBE 20. Intimate communication requires that the partners make explicit what they expect of each other.

Grin and Bear It   **By Lichty**

"Why do we have to have meaningful dialogues? . . . I feel much better if we merely yell at each other!"

"Grin and Bear It" by George Lichty
Courtesy of Publishers-Hall Syndicate

Tom Tracy

him to do or say something (perhaps, "Come on, let's go to the coffee shop");

3. transmitting meaningful information (perhaps, "I'm starved, but I can't stop to eat now").

Partner A, then, might well be putting his foot in his mouth if Partner B is saying, "You don't understand how busy I am" and "A" only shrugs and replies, "Why don't you go and have something to eat?" Maybe "B" wants "A" to bring him something to eat from the coffee shop so he can work and eat at the same time. Unfortunately, "A" can't divine this request — which "B" would never expect him to do if he were talking to a business colleague.

Many intimates stubbornly insist that there shouldn't be any communications problems between them. The folklore of romantic love leads lovers to believe that some sort of intuitive click or sensitivity links all intimates; that this should suffice to convey their deep mutual understanding; and that this miracle occurs simply because the partners love one another. So they demand to be divined. In effect, they say, "He ought to know how I feel" or, "You'll decode me correctly if you love me." This permits spouses to think they can afford to be sloppier in their intimate communications than they are in their nonintimate contacts.

Another reason why communications are such a problem is a psychological laziness that has many people in its grip. Encouraged by the romantic fallacy that the language of love falls into place as if by magic, they find it easy to shirk the task and shrug it off.

The third reason is that the popularity of game-playing and the role-taking in today's society

has encouraged the suspicion that transparency, even at home, may not be a good idea. This belief is usually grounded in the fear that candor would cause an intimate to reveal something about himself that might cool the partner. It creates still another temptation for partners to try to enjoy a free ride on the vague and often wrong presumption that they understand each other.

The easiest way to create communications problems is to withhold information from one's spouse. When partners don't confide in each other, they are likely to find themselves trying to tap their way through a vacuum, like blind people with white canes. The resulting fights can pop up at any time and place. For Herb and Lonnie Cartwright the place happened to be their kitchen. The time was the evening before they planned to give a big party:

LONNIE: I need another $30 for food for the party.

HERB: That's a lot of money for food.

LONNIE (*exasperated*): People have to eat!

HERB (*reasonable*): I know that.

LONNIE (*taking a deep breath before plunging into unaccustomed territory*): Ever since you bought that new insurance policy we're always strapped for cash.

HERB (*startled*): But it's in your name!

LONNIE (*vehemently*): I don't want you to die! Let's live a little now!

HERB (*shaken*): I resent that! After all, I was trying to do the right thing by you.

LONNIE (*with finality*): Then you shouldn't have bought the policy until after you get your next raise. I don't like to come to you like a beggar.

What happened here? These

Popeye by Bud Sagendorf

partners had kept each other in such ignorance over the years that they inevitably wound up poles apart on family financial policy. This wife, like so many others, thought of her husband as a money tree. One reason why she loved him was that he was such a good provider. She believed that, within reason, she could buy anything she wanted. But she carefully avoided a test of her notions by never expressing an interest in the family bank balance. To her, money was to spend, just like a child's pocket money. To her husband, on the other hand, money was the equivalent of security. He had told his wife that he had bought a big new insurance policy, but not how expensive it had been. The lesson of this case is that husbands would do well not to leave wives ignorant about personal finances or other basic realities of their life together.

When intimates refuse to impart strategic information that they possess, or when they refuse to react to information that is offered to them, they are asking for trouble. Sometimes a partner withholds information in the name of tact. This is especially true when it comes to sharing information about sexual preferences. There are times when the state of the union demands that transparency be tempered by tact. But much so-called tact is cowardice or deception—a cover-up to avoid confrontations and feedback from the opponent. The withholding of information only leads to worse explosions later.

Some husbands, for instance, don't tell their wives how broke they are. They "don't want her to worry." Suddenly a man from the loan company appears at home to repossess the wife's car. Not only is this crisis often unnecessary ("Honey, why didn't you tell me?

I could have borrowed the money from Dad!"). Often it leads to irreversible damage because it erodes the wife's trust in her spouse. In true intimacy stress is shared by partners.

There are partners, however, who, without knowing it, *cause* their spouses to withhold information. One such husband tended to get excited and be in the way when things went wrong at home. Then he lectured his wife that she should have managed better. When he went on business trips he called home daily and his wife always reassured him that things were fine. Usually they were, but one day the husband returned from a week's absence and was extremely upset to find that his wife had broken her ankle and hadn't said a word about it on the telephone. In her inner dialogue, the wife had said to herself, "He's no help in a crisis." The husband had brought this lack of trust upon himself.

When intimates are frustrated by their inability to communicate clearly and straightforwardly, they tend to confuse matters further by sending messages full of sarcasms, hyperboles, caricatures and exaggerations that befog or overdramatize. The list of these statics is almost endless, but here are some random examples:

"I'd just as soon talk to a blank wall." "You've got diarrhea of the mouth." "You did *not say that*; if you did, I didn't hear it!" "We have nothing to say to each other any more." "You always talk in riddles." "I've learned to keep my mouth shut." "You never say what you mean." "Why do you always interrupt me?" "You just like to hear the sound of your own voice." "You never stand up for yourself." "If I've told you once, I've told you a thousand times . . ."

When fight trainees are faced

George B. Fry III

with these statics as they try to communicate feelings and wishes to their partners, we sometimes tell them the ancient yarn about the Texas mule who was too stubborn to respond to commands. The owner decided to hire a famous mule trainer to cure the trouble. The trainer took one look at the mule and cracked him over the head with a two-by-four. The owner was appalled.

"That's dreadful," he said. "I thought you were going to train him!"

"Sure," said the trainer. "But first I have to get his attention."

Partners who must deal with statics need to review the techniques for getting a good fight started. The same goes for spouses who find themselves confronted with opponents who blanket out communications with jamming noises, the way the Communists used to jam Western radio broadcasts.

Some intimate jammers can be infuriatingly effective. Suppose a husband knows his wife wants to talk to him about his overspending. But the husband also knows his spouse loves to listen to gossip about his boss's sex life. The husband therefore rattles on interminably about fresh gossip he has just heard on the office grapevine and then dashes to the car to leave for work.

"Hey," shouts his wife. "We've got to talk about those bills!"

"Will do!" shouts the husband—and drives off.

Even partners who seem to appreciate the importance of open, unjammed communications rarely realize just how unambiguous their signals should be and how meticulously a message sender should solicit feedback from the recipient to check out whether his signal was understood as it was intended. Here is what often happens in the three

stages of message sending: (1) the intention of the message, (2) the framing of the message, and (3) the interpretation of the message at the other end of the line.

Case No. 1: The wife tells the kids not to bother Dad. He is listening.

> *How Meant*
> "I'm protecting you"
> *How Sent*
> "Don't bother him."
> *How Received*
> "She's fencing me in."

Case No. 2: The husband doesn't bring any of his buddies home from his club. She asks him about it.

> *How Meant*
> "It's too much work for you."
> *How Received*
> "He's ashamed of me."
> *How Sent*
> "Oh, let's skip it."

Husbands and wives who wish to extricate themselves from a jungle of unclear signals find it helpful to fix within their minds the seemingly simple fundamentals of communication:

Obtain the attention of your receiver. Prepare him to receive your message. Send out your message clearly and with a minimum of extraneous static. Make sure your information is beamed toward the receiver's wave length. Stake out your own area of interest and stick to its limits. Keep your self and your receiver focused on the joint interest area. Stimulate your receiver to respond by acknowledging reception. Obtain feedback to check how your message was received.

These principles are known to anyone who ever placed an important long-distance phone call. Yet intimates, especially while under the emotional stress of conflict and aggression, tend to

ignore the basics even though they "know better." Their resistance against forging a clear connection is a sign that they find conflict stressful and don't like to accept the fact that they are involved in one.

This is why noncommunicators lead each other around the mulberry bush with such round-robin jabs as these:

SHE: You never talk to me.
HE: What's on your mind?
SHE: It's not what's on *my* mind; it's that I never know what's on *your* mind.
HE (*slightly panicky*): What do you want to know?
SHE (*jubilantly*): Everything!
HE (*thoroughly vexed*): That's crazy!
SHE: Here we go again.

This game of hide-and-seek may also go like this:

HE: You talk too much!
SHE: About what?
HE: About everything.
SHE: One of us has to talk!
HE: You talk, but you never say anything.
SHE: That's crazy.
HE: You're darned right!
SHE (*thoughtfully*): What do you mean?
HE (*wearily*): You make a lot of noise, but that makes it impossible for us to have a real talk.
SHE: Here we go again. . . .

Here's what happened after the latter fight, between two unmarried young people:

DR. BACH (*to the girl*): What was he really telling you?
GIRL: That he doesn't like me.
DR. B (*to the boy*): Is that what you wanted to convey?
BOY: No! I love her!
DR. B: You two are starving for real communication. You're

using words like fog to hide your true feelings.

Here are some exercises that help:

1. Diagnose how efficient or inefficient your present level of communication is. Is each partner candid and transparent? Does each get a chance to tell the other what's "eating him"? Does each partner really understand what the other is after? Once shortcomings are identified, the fight techniques outlined in previous chapters should be used to negotiate settlements.

2. Locate some of the causes of poor communication by owning up to yourself and to each other that you occasionally or habitually use one of the statics discussed in this and the next two chapters. Try to catch each other in the use of static and aggressively eliminate its use. Calls of "Static!" or "Foul!" may help.

3. Stop blocking communication by explicitly renouncing the use of static maneuvers.

4. Start making communication flow more freely by deliberately making yourselves accessible, open, and crystal-clear. From time to time, take new readings of the quality of your communications. Has improvement taken place?

5. Respond with full resonance. Be sure you are sharing your private view of yourself and the world with your partner. Expressive communication enhances intimacy; reflective communication is useful but secondary. The more intimate two people are, the more they take turns expressing their views freely.

I know you believe you understood what you think I said, but I am not sure you realize that what you heard is not what I meant.

An Overview of Transactional Analysis

Muriel James and Dorothy Jongeward

The crazy person says, "I am Abraham Lincoln," and the neurotic says, "I wish I were Abraham Lincoln," and the healthy person says, "I am I, and you are you."   Frederick Perls[1]

PROBE 21.   You can use transactional analysis to understand yourself better and improve your intimate communication.

Many people come to a time in their lives when they are provoked to define themselves. At such a time transactional analysis offers a frame of reference that most people can understand and put to use in their own lives.

Introduction to Structural Analysis

Structural analysis offers one way of answering the questions: Who am I? Why do I act the way I do? How did I get this way? It is a method of analyzing a person's thoughts, feelings, and behavior, based on the phenomena of ego states.[2]

Berne defines an ego state as "A consistent pattern of feeling and experience directly related to a corresponding consistent pattern of behavior."[3] The findings of Dr. Wilder Penfield, neurosurgeon, support this definition. He found that an electrode applied to different parts of the brain evoked memories and feelings long forgotten by the person.[4]

The implications are that what happens to a person is recorded in his brain and nervous tissue. This includes everything a person experienced in his childhood, all that he incorporated from his parent figures, his perceptions of events, his feelings associated with these events, and the distortions that he brings to his memories. These recordings are stored as though on video tape. They can be replaced, and the event recalled and even reexperienced.

Each person has three ego states which are separate and distinct sources of behavior: the Parent ego state, the Adult ego state, and the Child ego state. These are not abstract concepts but realities. "Parent, Adult, and Child represent real people who now exist or who once existed, who have legal names and civic identities."[5]

The three ego states are defined as follows:

The *Parent ego state* contains the attitudes and behavior incorporated from external sources, primarily parents. Outwardly, it often is expressed toward others in prejudicial, critical, and nurturing behavior. Inwardly, it is experienced as old Parental messages which continue to influence the inner Child.

The *Adult ego state* is not related to a person's age. It is oriented to current reality and the objective gathering of information. It is organized, adaptable, intelligent, and functions by testing reality, estimating probabilities, and computing dispassionately.

The *Child ego state* contains

James-Jongeward, BORN TO WIN: Transactional Analysis with Gestalt Experiments, 1971, Addison-Wesley, Reading, Mass.

Andy Capp by Reg Smythe

By permission of Publishers-Hall Syndicate and
The Daily Mirror Newspapers Ltd., London

all the impulses that come naturally to an infant. It also contains the recordings of his early experiences, how he responded to them, and the "positions" he took about himself and others. It is expressed as "old" (archaic) behavior from childhood.

When you are acting, thinking, feeling, as you observed your parents to be doing, you are in your Parent ego state.

When you are dealing with current reality, gathering facts, and computing objectively, you are in your Adult ego state.

When you are feeling and acting as you did when you were a child, you are in your Child ego state.

According to structural analysis, each person may respond to a specific stimulus in quite distinct ways from each of his ego states; sometimes these ego states are in concert, sometimes in conflict. Let's look at the following examples.

To a stimulus of a piece of modern art

> *Parent:* Good grief! What's it supposed to be!
> *Adult:* That costs $350 according to the price tag.
> *Child:* Ooo, what pretty color!

To a request for an office report

> *Parent:* Mr. Brown is not cut out to be a supervisor.
> *Adult:* I know Mr. Brown needs these by five o'clock.
> *Child:* No matter what I do I can't please Mr. Brown.

Introduction to Analyzing Transactions

Anything that happens between people will involve a transaction between their ego states. When one person sends a message to another, he expects a response. All transactions can be classified as (1) complementary, (2) crossed, or (3) ulterior.[6]

Complementary Transactions

A complementary transaction occurs when a message, sent from a specific ego state, gets the predicted response from a specific ego state in the other person. Berne describes a complementary transaction as one which is "appropriate and expected and follows the natural order of healthy human relationship."[7] For example, if a wife who is grieving for her lost friend is comforted by a sympathetic husband, her momentary dependency need is answered appropriately.

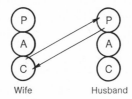

Wife   Husband

A complementary transaction can occur between any two ego states. For example, two people may transact Parent-Parent when lamenting their children's leaving home; Adult-Adult when solving a problem; Child-Child or Parent-Child when having fun together. A person from his Parent can transact with any of the ego states of another person. He can also do this with his Adult and Child. If the response is the expected one, the transaction is complementary. The lines of communication are *open* and the people can continue transacting with one another.

Gestures, facial expressions, body posture, tone of voice, and so forth, all contribute to the meaning in every transaction. If a ver-

bal message is to be completely understood, the receiver must take into consideration the nonverbal aspects as well as the spoken words.

Crossed Transactions

When two people stand glaring at each other, turn their backs on each other, are unwilling to continue transacting, or are puzzled by what has just occurred between them, it is likely that they have just experienced a *crossed transaction*. A crossed transaction occurs when an unexpected response is made to the stimulus. An inappropriate ego state is activated and the lines of transacting between the people are crossed. At this point, people tend to withdraw, turn away from each other, or switch the conversation in another direction. If a husband responds unsympathetically to his grieving wife, "Well, how do you think I feel!" he is likely to cause her to turn away from him.

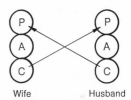

Wife   Husband

Crossed transactions are a frequent source of pain between people—parents and children, husband and wife, boss and employee, teacher and student, and so forth. The person who initiates a transaction, expecting a certain response, does not get it. He is crossed and often left feeling discounted.

Ulterior Transactions

Ulterior transactions are the most complex. They differ from complementary and crossed in that they always involve more than

© 1969, Publishers-Hall Syndicate and Daily Mirror, London TM ®

Knots

R. D. Laing

JILL *I am frightened*
JACK *Don't be frightened*
JILL *I am frightened to be frightened when you*
  tell me I ought not to feel frightened

  frightened
  frightened to be frightened
  not frightened to be frightened

  not frightened
  frightened not to be frightened
  not frightened to be not frightened

JILL *I'm upset you are upset*
JACK *I'm not upset*
JILL *I'm upset that you're not upset that I'm*
  upset you're upset
JACK *I'm upset that you're upset that I'm not*
  upset that you're upset that I'm upset,
  when I'm not.

JILL *You put me in the wrong*
JACK *I am not putting you in the wrong*
JILL *You put me in the wrong for thinking you*
  put me in the wrong.
JACK *Forgive me*
JILL *No*
JACK *I'll never forgive you for not forgiving me*

(continued on page 131)

two ego states. When an ulterior message is sent, it is disguised under a socially acceptable transaction. Such is the purpose of the old cliché: "Wouldn't you like to come up to see my etchings?" In this instance the Adult is verbalizing one thing while the Child, with the use of innuendo, is sending a different message.

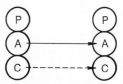

If a car salesman says to his customer with a leer, "This is our finest sports car, but it may be too racy for you," he is sending a message that can be heard either by the customer's Adult ego state or by his Child ego state. If the customer's Adult hears, he may respond, "Yes, you're right, considering the requirements of my job." If his Child responds, he may say "I'll take it. It's just what I want."

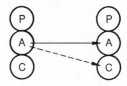

The Games People Play

People play psychological games with one another that are similar to games like monopoly, bridge, or checkers, that people play at social gatherings. The players must know the game in order to play— after all, if one person enters a card party ready to play bridge, and everyone else is playing pinochle, he can't very well play bridge.

All games have a beginning, a

given set of rules, and a concluding payoff. Psychological games, however, have an ulterior purpose. They are not played for fun. Of course, neither are some poker games.

Berne defines a *psychological game* as "a recurring set of transactions, often repetitive, superficially rational, with a concealed motivation; or, more colloquially, as a series of transactions with a gimmick."[8] Three specific elements must be present to define transactions as games: (1) an ongoing series of complementary transactions which are plausible on the social level, (2) an ulterior transaction which is the underlying message of the game, and (3) a predictable payoff which concludes the game and is the real purpose for playing. Games prevent honest, intimate, and open relationships between the players. Yet people play them because they fill up time, provoke attention, reinforce early opinions about self and others, and fulfill a sense of destiny.

Psychological games are played to win, but a person who plays games as a way of life is not a winner. Sometimes a person acts like a loser to win his game. For example, in a game of *Kick Me* a player provokes someone else to put him down.

Student: I stayed up too late last night and don't have my assignment ready.
(ulterior: I'm a bad boy, kick me.)

Instructor: You're out of luck. This is the last day I can give credit for that assignment.
(ulterior: Yes, you are a bad boy and here is your kick.)

(continued from page 130)

JILL *You think I am stupid*
JACK *I don't think you're stupid*
JILL *I must be stupid to think you think I'm*
stupid if you don't: or you must be lying
I am stupid every way:
to think I'm stupid, if I am stupid
to think I'm stupid, if I'm not stupid
to think you think I'm stupid, if you don't.

JILL *I'm ridiculous*
JACK *No you are not*
JILL *I'm ridiculous to feel ridiculous when I'm not.*
You must
be laughing at me
for feeling you are laughing at me
if you are not laughing at me.

How clever has one to be to be stupid?
The others told her she was stupid. So she made
herself stupid in order not to see how stupid
they were to think she was stupid,
because it was bad to think they were stupid.
She preferred to be stupid and good,
rather than bad and clever.

It is bad to be stupid: she needs to be clever
to be so good and stupid.
It is bad to be clever, because this shows
how stupid they were
to tell her how stupid she was.

WHAT'S THE MATTER WITH *HER?*

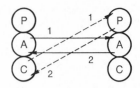

Recorded by JOE SOUTH on CAPITOL Records

GAMES PEOPLE PLAY

Words and Music by
JOE SOUTH

Moderately

Verse:

F

Oh, the games peo-ple play now, ev-'ry night and ev-'ry

oth - er cry; Break a heart then we
to you, Sing-in' Glo-ry Hal -le-
what you see, What's hap-pen-in' to

C

day, now. Nev - er mean - in' what they
say good - bye; Cross our hearts and we
lu - jah! And they're try'n' to sock it
you and me. God grant me the se -

Bb   C   F

say, now. Nev - er say - in' what they mean.
hope to die. That the oth - er was to blame.
to you. In the name of the Lord.
ren - i - ty, To re - mem-ber who I am.

And they while a - way the ho - urs In their i - vo - ry
Nei-ther one will ev - er give in. So, we gaze at an
They gon - na teach you how to me - di - tate; Read your hor-o-scope,
'Cause you're giv-in' up your san - i - ty For your pride and your

(continued on page 133)

Though he may deny it, a person who is used to this game tends to attract others who can play the complementary hand and are willing to "kick" him.

Every game has a first move. Some first moves are nonverbal: turning a cold shoulder, batting a flirty eye, shaking an accusative finger, slamming a door, tracking mud in the house, reading someone's mail, looking woebegone, not speaking. Other first moves are verbal statements such as:

You look so lonesome over here by yourself . . .
How could you go to school wearing that get-up!
He criticized you. Are you going to take that?
I have this terrible problem . . .
Isn't it awful that . . .

Barbara and Tom's favorite game was *Uproar*. They both knew the first move in the game so either could start it. Once it was started, a predictable set of transactions occurred which climaxed with a loud fight. The outcome was always the same—hostile withdrawal to avoid closeness. This was their payoff for playing the game, the avoidance of intimacy.

To set up the game either Barbara or Tom provoked the other with nonverbal behavior such as sulking, chain-smoking, withdrawing, or acting irritated. When the partner was "hooked" into playing, the game was under way. As the game continued he/she got a put-off or a put-down. After exchanging many angry words, they finally withdraw from each other.

The Born Loser by Art Sansom

When Barbara starts the game,
the transactions are:

Barbara: (Begins pouting and chain-smoking with exaggerated gestures)

Tom: "What's the matter? What's wrong?"

Barbara: "It's none of your business!"

Tom: (Goes out to the local bar)

Barbara: (Explodes in anger when he returns. A long battle ensues filled with accusations and counter-accusations. The payoff comes when Barbara breaks into tears, runs into the bedroom, and slams the door. Tom retreats to the kitchen for another drink. They make no further contact that evening.)

When Tom initiates the game,
the transactions are:

Tom: (Fixes a drink for himself, goes off to the den, and closes the door.)

Barbara: "Why didn't you fix a drink for me? Is something wrong?"

Tom: "Can't I even have a few minutes alone!"

Barbara: "If you want to be alone, I'll leave!" (Barbara goes shopping, buys things they can't afford, and returns carrying several packages.)

Tom: (Explodes in anger about the way she spends money. The game comes full circle when she stamps away mad and he fixes his bed in the den.)

Games tend to be repetitious. People find themselves saying the

(continued from page 132)

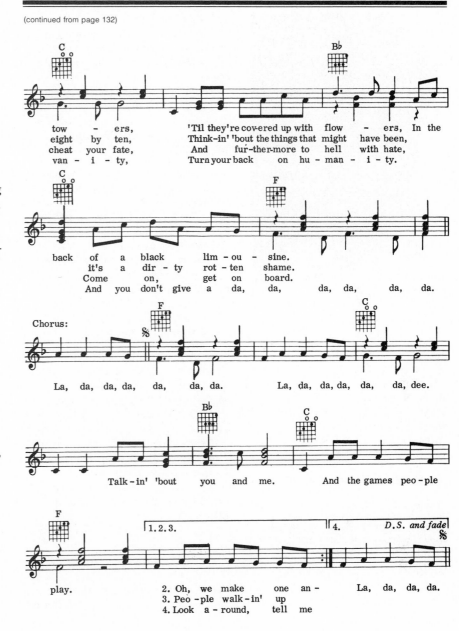

To Talk to You

Jean Itzin

the words
I want to say
fall cringing
to the floor,
scurrying into corners
seeking shadows,
hiding from your gaze.

"To Talk to You" by Jean Itzin. Photo by Dale Moyer. Reprinted by permission from SOUNDS OF SILENCE, Poems and Songs About Loneliness, Selected by Betsy Ryan. © 1972 by Scholastic Magazines, Inc.

same words in the same way, only the time and place may change. Perhaps the replay contributes to what is often described as "I feel as if I've done this before."

People play games with different degrees of intensity from the socially accepted, relaxed level to the criminal homicide/suicide level. Berne writes:

a) A First-Degree Game is one which is socially acceptable in the agent's circle.
b) A Second-Degree Game is one from which no permanent, irremediable damage arises, but which the players would rather conceal from the public.
c) A Third-Degree Game is one which is played for keeps, and which ends in surgery, the courtroom or the morgue.[9]

Games are individually programmed. They are played from the Parent ego state if the parent's games are imitated. They are played from the Adult ego state if they are consciously calculated. They are played from the Child ego state if they are based on early life experiences, decisions, and the "positions" that a child takes about himself and others.

Psychological Positions

When taking positions about themselves, people may conclude:

I'm smart.   I'm stupid.
I'm powerful.   I'm inadequate.
I'm nice.   I'm nasty.
I'm an angel.   I'm a devil.
I can't do anything right.   I can't do anything wrong.
I'm as good as anybody else.   I don't deserve to live.

When taking positions about others, people may conclude:

People will give me anything I want.   Nobody will give me anything.
People are wonderful.   People are no damn good.
Someone will help me.   People are out to get me.
Everybody likes me.   Nobody likes me.
People are nice.   Everybody's mean.

In general, the above positions are "I'm OK" or "I'm not-OK," and "You're OK" or "You're not-OK." The psychological positions taken about oneself and about others fit into four basic patterns.[10] The first is the winner's position, but even winners may occasionally have feelings that resemble the other three.

The First Position: I'm OK, You're OK

is potentially a mentally healthy position. If realistic, a person with this position about himself and others can solve his problems constructively. His expectations are likely to be valid. He accepts the significance of people.

The Second or Projective Position: I'm OK, You're not-OK

is the position of persons who feel victimized or persecuted. They blame others for their miseries. Delinquents and criminals often have this position and take on paranoid behavior which in extreme cases may lead to homicide.

The Third or Introjective Position: I'm not-OK, You're OK

is a common position of persons who feel powerless when they compare themselves to others. This position leads them to withdraw, to experience depression, and, in severe cases, to become suicidal.

The Fourth or Futility Position:
I'm not-OK, You're not-OK
is the position of those who lose
interest in living, who exhibit
schizoid behavior, and, in extreme cases, commit suicide or
homicide.

The person with the first position feels "Life is worth living."
With the second he feels "Your
life is not worth much." With the
third he feels "My life is not
worth much." With the fourth he
feels "Life isn't worth anything at
all."

---

1. Frederick S. Perls, *Gestalt Therapy Verbatim* (Lafayette, Calif.: Real People Press, 1969), p. 40.

2. Eric Berne, *Transactional Analysis in Psychotherapy* (New York: Grove Press, 1961), pp. 17–43.

Cf. Paul McCormick and Leonard Campos, *Introduce Yourself to Transactional Analysis: A TA Handbook* (Stockton, Calif.: San Joaquin TA Study Group, Distributed by Transactional Pub., 3155 College Ave., Berkeley, Calif., 94705, 1969).

Also see John M. Dusay, "Transactional Analysis," in *A Layman's Guide to Psychiatry and Psychoanalysis* by Eric Berne (New York: Simon & Schuster, 3rd ed., 1968), pp. 277–306.

3. Eric Berne, *Principles of Group Treatment* (New York: Oxford University Press, 1964), p. 364.

4. W. Penfield, "Memory Mechanisms," A.M.A. *Archives of Neurology and Psychiatry*, vol. 67 (1952), pp. 178–98.

5. Berne, *Transactional Analysis in Psychotherapy*, p. 32.

6. Eric Berne, *Games People Play* (New York: Grove Press, 1964), pp. 29–64.

7. Ibid., p. 29.

8. Eric Berne, "Transactional Analysis" in *Active Psychotherapy* by Harold Greenwald, ed. (New York: Atherton Press, 1967), p. 125.

9. Berne, *Games People Play*, p. 64.

10. Eric Berne, "Standard Nomenclature, Transactional Nomenclature," *Transactional Analysis Bulletin*, vol. 8, no. 32, October, 1969, p. 112.

Cf. Zelig Selinger, "The Parental Second Position in Treatment," *Transactional Analysis Bulletin*, vol. 6, no. 21, January, 1967, p. 29.

George B. Fry III

The Interview

William D. Brooks

The interview is a form of dyadic communication involving two parties, at least one of whom has a preconceived and serious purpose, and both of whom speak and listen from time to time.[1] This definition indicates clearly that the interview is a *bipolar communication situation*. Although it is possible to have more than two persons in an interview, i.e., the group interview, team interview, or board interview, yet even these interviews are essentially bipolar: there are *two* parties. Thus, the interview is different from a small, problem-solving group in which three, four, five, or some limited number of persons present several points of view and then cooperate to find a satisfactory solution. The interview is also unlike debate, even though debate is dyadic and bipolar, in that no third party renders a decision or acts as an arbiter in the interview, as is the case in debate.

A second element in the definition of the interview is that at least one person, and perhaps both, has a *preconceived and serious purpose*. Two persons getting together and talking with neither having thought in advance about the purpose or objective to be accomplished does not constitute an interview. It might be social conversation, but it is not an interview. The word *serious* helps to differentiate the interview from social conversation for enjoyment.

The third element in the definition is: *both of whom speak and listen from time to time*. This places the interview clearly within the category of interpersonal communication. This element also emphasizes the constant two-way interaction that is a characteristic of any successful interview. The situation in which one person does almost all the talking is not an interview. It may be a private lecture, or an interrogation, but it fails to become an interview. When a "high-pressure" salesman delivers a memorized fifteen-minute presentation to a trapped customer, he is not engaged in a sales interview, but in a public speech since, like public speaking, it is a one-way form of communication with one initiator of messages. Goyer, et al. have stated: "Indeed, it is probably safe to suggest that if an expository interviewer finds himself talking uninterruptedly for as long as *two minutes*, he very likely is failing to 'get through' to his interviewee."[2] Interviewing demands that each party be a skillful participator in both sending and receiving messages. Not only do both participants send and receive messages, but they are also constantly engaged in moment-to-moment adaptations — in checking on the meanings of messages through soliciting and sending feedback. The effective participant in interviewing cannot depend absolutely on an advance outline or memorized speech. Unlike the debate situation, the interviewer or interviewee cannot plan his response while his colleague talks. Neither can the participant in an interview stop the communication process while he interprets what the other person has said and its meaning. Nor can he depend on words alone. He must be sensitive to nonverbal communication, to feedback, to feelings and attitudes, to the interpersonal relationships that exist and are developing, and to his own accuracy and efficiency in *intrapersonal* communication. The interview is one of the most demanding and sophisticated forms of communication, as well as one of the most potentially productive forms of communication, and as such, it calls into practice all those elements of intrapersonal and interpersonal communication discussed in this text.

Interview Purposes

Interviews are of several types and take place in many different contexts with a variety of purposes. Nevertheless, it is possible to classify interviews in terms of the *dominant* purpose the interviewer (the person who has the chief responsibility for achieving a successful outcome) has in mind. Interviews have been classified into ten types: (1) information-getting, (2) information-giving, (3) advocating, (4) problem-solving, (5) counseling, (6) application for employment or job, (7) receiving complaints, (8) reprimanding or correcting, (9) appraising, and (10) stress interviewing.[3]

In the information-getting interview, the objective is usually to obtain beliefs, attitudes, feelings, or other data from the interviewee. Public opinion poll and research surveys are typical well-known examples, but in fact, most people participate frequently in essentially the same kind of communication situation.

The purpose of the information-giving interview is to explain or instruct. Giving work instructions to a new employee or explaining the procedures and policies of the organization to a new member are examples of information-giving interviews.

Sometimes, a person wishes to modify the beliefs or attitudes of another person and attempts to do so through the persuasive interview. The sales interview is a typical example of the interviewer (the persuader or salesman) attempting to sway the interviewee (the respondent or customer) towards adopting his point of view. Another example of the advocating interview is the attempt of a subordinate to persuade his chairman, foreman, or boss to accept a proposal; or when you go to the bank to secure a loan you are a persuader engaged in a persuasive interview. Throughout life each of us engages in interviews in which we try to persuade another person to agree with us.

The problem-solving interview involves both information and persuasion just as does the problem-solving small group. In fact, the problem-solving interview could be classified as a two-person discussion or problem-solving group.

The counseling interview may be directly persuasive as one person tries to get the other to change his behavior in a prescribed manner, or it may be relatively non-persuasive (i.e., non-directive) in that its objective is to provide a situation in which the client can gain insight into his own problems. Counseling interviews focus on the *personal* problems of the person being advised. This type of interview requires a high degree of skill and psychological sophistication on the part of the counselor.

The employment interview, an interview in which virtually every member of society participates sooner or later, is a special type of interview that utilizes information-getting, information-giving, and persuasion as each party tries to get information from the other party and, perhaps, tries to persuade the other party.

Receiving complaints and reprimanding are specialized interviews which require the combination of several skills—persuading, problem-solving, counseling, information-giving, and information-getting. The purpose of the receiver of complaints is to do as much as possible to satisfy grievances. The purpose of the reprimand interview is to change the behavior of the interviewee favorably by helping him acquire new insight and motivation.

The appraising interview aims to inform the interviewee as to how well he is doing at his job and to give guidelines relative to his future performance. This interview of appraisal is related, in part, to the counseling interview.

Stress interviewing is often used as a testing procedure in which an opportunity is provided to observe how the interviewee reacts or behaves under pressure.

Participants in the Interview

The participants in interviews generally are most commonly referred to as *interviewer* and *interviewee*, although these terms are not the most appropriate for some interview situations. Terms such as counselor/counselee or persuader/persuadee are, for example, better terms for the

B.C. *by Johnny Hart*

By permission of Johnny Hart and Field Enterprises, Inc.

counseling situation and the persuasive interview. However, regardless of the term used—counselor, persuader, or interviewer—it refers to the party that carries the chief responsibility for achieving a successful outcome of the interview. It should be recognized, of course, that in many interviews both parties accept a responsibility for the successful outcome of the interview. This is especially true of the employment interview in which the employer wishes to "sell" his company and the applicant attempts to "sell" his qualifications.

The interviewee in most interview situations has the power of decision. In the information-getting interview the respondent (interviewee) decides whether to provide the information or not; in the reprimand and appraisal interviews the interviewee decides whether he will accept the correction or evaluation; and in the persuasive interview the respondent has the power of accepting or rejecting the persuasive attempt. In the employment interview, however, both parties share the decision-making power.

There are role-relationships in every interview as there are in other communication situations. Normally, it is the responsibility of the interviewer to take the initiative in the interview and to clarify role-relationships if such clarification is needed. It is not unusual in the employment interview for roles to change as the interview develops: e.g., at one time the applicant is the respondent and at another time the em-

ployer is the respondent. Since the functions of each interview participant vary widely among types of interviews as well as from specific interview to specific interview, it is unwise to think in terms of rigid, universal duties.

The Question-Answer Process

There are many ways of classifying the various types of questions. Regardless of the classification system used, it appears to be a useful first step in developing skill in the question-answer process to be able to identify types of questions and their uses as well as types of answers. Our system calls for classifying interview questions into five basic types: open, closed, mirroring, probing, and leading.

Open Questions

Open questions call for a response of more than a few words. One type of open question, the open-ended question, is extremely vague in that it may do nothing more than specify a topic and ask the respondent to talk. An example is "What do you think about life?" or "Tell me a little about yourself."

A second kind of open question is more direct in that it identifies a more restricted topic area and asks for a reply on that restricted topic. In some classification systems this question is classified separately from open questions and is called the direct question. An example is "What did you do on your weekends last winter?"

Closed Questions

A second category of questions is the closed question. The closed question calls for a specific re-

The heart of the interviewing process is the quality of the questioning.

sponse of a few words. One type of closed question is the yes-no, or bipolar question. It calls for a "yes" or a "no" answer—or, perhaps, an "I don't know" reply. "Did you attend the last home basketball game last winter?" is a closed question. Similarly, "What two courses did you like most, and what two courses did you like least in high school?" is a closed question, though not a yes-no question.

One important principle related to the use of open or closed questions is that these types of questions tend to influence the length of the interviewee's responses. Open questions encourage the respondent to talk more, while closed questions discourage participation by the respondent.[4] Since one of the problems in most interviews is getting the interviewee to become freely involved and to participate in the interview, it is unwise for the interviewer to plan and use only closed questions. Neither should an interviewer in the informative, persuasive, or employment interview rely solely on open questions. Doing so, he may discover that, even though the interviewee does talk a lot he gives up very little specific information about himself. Further, the exclusive use of open questions often results in covering fewer topics than might have been possible with more direction and specificity. It is desirable to learn to use both types of questions. Generally speaking, open questions are more likely to be used in the early part of the interview or at the introduction of each new topic area, while closed questions are used as follow-ups for the responses to open questions.

Mirror Questions

Mirror questions are nondirective

techniques. The reason for using a mirror question is to encourage the interviewee to expand on a response that the interviewer believes was incomplete. Mirror questions are often restatements of what the interviewee has just said. If the interviewee has said: "I don't approve of legalizing abortion," a mirror question might be: "You say that abortion should not be legalized?" Closely related to the mirror question is the probe.

Probing Questions

Some questions are asked in order to probe more deeply into the reasons for an attitude or belief, or to elicit more specific information. Not all probes are questions of *why* or *how*, although those are common probing questions. There are a variety of other vocalizations that act effectively as probes and encouragements. Brief sounds or phrases such as "Uh-huh," "I see," "That's interesting," "Oh?" "Good," "I understand," and "Go on" have the effect of requesting further comment from the respondent. Probes and encouragements are introduced at any time—during pauses or while the interviewee is speaking. They indicate careful attention and interest, and they have the function of encouraging the respondent to "tell more" without specifying in a closed way the further response. It is important that an interviewer avoid the habit of relying on one reinforcing or probing word.

Equally as important as direct probing questions and sounds or phrases of encouragement is the use of silence. The inexperienced interviewer is often afraid of pauses and silences. He tends to fill every silence, and so doing, rushes through the interview.

Tom Tracy

Sometimes, if the respondent is slow in answering a question, the inexperienced interviewer may rush in to rephrase the question or to ask a new question. With experience, interviewers can learn when to use silence as a means of communication—as a probe, for example. Silences, if they are effective as probes, must be terminated by the respondent. Research findings indicate that silences of three to six seconds are most effective in getting the respondent to provide more information.[5] If the respondent does not terminate the silence within that time, the chances of his remaining silent increase. This means not only that the interviewer will have to speak, but that the use of silence will have been ineffective and that it will have had a damaging effect upon the interview situation. Hence, when one uses silence as a probe, he should be prepared to terminate the silence within six seconds or at such time as it seems destined to fail as a probing technique.

Leading Questions

Leading questions strongly imply or encourage a specific answer. They "lead" the respondent to an answer the interviewer expects. The leading question can be quite *detrimental* to the interview when used for the wrong reasons. If the interviewer wants straightforward, valid, and reliable information from the respondent, he will want to carefully avoid using leading questions. Cannell and Kahn state: "Questions should be phrased so that they contain no suggestion as to the most appropriate response,"[6] and Bingham, Moore, and Gustad state: "Avoid implying the answer to your own question."[7] If, however, the interviewer wishes to *test* the respond-

ent, to see if he *really* understands, or is *genuinely* committed, then the leading question may be quite useful. For example, when the speech therapist asks the mother of a stuttering child, "You are slapping his hands every time he starts to stutter, aren't you?" he is leading her to an incorrect answer unless she clearly understands that slapping the child for stuttering is inappropriate behavior. When this tactic is taken by the interviewer, he is sometimes referred to as the *devil's advocate*.

One type of leading question is the *yes-response* question, or the *no-response* question. "Naturally, you agreed with the decision, didn't you?" is an example of a yes-response question. One of the components of leading questions is *expectation*. If the interviewer asks, "Are you twenty-one years old?" the question is a direct, closed question, but it is not leading. If the interviewer, however, asks, "Of course, you are twenty-one years old, aren't you?" he indicates an expectation. Expectations can be identified by the syntax and logic of the question, but intonation can communicate doubt, confidence, and *expectation*. Through intonation and emphasis one might make the question, "Did *you* agree with that decision?" a leading question. The intonation and emphasis could register surprise and incredulity at anything other than the expected answer.

Another form of the leading question is the loaded question, which uses loaded words and has high emotional connotations. It reaches "touchy spots" and strikes strong feelings. It may present a dilemma from which it is difficult for the respondent to escape. Questions that are not stated objectively are considered loaded. Various techniques are

...THE ART OF COMMUNICATION SUFFERS SOMEWHAT AT THE CONVERSATIONAL LEVEL.

used to indicate the bias or expectation. Prestige may be used. "The President of the United States believes that the problem is serious. Do you agree?" is an example of using prestige to indicate the bias. The interviewer may also associate positive stereotypes with responses that are desired or negative stereotypes with responses that are not desired. It is apparent that loaded questions should be used with extreme caution, and probably not at all by the inexperienced interviewer. When used by an insightful and skilled interviewer, the loaded question may uncover important hidden information, attitudes, or feelings.

To gain an understanding of the question-answer process, one needs to become familiar with and be able to recognize the various types of questions that may be used. Through guided practice, he can develop skill in using questions. He must also develop skill

in recognizing inadequate answers to his questions.

Inadequate Answers

One kind of inadequate response is the *ooververbalized response*. In one trial situation, the lawyer asked a witness how she came to be at a certain place at 1:30 A.M. She proceeded to tell in detail how she had spent the preceding twenty-four hours. After five minutes in relating what she had done between 7:00 A.M. and noon, the attorney was finally successful in interrupting her and requesting her to skip those details and tell why she was at that certain place at 1:30.

Another kind of inadequate response is the *irrelevant answer*. It simply has nothing to do with the question asked. It has no bearing on the subject or purpose of the interview.

A third unacceptable response is the *inaccurate response*. The

information may be purposely or accidentally false, but it is inaccurate, detrimental, and unacceptable. Inaccurate responses are often difficult to detect, but when inaccuracy is suspected related questions and delayed, repeated questions may be asked to check consistency.

The *partial response* is a fourth kind of inadequate answer. Partial responses are easily detected if the interviewer is alert and thinking. If the interviewer is hastily taking the first small answer and rushing on to his next question, he may settle for partial responses when he should have probed and elicited more information.

Nonresponse is the fifth inadequate response. It is a rather serious response which may be ignored and the question dropped, or which may be probed if the interviewer thinks it would be profitable to do so. One of the most common weaknesses related to using questions in the interview is the tendency to take too much for granted, i.e., the interviewer too easily assumes that his interpretations of the interviewee's responses are accurate. He jumps to conclusions too quickly. He fails to check the meanings of the messages. The interviewer also assumes too quickly that the interviewee understands the question—that the respondent has the same frame of reference as does the interviewer. Such assumptions are not warranted, as has been stressed throughout this text. As interviewers and as interviewees we need to develop a critical attitude toward our questions and answers. We must curb the tendency to accept the first meaning that pops into our heads. The

tendency to take things for granted, to presume, is not easy to correct. It is a common characteristic we all share. It is a subtle fault, and for this reason, we need to discipline ourselves—to stop and ask ourselves, "Now, what am I taking for granted here?" Successful interviewing requires effective interpersonal and intrapersonal communication.

We must remember that in the informational interview, information is forfeited when we omit data and meanings, when we distort statements (sometimes we mistake qualified statements for definite statements), and when we make additions to what the other person has said. We can prevent some of this forfeiting of information if we are systematic, if we employ verbal emphasis and attention factors, if we encourage and use feedback, if we summarize frequently, and if we are sensitive to the other person's viewpoint, frame of reference, experience, and intended meaning. We must remember that role differences, interpersonal attraction, thinking habits, attitudes, and poor listening habits can act as barriers to effective informational interviewing.

The Structure of the Interview

There are at least three parts to all interviews—the opening, the substantive part, and the closing. The initial stage, opening the interview, is quite important, for during this time the relationship between the interviewer and the respondent is established. The objectives of the opening are to establish confidence, trust, clarity

of the purpose of the interview, and the identification of mutual goals. Rapport, an important element throughout the interview, is largely established in the opening stage of the interview. Some preinterview acts also relate to the establishment of rapport. The request for an interview should *never* be made in terms that alarm or threaten the interviewee, for example; and the place selected for the interview should be private, comfortable, and conducive to a smooth and satisfactory interview operation. In addition to pre-interview planning, certain behavior during the opening of the interview can help to establish good rapport, confidence, and relaxation for the interview. The purpose of the interview should be clearly explained and the procedures indicated and mutually agreed to or adjusted.

The second phase of the interview is the substantive part of the interview that relies heavily upon the question-answer process previously discussed.

The final part of the interview is the closing. Some interviews come to natural closings as a result of the nature of the progress of the discussion or as a result of the inclination of the participants. Other interviews need to be continued, but circumstances dictate that they must be closed. Still other interviews could be continued profitably because things are going so well, but time dictates that they must be ended. Regardless of the reasons or conditions, the interview closing ought to contain a short summary by the interviewer, an opportunity for the interviewee to make additions and corrections, and an indication of the next steps, or where-to-go-from-here.

1. Robert S. Goyer, W. Charles Redding, and John T. Rickey, *Interviewing Principles and Techniques* (Dubuque, Iowa: Wm. C. Brown Book Company, 1968), p. 6.

2. Ibid., p. 14.

3. Ibid., pp. 7–8.

4. Stephen A. Richardson, Barbara S. Dohrenwend, and David Klein, *Interviewing: Its Forms and Functions* (New York: Basic Books, Inc., 1965), p. 147.

5. See: R. L. Gordon, "An Interaction Analysis of the Depth-Interview" (Ph.D. diss., University of Chicago, 1954); and G. Saslow et al. "Test-Retest Stability of Interaction Patterns During Interviews Conducted One Week Apart," *Journal of Abnormal Social Psychology* 54 (1957): 295–302.

6. C. F. Cannell and R. L. Kahn, "The Collection of Data by Interviewing," in *Research Methods in the Behavioral Sciences*, ed L. Festinger and D. Katz (New York: Dryden Press, 1953), p. 346.

7. W. V. D. Bingham, B. V. Moore, and J. W. Gustad, "How to Interview" (New York: Harper & Brothers, 1959), p. 74.

Prods

1. How does a conversation with a friend differ from a public speech? Be as specific as you can; consider type of language, kinds of nonverbal behavior, and amount of risk involved.

2. Talk with the personnel director of a large organization about his or her interviewing style—the purpose of an interview, the criteria for judging its success, and the kinds of questions used.

3. Think of a conversation you recently had with a close friend. How might you have helped improve the conversation? What might the other person have done to improve it?

4. List five parent messages you received today. How have they influenced your behavior? Think of the way in which you use your Adult and Child. Describe two situations where both were used.

5. What TA games do you like to play? How do you know when you're playing them? What can you do to stop them?

6. With whom do you have intimate communication? Describe the relationships and explain how they differ from other relationships.

7. Refer to the exercises on assertive responses. Write an exercise for developing an assertive behavior for yourself.

2

SERIAL

PROBE 23 Serial communication of information involves the reproduction of a message through a network of individuals.

PROBE 24 Differences in sender-receiver backgrounds, personalities, and expectations are likely to distort any message — especially one that is transmitted serially.

PROBE 25 Alterations, omissions, and additions can occur in serially reproduced messages because of the motives and assumptions of communicators.

PROBE 26 In organizations the grapevine distributes information to members through serial reproduction.

Relationship 2: Serial

When information is communicated by means of a series of dyads or one-to-one contacts, we call the process serial communication. That is, relationships in which messages are reproduced in one-to-one-to-one-to-one encounters are referred to as serial. As you reflect on the situations you are involved in that require getting information from one person to another through *someone else,* the widespread use of serial communication becomes apparent. For example, at home you may want to get a message to your mother, who is not at home, so you ask your brother, who is at home, to tell her when she comes in. The three of you constitute the basic unit of serial communication: the first person's message (you) was reproduced by a second person (your brother) for a third person (your mother).

Serial communication occurs in a multitude of places, including day-to-day contacts at school, at work, at church, in social clubs, and in community and government organizations. The messages that determine most of our daily decisions come to us secondhand, through the serial process. We learn little information about what has happened across the country directly; most of the time, we listen to what a newscaster has received from someone who has written about a report that was received by someone who may have been at the scene. Walking around campus, you may chat with a friend who tells you what she heard from a neighbor about an event that happened across town. Remember, that is a serial communication situation.

Problems that develop from difficulties in dyadic relationships may also affect serial communication. In addition, the rate at which information changes is accelerated by the person-to-person-to-person reproduction process. Being sensitive to the possibility of distortion creeping into serially reproduced messages may help you guard against or at least take steps to minimize the effects of changes. You may want to develop some special skills in reducing information loss in serial situations. Since serial communication is so widespread in our organizational society, ways of improving the quality of serial communication are some of the most important communication skills we need today.

Serial Communication

R. Wayne Pace and Robert R. Boren

Information is diffused throughout complex organizations, e.g., university, business, governmental agency, hospital, or church, by a process in which the person in charge or at the top of the hierarchy (dean, manager, section head, administrator, or bishop) sends a message to a second person who is required, in turn, to reproduce the message for a third person. The *reproduction* of the first person's message becomes the message of the second person, and the reproduction of the reproduction becomes the message of the third person. Strictly interpreted, the "flow" of information in an organization occurs in this serial, reproductive fashion. Information itself does not flow; but, through successive reproductions, messages become subject to modifications that give communicators the impression that messages are constantly changing like the flow of water down the tumultuous Missouri River as it surges toward the Mississippi. Messages in serial reproduction, like water in a great river, change through losses, gains, absorptions, and combinations along the route from the headwaters to their final destination.

Networks

The serial reproduction of a message is a way of disseminating information by means of successive dyadic encounters involving—eventually—a large number of individuals. Since the sequence of reproduced messages represents a pattern of "who-talks-to-whom," serial communication has, as one of its most significant features, a *communication network*. Keith Davis, Daniel Katz, Robert L. Kahn, and Paul Lazarsfeld—among others—have summarized, in different contexts and for different purposes, a number of attributes and designs of networks of interpersonal communication.[1] Among some of the more important characteristics to be noted are: (1) Networks vary in terms of the message-content that they carry; (2) each network has a sequence for the distribution of messages; (3) restrictions influence the number of links in a network; and (4) networks must exhibit an adaptability for handling the required number of messages at the rate at which they enter the system.

Message-Content

As the name *chain-of-command* implies, directives, orders, and other types of authoritative messages are carried through communication networks, usually in an ascending order or rank. This network is often referred to as the "lines of authority" and should be structured so as to link and establish contact with every member of the organization in some official manner. These lines of contact should be clearly understood by all individuals in the organi-

---

PROBE 23. Serial communication of information involves the reproduction of a message through a network of individuals.

---

zation and should be as direct and short as possible. With only rare exceptions, the complete sequence of contacts should be used to disseminate messages having authoritative content.[2] Sometimes a different network is utilized in the diffusion of information about the overall functioning of the organization. Although the network that disseminates orders and directives may also carry *messages about how the organization is operating*, the two networks are often quite different.

Another communication network allows specialized *messages relevant to the accomplishment of technical jobs* to be distributed to the limited number of receiver/sources who can use them most advantageously. Messages concerning equipment, procedures, and research data may be made available to specific individuals without employing either the authority lines or the operational lines of communication. Most of us are involved in one or more quite restricted networks that consist of our friendship contacts. *Messages about the extra-organizational lives of individuals* are usually diffused along friendship communication networks. Family events, church and social experiences, and community activities generally travel in serially reproduced chains in these kinds of friendship networks. Stanley Milgram described an experiment in which several individuals were asked to use only friendship contacts to move a message from a town in Kansas to a specific unknown person in Massachusetts. In one case, the message arrived four days later and had involved only four people, including the initiator and the recipient.[3] Finally, in most organizations, *messages about*

important contributions, recognitions, and reputations are diffused in a prestige network. Although usually this network may be rather small, there frequently exists a chain of individuals who have information about and bestow prestige upon other members of the organization.

Message-Sequence

The sequence in which messages are diffused in a network chain may be determined by the content of the message to be disseminated or by some other factor. Broadly speaking, however, three basic arrangements or "sequence-systems" prevail: the single strand, the cluster pattern, and the repetitive system. The *single strand* involves a series of message reproductions along a well-defined chain from A to B to C to D to E. *The cluster pattern*, a more complex system, involves single strands of varying lengths. Each strand has one or more dyadic contacts with some end-points and some "liaison" individuals who provide linkages between groups of people and who cross networks to transmit messages actively to several others. The *repetitive system* is one in which the initiator of the message reiterates or reproduces the message several times—in each instance to different individuals in different locations.

Network Restrictions

Obviously, the size and complexity of communication networks are determined by the number of links necessary and desirable to make contact with each individual who should be part of the network. Although a network may be

Blondie by Chic Young

© King Features Syndicate, Inc., 1971.

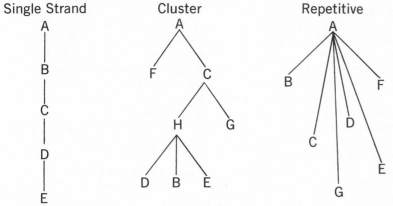

Fig. 1. *Three basic, sequential communication-network systems*

designed, for instance, to contact all fifty members of an organization, the actual network may be considerably smaller. Both research scholars and managers agree that a network will tend to be more efficient if it has a limited number of links. Alex Bavelas and Dermot Barrett, for example, experimented with three networks similar to those shown in Figure 1, and they discovered that the restricted *repetitive* network seemed to function the fastest and with the highest degree of accuracy.[4] The most efficient communication network will be the one which (1) allows each individual link to receive just the proper number of messages to do his or her work satisfactorily and keep informed, and (2) restricts entry of irrelevant and unnecessary messages into the system.

Network Adaptability

Sometimes the number of incoming messages exceeds the level at which the network and/or the individuals of which it is composed can handle them. When too many messages enter the system or the messages come too fast to be processed, the outside limits of network adaptability have been reached. The effectiveness with which an organization and its communication network function is a measure of its ability to handle messages. Unfortunately, messages enter a network at varying rates, creating fluctuations and high and low periods of message-intake. When a network loses its capability to adapt to these fluctuations and intake-variations and when it fails to hold in reserve a capacity for processing the unpredictable entry of unanticipated messages, the network or one or more of its components will experience *overload*.

Networks and individuals alike develop ways of adjusting to and avoiding messages when an overload appears to be developing. To maintain an uninterrupted sequence in the handling of messages, we may ignore some messages, delay responding to unimportant messages, answer only parts of other messages, respond inaccurately to certain messages, take less time with each message, work with messages at only superficial levels, block messages before they can enter the system (by keeping the telephone off the hook, for instance), have a surrogate (secretary) give answers, create a new position to handle specialized kinds of messages, or reduce standards to allow for more errors in the handling of messages.[5]

Reproduction Inaccuracies

The serial reproduction of messages in communication networks is, of course, susceptible to a number of problems and possible shortcomings. Many of these difficulties relate to the way in which the network is devised and structured. We must, therefore, continuously ask: (1) Are all members of the organization adequately included in appropriate networks? (2) Is each individual properly linked to others in the network so as to provide information when he or she needs it to work efficiently? (3) Does the network in question contain an adequate number of linkages to restrict unnecessary and irrelevant messages? (4) Do the network and the individuals involved in it have functional ways of adapting to messages that enter the system too fast and for coping with a larger-than-usual number of incoming messages?

The serial reproduction of messages is also subject to the losses, gains, and distortions that are likely to occur when a message is relayed, rephrased, or completely restructured as it is disseminated through a communication network. Most investigators of the serial reproduction process agree that changes take place in messages as they are reproduced by each succeeding individual in the network. Frederic Bartlett, for example, reported that in the re-

production of folk stories, argumentative prose, and simple drawings, details were usually grouped around a central theme, with inconsistent details being forgotten or modified to fit the theme. He also noted that certain elements were sharpened until they dominated the entire plot and that the changes and loss of important information tended generally to be quite radical. The individual interests of the message-reproducer, as well as idiosyncrasies of subject matter, tended to be reflected in the reproduced messages.[6] M. E. Tresselt and S. D. Spragg arrived at conclusions similar to Bartlett's; but, in addition, they discovered that the accuracy of reproduction was improved by inducing—prior to the individual's engaging in the serial process—a "mental set" relevant to the materials to be reproduced.[7] F. L. Brissey[8] and—later—Curtis Stadstad[9] employed a mental set and found that a progressive loss of information occurred, but that the information that was retained tended to be that which was most relevant to the main theme of the original message. Brissey concluded, however, that "the decline in information is a result of *omission* rather than of *distortion*."[10]

Using a test designed to determine degrees of prejudice, Wendell Johnson and Carolyn Wood categorized subject-persons and had them serially reproduce written passages containing both positive and negative information about blacks.[11] Subjects who held positive attitudes tended to abstract and reproduce positive information, whereas subjects with negative attitudes tended to select and reproduce negative information. Johnson and Wood concluded that information was lost when it was not in agreement with the attitudes of the subjects,

thus supporting the idea that in serial communication the information that is gleaned from a message for further reproduction will be significantly influenced by the past experiences, attitudes, and beliefs of the person who reproduces it.

Several investigations involving serial reproduction procedures have discovered that a number of fairly consistent changes occur throughout the process.[12] In brief, the investigators have found that when messages are serially reproduced (*a*) details become omitted, declining sharply in number at the beginning of the series and continuing throughout thereafter—but at a somewhat slower rate (sometimes called leveling); (*b*) details, when retained, become highlighted, allowing them to gain in importance and meaningfulness (sometimes called sharpening); (*c*) details become added for the purpose of embellishing the description or message; (*d*) details become modified to conform to the predispositions of the interpreter (sometimes called assimilation); (*e*) statements that were previously qualified tend to become definite statements in later reproduction; (*f*) details tend to be combined into a single, unitary concept—for example, what starts out as three different individuals becomes, in a later reproduction, a "group" (sometimes called condensation); (*g*) details of events or happenings are described in the order in which one would *expect* them to occur rather than as they actually *did* occur; (*h*) details are adapted so as to make the entire message or event seem plausible; and (*i*) finally, certain phrases are adjusted to reflect the accepted style of expression used by the social level and stratum of the individuals collectively involved in the serial reproduction of the message.

1. Keith Davis, "Management Communication and the Grapevine," *Harvard Business Review* 31, No. 5 (September–October 1953): 43–49. Daniel Katz and Robert L. Kahn, "Communications: The Flow of Information," *The Social Psychology of Organizations* (New York: John Wiley & Sons, Inc., 1966), pp. 235–239. Elihu Katz and Paul F. Lazarsfeld, "Interpersonal Networks: Communicating Within the Group," in *Personal Influence* (New York: The Free Press, 1955), pp. 82–115.

2. For a discussion of the organization as a communication network, see Chester I. Barnard, *The Functions of an Executive* (Cambridge, Mass.: Harvard University Press, 1938).

3. Stanley Milgram, "The Small-World Problem," *Psychology Today* 1, No. 1 (May 1957): 61–67.

4. Alex Bavelas and Dermot Barrett, "An Experimental Approach to Organizational Communication," *Personnel* 27 (March 1951): 367–371.

5. J. G. Miller, "Information Input Overload and Psychopathology," *American Journal of Psychiatry* 116, No. 8 (February 1960): 695–704. R. L. Meier, "Communication Overload: Proposals from the Study of a University Library," *Administrative Science Quarterly* 7, No. 4 (March 1963): 521–544. Stanley Milgram, "The Experience of Living in Cities," *Science* 167, No. 3924 (March 13, 1970): 1461–1468.

6. Frederic C. Bartlett, *Remembering* (London: Cambridge University Press, 1932), pp. 118–176.

7. M. E. Tresselt and S. D. Spragg, "Changes Occurring in the Serial Reproduction of Verbally Perceived Messages," *Journal of Genetic Psychology* 58–59 (1941): 255–264.

8. F. L. Brissey, "The Factor of Relevance in the Serial Reproduction of Information," *The Journal of Communication* 11, No. 4 (December 1961): 211–219.

9. Curtis A. Stadstad, "The Factor of Relevance in the Serial Reproduction of Orally Transmitted Information," (M.A. diss., University of Montana, 1969), pp. 25–26.

10. Brissey, p. 218

11. Wendell Johnson and Carolyn Wood, "John Told Jim What Joe Told Him," *Etc.: A Review of General Semantics* 2 (1944–1945): 10–28.

12. See, for example, Gordon Allport and Leo Postman, *The Psychology of Rumor* (New York: Holt, Rinehart & Winston, Inc., 1947); T. M. Higham, "The Experimental Study of the Transmission of Rumor," *British Journal of Psychology* 42 (1951): 42–55; Irving J. Lee and Laura L. Lee, *Handling Barriers in Communication* (New York: Harper & Row, Publishers, 1957), pp. 64–70; and William V. Haney, "Serial Communication of Information in Organizations," in *Concepts and Issues in Administrative Behavior*, Sidney Mailick and Edward H. Van Ness, eds. (Englewood Cliffs, N.J.: Prentice-Hall, Inc., 1962), pp. 150–163.

Distortion in Communication

John R. Freund and Arnold Nelson

There is a children's game called "Telephone," in which a word or phrase is whispered from one child to another through a long series until, at the "end of the line," words emerge which generally bear little resemblance to the original message. Anyone who has played the game tends to attribute the distortion of the message either to the means of communication (whispering) or to the impulses of the children participating, which might lead them to distort the message deliberately in order that the game may be successful.

Few people realize that similar distortion occurs when adults participate, speak in normal tones and seek wholeheartedly to get the message through the series intact. . . . The distortion is not confined to superficial changes in wording, but works as much havoc upon the ideas contained in the original message as could be expected if they were to be subjected to deliberate misrepresentation. . . . The changes made by any one speaker are small in comparison to the cumulative effect of these changes. . . .

In ordinary communication between one sender and one receiver no message is transmitted without some change, however small. Frequently, though, the changes are so small as to go undetected, and their very existence rests upon deductions about what must be true rather than

what can be seen to be true. If someone insists, for instance, that he knows exactly what I mean when I say, "I had a flat tire yesterday," I cannot dissuade him by pointing to a tangible change in the uttered message, or signal, as he repeats it. If, however, the communication process can be "stretched out" through serial reproduction of the message, the otherwise invisible changes in meaning can be detected in visible alterations in the reproduced signals. The process is somewhat like that by which plants and flowers can be "seen" growing in fast-motion movies.

A closer analogy exists in the occurrence of noise in high fidelity recording equipment. An expensive high fidelity set reduces noise to levels that cannot be detected by the ear. But that it still exists can be demonstrated by recording from one such set to another and back again several times. Each successive recording acquires all of the preceding noise and adds its own. The original signal, however, remains unreinforced; and if this process is carried on long enough, the signal will be lost in the accumulated noise.

But distortion in communication between human beings is more than just the effects of the accumulation of noise, as a brief analysis of the process will show. When one person talks to another, the message (which is transmit-

From "Distortion in Communication" by John R. Freund and Arnold Nelson in READINGS FOR COMMUNICATION, ed. Ralph N. Miller. © Communication Staff, Western Michigan University.

ted as a signal only once) occurs in at least four different forms:

1. The message at its source (in the mind of the speaker before it is uttered)

2. The message as it is uttered (altered from its first form to fit the speaker's preconception of his listener's ability to understand him)

3. The message as it is perceived and retained by the listener (altered from its second form by the listener's individual background of experience)

4. The message as it is remembered by the listener (altered from its third form by the activity of selection and rejection)[1]

It can be seen, consequently, that the distortion that occurs in any particular message may be the result of a number of causes which are locked in the minds of the sender and the receiver and have nothing whatsoever to do with external "noise." Furthermore, we can see that by examining a serially reproduced message we will be able to see the results of an accumulation of these invisible changes, which frequently take the form of a definite change in the signal at the end of the series.

In order to understand the way in which a serially reproduced message is related to the normal communication process, the reader may wish to examine the following diagram. Here, the four forms of the message are represented by their numbers, as above.

Speaker	Speaker	Speaker	Speaker
A	B	C	D
3–4	1–2 --→ 3–4		1–2
	1–2 --→ 3–4		1–2 --→ 3–4

Three things should be observed: first, only one form of the message (number 2) exists as an observable signal; second, each speaker is involved in all four forms of the message; and third, two forms of the message (numbers 1 and 4) are merged. This third point means that Speaker B in the diagram makes use of the fourth form of the message as the raw material out of which he frames his signal to Speaker C. Some interesting things happen in this merger but exactly how they happen is a complicated affair, more complicated than the terms "remembering" and "forgetting" suggest. Three causes of distortion that have impressed us are these:

1. The influence of the speaker's and listener's background of experience.

2. The influence of the personality of the speaker or listener.

3. The influence of faulty prediction on the part of speaker or listener.

The last item may need some clarification. Any kind of communication involves prediction on the part of both the speaker and listener. A speaker may have a faulty "image" of his listener and alter the signal on the basis of that image. This alteration could easily yield a confused impression for the listener. Or the listener may have a very fixed notion of what the speaker is going to say, and this predictive "set" will cause him to fail to perceive or recall the actual signal.

One further cause of distortion ought to be mentioned inasmuch as it is very nearly confined to serially reproduced messages: this is the sweeping, structural change that occasionally alters a message so drastically that we are at a loss to explain the

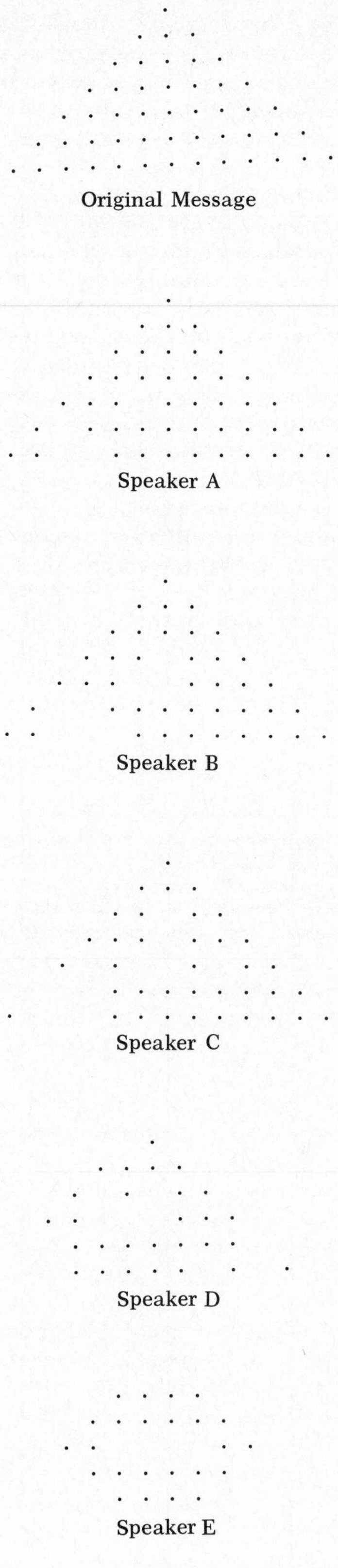

Original Message

Speaker A

Speaker B

Speaker C

Speaker D

Speaker E

change in terms of what was contained in the message immediately preceding it. Our first guess is likely to be that we have come upon a very weak link in a chain of listeners. The explanation becomes clear, however, when we examine the whole series. If we do so, we can see that in every retelling of the message more details of varying importance are lost or altered slightly. As a result of the steady, somewhat random loss of details, the structure of the whole message tends to become imbalanced and finally unstable. This is accompanied by a corresponding strain upon the mind of the listener. The results of the strain are finally manifested in a reordering of all the details into a new form which "makes sense" and is structurally satisfying, even though it is an extreme distortion of the original message. The diagram at left attemps to illustrate this kind of structural change. Imagine that the geometric figures represent the "meaning" of the whole message and that each dot stands for a detail.

It can be seen that the original triangle slowly loses one of its supporting corners. To us, it still vaguely resembles the original triangle, but we must remember that Speaker E receives only what is sent by Speaker D. To him, apparently, it resembles nothing, and therefore he feels obliged to alter it into the neat little symmetrical figure that becomes his message.

This brings us to a final question. What can be learned from observing the process of serial reproduction besides the somewhat dismal generalization that all communication tends toward distortion? Can anything be done to halt—or at least to retard—distortion? A few general principles may be offered, which, however,

B.C. by Johnny Hart

By permission of Johnny Hart and Field Enterprises, Inc.

are not easily observed in practice.

First, if there is an opportunity for feedback to be employed, it helps to diminish distortion. A better term, perhaps, is "reverberation," for feedback from the listener must be coupled with "feed forward" on the part of the speaker, an attitude which anticipates verbally difficulties which the listener may not realize he is encountering. Successful reverberation—immensely difficult to achieve—is probably the greatest single deterrent to distortion in any kind of communication.

The two final principles are somewhat related to reverberation. The first applies to the sender of the message. He must endeavor to exercise forward responsibility. Speaker B has a powerful urge to feel responsible to Speaker A—to deliver A's message intact. This urge frequently overwhelms the much more important responsibility that B has to Speaker C. The result of a failure to exercise forward responsibility is loss of contact with the listener—and, of course, distortion.

Finally, the listener has the responsibility of maintaining the faculties of prediction and recall in a state of equilibrium. While he is listening he must constantly predict what he thinks the message is going to be, and just as constantly check his predictions and alter them on the basis of what he can recall of what has actually been said.

In spite of everything, something of the original message will be lost if the signal is not short enough to be memorized. Paradoxically, an awareness of this fact is often of aid in bringing about the attitude that is most conducive to the preservation of the message.

---

1. Ian M. L. Hunter, in *Memory: Facts and Fallacies* (Baltimore, Penguin Books Inc., 1957), pp. 14–16, distinguishes "retention" from "remembering" in the following way: Retention is an unobservable brain process which is "a necessary condition for remembering for, without it, there would be nothing to remember." Remembering is a process "by means of which the effects of past learning manifest themselves in the present," and is able to be observed, at least somewhat.

PROBE 25. Alterations, omissions, and additions can occur in serially reproduced messages because of the motives and assumptions of communicators.

Serial Communication of Information in Organizations

William V. Haney

An appreciable amount of the communication which occurs in business, industry, hospitals, military units, government agencies — in short, in chain-of-command organizations — consists of serial transmissions. *A* communicates a message to *B*; *B* then communicates *A*'s message (or rather his *interpretation* of *A*'s message) to *C*; *C* then communicates his interpretation of *B*'s interpretation of *A*'s message to *D*; and so on. The originator and the ultimate recipient of the message[1] are separated by "middle men."

"The message" may often be passed down (but not necessarily all the way down) the organization chain, as when in business the chairman acting on behalf of the board of directors may express a desire to the president. "The message" begins to fan out as the president, in turn, relays "it" to his vice presidents; they convey "it" to their respective subordinates; and so forth. Frequently "a message" goes up (but seldom all the way up) the chain. Sometimes "it" travels laterally. Sometimes, as with rumors, "it" disregards the formal organization and flows more closely along informal organizational lines.

Regardless of its direction, the number of "conveyors" involved, and the degree of its conformance with the formal structure, serial transmission is clearly an essential, inevitable form of communication in organizations.

It is equally apparent that serial transmission is especially susceptible to distortion and disruption. Not only is it subject to the shortcomings and maladies of "simple" person-to-person communication but, since it consists of a series of such communications, the anomalies are often *compounded*.

This is not to say, however, that serial transmissions in organizations should be abolished or even decreased. We wish to show that such communications *can be improved* if communicators are able (1) to recognize some of the patterns of miscommunication which occur in serial transmissions; (2) to understand some of the factors contributing to these patterns; (3) to take measures and practice techniques for preventing the recurrence of these patterns and for ameliorating their consequences.

I shall begin by cataloguing some of the factors which seemingly influence a serial transmission.

Motives of the Communicators

When *B* conveys *A*'s message to *C* he may be influenced by at least three motives of which he may be largely unaware.

The Desire to Simplify the Message

We evidently dislike conveying detailed messages. The responsi-

William V. Haney, "Serial Communication of Information in Organizations" in CONCEPTS AND ISSUES IN ADMINISTRATIVE BEHAVIOR, Sidney Mailick and Edward H. Van Ness, Eds., © 1962. Reprinted by permission of Prentice-Hall, Inc., Englewood Cliffs, New Jersey.

bility of passing along complex information is burdensome and taxing. Often, therefore, we unconsciously simplify the message before passing it along to the next person. It is very probable that among the details most susceptible to omission are those we already knew or in some way presume our recipients will know without our telling them.

The Desire to Convey a "Sensible" Message

Apparently we are reluctant to relay a message that is somehow incoherent, illogical, or incomplete. It may be embarrassing to admit that one does not fully understand the message he is conveying. When he receives a message that does not quite make sense to him he is prone to "make sense out of it" before passing it along to the next person.

The Desire to Make the Conveyance of the Message as Pleasant and/or Painless as Possible for the Conveyor

We evidently do not like to have to tell the boss unpleasant things. Even when not directly responsible, one does not relish the reaction of his superior to a disagreeable message. This motive probably accounts for a considerable share of the tendency for a "message" to lose its harshness as it moves up the organizational ladder. The first line supervisor may tell his foreman, "I'm telling you, Mike, the men say that if this pay cut goes through they'll strike—and they mean it!" By the time "this message" has been relayed through six or eight or more echelons (if indeed it goes that far) the executive vice president might express it to the president as, "Well, sir, the men seem a little concerned over the projected wage reduction but I am confident that they will take it in stride."

One of the dangers plaguing some upper managements is that they are effectively shielded from incipient problems until they become serious and costly ones.

Assumptions of the Communicators

In addition to the serial transmitter's motives we must consider his assumptions—particularly those he makes about his communications. If some of these assumptions are fallacious and if one is unaware that he holds them, his communication can be adversely affected. The following are, in this writer's judgment, two of the most pervasive and dangerous of the current myths about communication.

The Assumption That Words Are Used in Only One Way

A study indicates that for the 500 most commonly used words in our language there are 14,070 different dictionary definitions— over 28 usages per word, on the average.[2] Take the word *run*, for example:

> Babe Ruth scored a *run*.
> Did you ever see Jesse Owens *run*?
> I have a *run* in my stocking.
> There is a fine *run* of salmon this year.
> Are you going to *run* this company or am I?
> You have the *run* of the place.
> Don't give me the *run* around.
> What headline do you want to *run*?
> There was a *run* on the bank today.
> Did he *run* the ship aground?
> I have to *run* (drive the car) downtown.
> Who will *run* for President this year?
> Joe flies the New York-Chicago *run* twice a week.
> You know the kind of people they

12·15

WHY YOU @X⊛☆!! @X⊛☆!!

A TRUE POET ALWAYS RHYMES HIS CUSS WORDS.

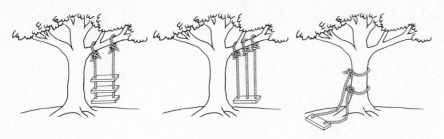

As Teachers Requested It	***As Coordinators Ordered It***	***As Curriculum Staff Wrote It***

As the Art Department Designed It	***As Teachers Implemented It***	***What the Student Wanted***

From a mimeographed school publication in a Utah school district.

run around with.
The apples *run* large this year.
Please *run* my bath water.

We could go on at some length — my small abridged dictionary gives eighty-seven distinct usages for *run*. I have chosen an extreme example, of course, but there must be relatively few words (excepting some technical terms) used in one and in only one sense.

Yet communicators often have a curious notion about words *when they are using them*, i.e., when they are speaking, writing, listening, or reading. It is immensely easy for a "sender" of a communication to assume that words are used in only one way — the way he intends them. It is just as enticing for the "receiver" to assume that the sender intended his words as he, the receiver, happens to interpret them at the moment. When communicators are unconsciously burdened by the assumption of the mono-usage of words they are prone to become involved in the pattern of miscommunication known as *bypassing*.

Bypassing: Denotative and Connotative. Since we use words to express at least two kinds of meanings there can be two kinds of bypassings. Suppose you say to me, "Your neighbor's grass is certainly green and healthy looking, isn't it?" You could be intending your words merely to *denote*, i.e., to point to or to call my attention, to the appearance of my neighbor's lawn. On the other hand, you could have intended your words to *connote*, i.e., to imply something beyond or something other than what you were ostensibly denoting. You might have meant any number of things: that my own lawn needed more care;

that my neighbor was inordinately meticulous about his lawn; that my neighbor's lawn is tended by a professional, a service you do not have and for which you envy or despise my neighbor; or even that his grass was not green at all but, on the contrary, parched and diseased; and so forth.

Taking these two kinds of meanings into account it is clear that bypassing occurs or can occur under any of four conditions:

1. *When the sender intends one denotation while the receiver interprets another.*

2. *When the sender intends one connotation while the receiver interprets another.*

   A friend once told me of an experience she had had years ago when as a teenager she was spending the week with a maiden aunt. Joan had gone to the movies with a young man who brought her home at a respectable hour. However, the couple lingered on the front porch somewhat longer than Aunt Mildred thought necessary. The little old lady was rather proud of her ability to deal with younger people so she slipped out of bed, raised her bedroom window, and called down sweetly, "If you two knew how pleasant it is in bed, you wouldn't be standing out there in the cold."

3. *When the sender intends only a denotation while the receiver interprets a connotation.*

   For a brief period the following memorandum appeared on the bulletin boards of a government agency in Washington: *Those department and sections heads who do not have secretaries assigned to them may take advantage of the stenographers in the secretarial pool.*

4. *When the sender intends a connotation while the receiver interprets a denotation only.*

The Assumption That Inferences Are Always Distinguishable from Observations

It is incredibly difficult, at times, for a communicator (or anyone) to discriminate between what he "knows" (i.e., what he has actually observed — seen, heard, read, etc.) and what he is only inferring or guessing. One of the key reasons for this lies in the character of the language used to express observations and inferences.

Suppose you look at a man and observe that he is wearing a white shirt and then say, "That man is wearing a white shirt." Assuming your vision and the illumination were "normal" you would have made a statement of *observation* — a statement which directly corresponded to and was corroborated by your observation. But suppose you now say, "That man bought the white shirt he is wearing." Assuming you were not present when and if the man bought the shirt that statement would be *for you a statement of inference.* Your statement went *beyond* what you observed. You inferred that the man bought the shirt; you did not observe it. Of course, your inference may be correct (but it could be false: perhaps he was given the shirt as a gift; perhaps he stole it or borrowed it; etc.).

Nothing in the nature of our language (the grammar, spelling, pronunciation, accentuation, syntax, inflection, etc.) prevents you from speaking or writing (or thinking) a statement of inference *as if* you were making a statement of observation. Our language permits you to say "Of course, he bought the shirt" with certainty and finality, i.e., with as much confidence as you would make a statement of observation.

Permutation Personified

Despite telemetering advances, improvements in mechanical transmission of data and collating total knowledge, there are occasional breakdowns in communication. We're indebted to a traveler recently returned from Miami for this example.

Operation: Halley's Comet

A COLONEL issued the following directive to his executive officer:

"Tomorrow evening at approximately 2000 hours Halley's Comet will be visible in this area, an event which occurs only once every 75 years. Have the men fall out in the battalion area in fatigues, and I will explain this rare phenomenon to them. In case of rain, we will not be able to see anything, so assemble the men in the theater and I will show them films of it."

EXECUTIVE OFFICER to company commander:

"By order of the colonel, tomorrow at 2000 hours, Halley's Comet will appear above the battalion area. If it rains, fall the men out in fatigues. Then march to the theater where the rare phenomenon will take place. something which occurs only once every 75 years."

COMPANY COMMANDER to lieutenant:

"By order of the colonel in fatigues at 2000 hours tomorrow evening. the phenomenal Halley's Comet will appear in the theater. In case of rain in the battalion area, the colonel will give another order, something which occurs once every 75 years."

LIEUTENANT to sergeant:

"Tomorrow at 2000 hours, the colonel will appear in the theater with Halley's Comet, something which happens every 75 years. If it rains, the colonel will order the comet into the battalion area."

SERGEANT to squad:

"When it rains tomorrow at 2000 hours, the phenomenal 75-year-old General Halley, accompanied by the Colonel, will drive his Comet through the battalion area theater in fatigues."

Reprinted from "Permutation Personified" in *Boles Letter*. Copyright 1962 by Edmond D. Boles & Associates. Used by permission of Edmond D. Boles.

The effect is that it becomes exceedingly easy to confuse the two kinds of statements and also to confuse inference and observation on nonverbal levels. The destructive consequences of acting upon inference as if acting upon observation can range from mild embarrassment to tragedy. . . .

Trends in Serial Transmission

These assumptions,[3] the monousage of words, and the inference-observation confusion, as well as the aforementioned motives of the communicators, undoubtedly contribute a significant share of the difficulties and dangers which beset a serial transmission. Their effect tends to be manifested by three trends: omission, alteration, and addition.

Details Become Omitted

It requires less effort to convey a simpler, less complex message. With fewer details to transmit the fear of forgetting or of garbling the message is decreased. . . . The essential question, perhaps, is which details *will be retained?*

1. Those details the transmitter wanted or expected to hear.

2. Those details which "made sense" to the transmitter.

3. Those details which seemed important *to the transmitter.*

4. Those details which for various and inexplicable reasons seemed to stick with the transmitter—those aspects which seemed particularly unusual or bizarre; those which had special significance to him; etc.

Blondie by Chic Young

© King Features Syndicate, Inc., 1972.

Details Become Altered

Among the details most susceptible to change were the qualifications, the indefinite. Inferential statements are prone to become definite and certain. What may start out as "The boss seemed angry this morning" may quickly progress to "The boss was angry."

A well-known psychologist once "planted" a rumor in an enlisted men's mess hall on a certain Air Force base. His statement was: "Is it true that they are building a tunnel big enough to trundle B-52's to—(the town two miles away)?" Twelve hours later the rumor came back to him as: "They are building a tunnel to trundle B-52's to—." The "Is-it-true" uncertainty had been dropped. So had the indefinite purpose ("big enough to").

Details Become Added

Not infrequently details are added to the message to "fill in the gaps," "to make better sense," and "because I thought the fellow who told it to me left something out."

Distortion in serial communication can be reduced by being aware of sources of change and by systematically using ways to maintain accurate reproduction of messages.

The psychologist was eventually told that not only were they building a tunnel for B-52's but that a mile-long underground runway was being constructed at

A Communications Problem

A U.S. Navy court of inquiry has reported its finding on the Israeli attack June 8 on the *USS Liberty,* and it is an amazing document, not so much for what it says as for what is left unsaid.

It should not be surprising that the court of inquiry did not make a judgment, for it could not, on the reasons for the attack, which killed 34 Americans and wounded 75. Israel has apologized and said the attack was made in error, and a final judgment must await the evidence from her side which was outside the naval court of inquiry's jurisdiction.

But surely it is most surprising to learn from the Navy's finding that hours before the *Liberty* was hit the Joint Chiefs of Staff had ordered her to move farther from the Sinai coast, and that "the messages were misrouted, delayed and not received until after the attack." The *Liberty* at the time was in international waters, but no closer than 13.6 nautical miles from land.

Our government has said that the *Liberty* was there to provide radio communications in case an American evacuation from the Middle East became necessary. That seems fair enough—but is it all?

The *Liberty* was not just another communications ship. She contained all the latest, sophisticated electronic gear, and may well have had the capacity to eavesdrop on land communications near by. The Pentagon has declined comment on reports that her mission was to monitor Israeli and Egyptian radio transmissions from the battlefield.

Readers will recall that after the war began, Israel was able to quote portions of a phone conversation between Egypt's Nasser and Jordan's King Hussein in which they discussed plans, later carried out, to try to blame the United States for the destruction of their planes. Here was another example of the fruits of electronic monitoring.

But the shocking thing in the court of inquiry's finding was the failure, somewhere between the Joint Chiefs of Staff in Washington and the eastern Mediterranean, to communicate quickly with the most modern communications ship in the world.

The warning implicit in this applies not merely to the Navy's communications system, but to the communications network whose use or misuse can control all of our many terrible weapons of destruction.

Congress ought to find out more about it, and sooner than it took the Pentagon to get a message to the *Liberty*.

Courtesy of the Boston Globe: Editorial "A Communications Problem" June 30, 1967.

the end of it! The runway was to have a ceiling slanting upward so that a plane could take off, fly up along the ceiling and emerge from an inconspicuous slit at the end of the cavern! This, he admitted, was a much more "sensible" rumor than the one he had started, for the town had no facilities for take-offs and thus there was nothing which could have been done with the B-52's once they reached the end of the tunnel!

Correctives[4]

Even serial transmissions, as intricate and as relatively uncontrolled communications as they are, can be improved. The suggestions below are not sensational panaceas. In fact, they are quite commonplace, common sense, but uncommonly used techniques.

1. *Take notes.*

2. *Give details in order.*
   Organized information is easier to understand and to remember. Choose a sequence (chronological, spatial, deductive, inductive, etc.) appropriate to the content and be consistent with it. For example, it may suit your purpose best to begin with a proposal followed by supporting reasons or to start with the reasons and work toward the proposal. In either case take care to keep proposals and reasons clearly distinguished rather than mixing them together indiscriminately.

3. *Be wary of bypassing.*
   If you are the receiver, query (ask the sender what he meant) and paraphrase (put what you think he said or wrote into your own words and get the sender to check

you). These simple techniques are effective yet infrequently practiced, perhaps because we are so positive we *know* what the other fellow means; perhaps because we hesitate to ask or rephrase for fear the other fellow (especially if he is the boss) will think less of us for not understanding the first time. Querying and paraphrasing are *two-way* responsibilities and the sender must be truly approchable by his receivers if the techniques are to be successful.

This checklist may be helpful in avoiding bypassing:

Could he be denoting something other than what I am?
Could he be connoting something other than what I am?
Could he be connoting whereas I am merely denoting?
Could he be merely denoting whereas I am connoting?

4. *Distinguish between inference and observation.*
   Ask yourself sharply: Did I *really* see, hear, or read this—or am I guessing part of it? The essential characteristics of a statement of observation are these:

   1. It can be made only by the observer.
      (What someone tells you as observational is still inferential for you if you did not observe it.)
   2. It can be made only *after* observation.
   3. It stays with what has been observed; does not go beyond it.

This is not to say that inferential statements are not to be made—we could hardly avoid doing so. But it is important or even vital at times to know *when* we are making them.

5. *Slow down your oral transmissions.*
By doing so, you give your listener a better opportunity to assimilate complex and detailed information. However, it is possible to speak too slowly so as to lose his attention. Since either extreme defeats your purpose, it is generally wise to watch the listener for clues as to the most suitable rate of speech.

6. *Simplify the message.*
This suggestion is for the *originator* of the message. The "middle-men" often simplify without half trying! Most salesmen realize the inadvisability of attempting to sell too many features at a time. The customer is only confused and is unable to distinguish the key features from those less important. With particular respect to oral transmission, there is impressive evidence to indicate that beyond a point the addition of details leads to disproportionate omission.

7. *Use dual media when feasible.*
A message often stands a better chance of getting through if it is reinforced by restatement in another communication medium. Detailed, complex, and unfamiliar information is often transmitted by such combinations as a memo follow-up on a telephone call; a sensory aid (slide, diagram, mockup, picture, etc.) accompanying a written or oral message, etc.

8. *Highlight the important.*
Presumably the originator of a message knows which are its important aspects. But this does not automatically insure that his serial transmitters will similarly recognize them. There are numerous devices for making salient points stand out as such; e.g., using underscoring, capitals, etc., in writing; using vocal emphasis, attention-drawing phrases ("this is the main point . . . ." "here's the crux . . .," "be sure to note this . . ."), etc., in speaking.

9. *Reduce the number of links in the chain.*
This suggestion has to be followed with discretion. Jumping the chain of command either upward or downward can sometimes have undesirable consequences. However, whenever it is possible to reduce or eliminate the "middlemen," "the message" generally becomes progressively less susceptible to aberrations. Of course, there are methods of skipping links which are commonly accepted and widely practiced. Communication downward can be reduced to person-to-person communication, in a sense, with general memos, letters, bulletins, group meetings, etc. Communication upward can accomplish the same purpose via suggestion boxes, opinion questionnaires, "talk-backs," etc.

10. *Preview and review.*
A wise speech professor of mine used to say: "Giving a speech is basically very simple if you do it in three steps: First, you tell them what you're going to tell them; then you tell; then, finally, you tell them what you've told them." This three step sequence is often applicable whether the message is transmitted by letter, memo, writ-

ten or oral report, public address, telephone call, etc.

Summary

After the last suggestion I feel obliged to review this article briefly. We have been concerned with serial transmission—a widespread, essential, and yet susceptible form of communication. Among the factors which vitiate a serial transmission are certain of the communicator's motives and fallacious assumptions. When these and other factors are in play the three processes— omission, alteration, and addition —tend to occur. The suggestions offered for strengthening serial transmission will be more or less applicable, of course, depending upon the communication situation.

An important question remains: What can be done to encourage communicators to practice the techniques? They will probably use them largely to the extent that they think the techniques are needed. But do they think them necessary? Apparently many do not. When asked to explain how the final version came to differ so markedly from the original, many of the the serial transmitters in my studies were genuinely puzzled. A frequent comment was "I really can't understand it. All I know is that I passed the message along the same as it came to me." If messages were passed along "the same as they came," of course, serial transmission would no longer be a problem. And so long as the illusion of fidelity is with the communicator it is unlikely that he will be prompted to apply some of these simple, prosaic, yet effective techniques to his communicating. Perhaps a first step would be to induce him to question his unwarranted assurance about his communication. The controlled serial transmission experience appears to accomplish this.

---

1. "The message," as already suggested, is a misnomer in that what is being conveyed is not static, unchanging, and fixed. I shall retain the term for convenience, however, and use quotation marks to signify that its dynamic nature is subject to cumulative change.

2. Lydia Strong, "Do You Know How to Listen?" *Effective Communication on the Job*, Dooher and Marquis, eds. (New York: American Management Association, 1956), p. 28.

3. For a more detailed analysis of these assumptions and for additional methods for preventing and correcting their consequences, see Willian V. Haney, *Communication: Patterns and Incidents* (Homewood, Ill.: Irwin, 1960), chs. III, IV, V.

4. Most of these suggestions are offered by Irving J. and Laura L. Lee, *Handling Barriers in Communication* (New York: Harper & Bros., 1956), pp. 71–74.

Management Communication and the Grapevine

Keith Davis

Professor of Management, Arizona State University, Tempe, Arizona

A particularly neglected aspect of management communication concerns that informal channel, the grapevine. There is no dodging the fact that, as a carrier of news and gossip among executives and supervisors, the grapevine often affects the affairs of management. The proof of this is the strong feelings that different executives have about it. Some regard the grapevine as an evil — a thorn in the side which regularly spreads rumor, destroys morale and reputations, leads to irresponsible actions, and challenges authority. Some regard it as a good thing because it acts as a safety valve and carries news fast. Others regard it as a very mixed blessing.

Whether the grapevine is considered an asset or a liability, it is important for executives to try to understand it. For one thing is sure: although no executive can absolutely control the grapevine, he can *influence* it. And since it is here to stay, he should learn to live with it.

As for the research basis of the analysis, the major points are these:

1. *Company studied* — The company upon which the research is based is a real one. I shall refer to it as the "Jason Company." A manufacturer of leather goods, it has 67 people in the management group (that is, all people who supervise the work of others, from top executives to foremen) and about 600 employees. It is located in a rural town of 10,000 persons, and its products are distributed nationally.

2. *Methodology* — The methods used to study management communication in the Jason Company are new ones. Briefly, the basic approach was to learn from each communication recipient how he first received a given piece of information and then to trace it back to its source.

Significant Characteristics

In the Jason Company many of the usual grapevine characteristics were found along with others less well known. For purposes of this discussion, the four most significant characteristics are these:

1. *Speed of transmission* — Traditionally the grapevine is fast, and this showed up in the Jason Company.

2. *Degree of selectivity* — It is often said that the grapevine acts without conscious direction or thought — that it will

> **PROBE 26. In organizations the grapevine distributes information to members through serial reproduction.**

carry anything, any time, anywhere. This viewpoint has been epitomized in the statement that "the grapevine is without conscience or consciousness." But flagrant grapevine irresponsibility was not evident in the Jason Company. In fact, the grapevine here showed that it could be highly selective and discriminating. Whether it may be *counted on* in that respect, however, is another question. The answer would of course differ with each case and would depend on many variables, including other factors in the communication picture having to do with attitudes, executive relationships, and so forth.

3. *Locale of operation* — The grapevine of company news operates mostly at the place of work. Since management has some control over the work environment, it has an opportunity to influence the grapevine. By exerting such influence the manager can more closely integrate grapevine interests with those of the formal communication system, and he can use it for effectively spreading more significant items of information than those commonly carried.

4. *Relation to formal communication* — Formal and informal communication systems tend to be jointly active, or jointly inactive. Where formal communication was inactive at the Jason Company, the grapevine did not rush in to fill the void; instead, there simply was lack of communication. Similarly, where there was effective formal communication, there was an active grapevine.

Informal and formal communication may supplement each other. Often formal communication is simply used to confirm or to expand what has already been communicated by grapevine. This necessary process of confirmation results partly because of the speed of the grapevine, which formal systems fail to match, partly because of its unofficial function, and partly because of its transient nature. Formal communication needs to come along to stamp "Official" on the news and to put it "on the record," which the grapevine cannot suitably do.

Spreading Information

Human communication requires at least two persons, but each person acts independently. Person A may talk or write, but he has not *communicated* until person B receives. The individual is, therefore, a basic communication unit. That is, he is one "link" in the communication "chain" for any bit of information.

The formal communication chain is largely determined by the chain of command or by formal procedures, but the grapevine chain is more flexible. There are four different ways of visualizing it, as Exhibit I indicates:

1. *The single-strand chain* — A tells B, who tells C, who tells D, and so on; this makes for a tenuous chain to a distant receiver. Such a chain is usually in mind when one speaks of how the grapevine distorts and filters information until the original item is not recognizable.

2. *The gossip chain* — A seeks and tells everyone else.

Blondie by Chic Young

© King Features Syndicate, Inc., 1969.

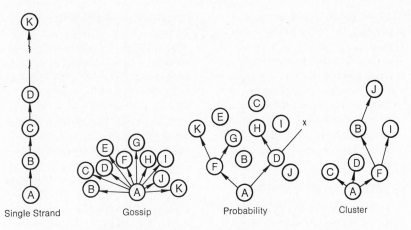

Exhibit I. *Types of communication chains*

3. *The probability chain* — A communicates randomly, say, to F and D, in accordance with the laws of probability; then F and D tell others in the same manner.

4. *The cluster chain* — A tells three selected others; perhaps one of them tells two others; and then one of these two tells one other. This was virtually the only kind of chain found in the Jason Company, and may well be the normal one in industry generally.

Active Minority

The predominance of the cluster chain at the Jason Company means that only a few of the persons who knew a unit of information ever transmitted it — what Jacobson and Seashore call the "liaison" individuals.[1] All others who received the information did not transmit it; they acted merely as passive receivers.

For example, when a quality-control problem occurred, 68% of the executives received the information, but only 20% transmitted it. Again, when an executive

planned to resign to enter the insurance business, 81% of the executives knew about it, but only 11% passed the news on to others. Those liaison individuals who told the news to more than one other person amounted to less than 10% of the 67 executives in each case.

These active groups varied in membership. There was no evidence that any one group consistently acted as liaison persons; instead, different types of information passed through different liaison persons. However, as will be shown later, some individuals were invariably communication "isolates"; they received and transmitted information poorly or not at all.

The above findings indicate that if management wants more communication, it should increase the number and/or effectiveness of its liaison individuals. Liaison individuals tend to act in a predictable way. If an individual's unit of information concerns a job function in which he is interested, he is likely to tell others. If his information is about a person with whom he is associated socially, he also is likely to tell others. Furthermore, the sooner

he knows of an event after it happened, the more likely he is to tell others.

In other words, three well-known communication principles which are so often mentioned in relation to attitudes also have a major influence on the spread of information by liaison individuals:

1. Tell people about what will affect them (job interest).

2. Tell people what they want to know, rather than simply what you want them to know (job and social interest).

3. Tell people soon (timing).

Conclusion

If management wants to do a first-class communication job, at this stage it needs fewer medicines and more diagnoses. Communication analysis has now passed beyond "pure research" to a point where it is immediately useful to top management in the individual firm. The patterns of communication that show up should serve to indicate both the areas where communication is most deficient and the channels through which information can be made to flow most effectively.

In particular, no administrator in his right mind would try to abolish the management grapevine. It is as permanent as humanity is. Nevertheless, many administrators have abolished the grapevine from *their own minds*. They think and act without giving adequate weight to it or, worse, try to ignore it. This is a mistake. The grapevine is a factor to be reckoned with in the affairs of management. The administrator should analyze it and should consciously try to influence it.

---

1. Eugene Jacobson and Stanley E. Seashore, "Communication Practices in Complex Organizations," *The Journal of Social Issues*, vol. VII, no. 3, 1951, p. 37.

Prods

1. What can happen in a conversation with a friend when either or both of you assume that you know what the other is talking about? What can you do to check your assumptions? Try one of them.

2. Ask a friend who works in a large organization to describe to you the number and order of steps in which a message travels from a high-ranking manager to a low-ranking employee. What are the potential sources of distortion in that network?

3. Identify an instance where distortion in the serial reproduction of a message was caused by differences in the backgrounds or personalities (or both) of the people involved.

4. Look up *fast* in the dictionary. How many meanings are listed? Write five sentences using a different sense of *fast* in each one. What implications for serial communication can be drawn from this exercise?

5. You and a friend see a man wearing a dark blue suit and carrying a briefcase get into a shiny limousine. You say to your friend, "He's probably a wealthy businessman." What two elements of communication are you confusing in this statement? What might you have said differently?

6. Talk to the director of communication, personnel director, or some other manager in a large organization about the operation of the grapevine in his or her company. How fast is it? How accurate is it? What does the manager do to improve its accuracy? Do certain individuals in the company tend to contribute to the flow of the grapevine more than others?

7. Select three friends who are likely to spread a rumor fast and far, and tell them that the university is about to adopt a new policy on grading. After three days ask some other friends whether they heard about the new policy and, if so, who told them, when and where, and whether they believe it's true.

Relationship 1: **Dyadic**

Relationship 2: **Serial**

Relationship 3: **Small Group**

Relationship 4: **Speaker-Audience**

3
RELATIONSHIP

SMALL GROUP

PROBE 27 A small group is a collection of individuals who communicate face-to-face and depend on each other to a significant degree.

PROBE 28 The climate of a group can develop defensively or supportively, depending upon the verbal and nonverbal behaviors of its members.

PROBE 29 Leadership in a group involves the interaction between a person and the members of the group, all of whom assume various roles at various times.

PROBE 30 Problem solving in your group will be more efficient if you follow a pattern or sequence.

Relationship 3: Small Group

A small group may consist of anywhere from three to twenty individuals. The point at which the individuals involved find difficulty interacting face-to-face with one another is where the relationship moves from one of a small group to one between speaker and audience. For purposes of problem solving in groups, about five to nine individuals seems optimal. With a group of that size, some members are able to remain silent without seriously jeopardizing the productivity of the group while at the same time all members, if they wish to participate, have an opportunity to make a fair contribution.

The small group is probably as common a communication setting as any you will ever experience. People interact and attempt to accomplish things in groups wherever they go: members of the family meet, a committee is appointed, an afternoon social is organized in the park, a student government task group is appointed, and a dormitory discussion group meets. Some groups meet to solve problems, others to share information, while others meet for self-improvement and to learn about themselves. Hardly a day passes that most of us fail to meet in some type of group.

Effective group work depends on being able to recognize when group interaction begins to fail. Information about and sensitivity to patterns of interaction, factors that affect group climate and productivity, problem-solving procedures and processes, leadership and participant behaviors, brainstorming, and decision making may help you work productively with people in groups.

Human Interaction in the Small Group Setting

Introduction

Lawrence B. Rosenfeld

Without talking, form groups with no more than four members. Once your group is formed, discuss the following questions:

1. What is a group?
2. What effect does the classroom environment have on the group?
3. What cues did the members give each other to indicate that they were part of the group that was formed?
4. What effect does the lack of oral verbal communication have on interaction?
5. Have you attained a group identity?
6. Can you describe the personalities of each of the members?
7. Can you differentiate among the roles that are being enacted? Who is the leader?
8. What problems are encountered, and how are they handled? . . .

Human existence is dependent upon society; without social life no human life would be possible. Society is sustained by communication; communication makes human life possible. Social life and communication are two words which imply sharing and participating, but the 1970s is witnessing the rise of existential loneliness, the increased use of the word *alienation*. As interaction decreases, as we find ourselves farther and farther apart, we become less than social, and human life becomes less than what it could be.

One reason for decreased human contact may be the increased technological sophistication of our generation. Why take the time to walk to a friend's house when it is so much easier to call on the telephone? But the telephone is not real human contact. Human contact is replaced by the telephone voice. Similarly, radio, television, and the movies have separated us from each other, formed barriers between us, eliminated the necessity for human contact. Without human contact communication is curtailed, aborted. We sit and listen, or sit and watch, and realize that we cannot affect the course of action in what we observe. In a sense, communication has not taken place, if, indeed, communication is a form of exchange through which people can come into contact with each other's minds (Newcomb, Turner, and Converse 1965).

Our age, though, may be coming to realize the necessity for human contact. The rise of sensitivity groups, training groups, group marathons, human relations workshops, and the increased use of groups in academic and business settings, all provide evidence that the most efficient means for insuring "survival" is in human contact, face-

PROBE 27. A small group is a collection of individuals who communicate face-to-face and depend on each other to a significant degree.

Tom Tracy

to-face interaction: interpersonal communication.

Generally, groups provide a variety of experiences. Whether the specific purpose is to provide companionship, share information, solve a particular problem, or provide the group members with therapy, all groups are valuable because they serve the following purposes:

1. Encourage meaningful interaction. Meaningful interaction can best take place when there is face-to-face contact, when individuals acknowledge and adjust to each other's presence. What constitutes meaningful interaction varies from group to group. For example, *casual groups* are not established to solve a particular problem, but rather to provide members with friendship, interesting conversation, and companionship. To the extent that these things are provided, the interaction is meaningful.

2. Facilitate the learning of problem-solving procedures. Working in groups provides individuals with the opportunity to better understand a variety of views as members present and defend opposing views. During idea development members learn to critically evaluate the ideas of others. Problem solving also entails learning how to deal with conflicts, and how to affect a compromise. Individuals in *problem-solving groups* discover alternatives which are not possible under circumstances where directives and orders are the usual methods for solving problems. Although all groups are problem-solving groups to some extent, the main characteris-

tic of the problem-solving group is that a group goal is established which centers on a problem, goal, or task, and interaction results in a group-generated solution.

3. Facilitate the development of commitments. Individuals in a group normally develop commitments to both the group and its decisions. Group members feel a sense of responsibility and loyalty to one another; as a consequence, group-generated decisions have a higher probability of being enacted than decisions derived from authority figures. *Consciousness-raising groups*, which concentrate on creating an intense group identity, develop strong commitments in group members for each other, as well as for the group's decision to end oppression. Women's Liberation is an example of a consciousness-raising group (Chesebro, Cragan, and McCullough 1971).

4. Provide a background for understanding the impact of communication, and developing awareness of other people. We affect one another by communicating, and in the small group setting we have the opportunity to learn what our impact as communicators is on others. The small group can provide a means whereby we observe our own behavior, and where we can see how different forms of behavior elicit different responses.

The information flow in the small group setting is intense: not only is factual information presented, but each participant also is bombarded with his own and others' feelings, wishes, commands, desires, and needs. This information may be imparted verbally, nonverbally, intentionally, or unintentionally. The more directly individuals work with others, the better opportunity they will have to become aware of and sensitive to the feelings and emotions of others. *Therapy groups*, such as sensitivity training groups, function with the expressed intent of helping individuals by increasing their awareness. This awareness helps group members to build an individual identity which will facilitate social interaction (Rogers 1970). . . .

Groups may be defined according to certain attributes. Homan's (1950) definition focuses exclusively on *interaction*: "A group is defined by the interaction of its members. [Each member of the group] interacts more often with [the other members] than he does with outsiders" (p. 84). A group may be defined in terms of the *patterns* of its interaction. The definition offered by Merton (1957) specifies that there is patterned interaction which can be identified, and that members have expectations of each other in terms of adherence to the patterns of interaction. These patterns of interaction are usually the result of established norms. Other definitions focus upon *perceptions*: a group is a group if individuals outside the group perceive it to be a group, and if group members themselves perceive the group. Smith (1945) offers such a definition when he writes that a group consists of individuals "who have a collective perception of their unity and who have the ability or tendency to act and/or are acting in a unitary manner toward the environment" (p. 227).

Cartwright and Zander's (1968) definition of "group," the one used to guide this study of small

group behavior, is broad enough to encompass the many diverse definitions already presented, yet specific enough to help focus our attention. They define a group as "a collection of individuals who have relations to one another that make them interdependent to some significant degree" (p. 46). This definition provides parameters for group size (as the size increases the opportunity to influence other members decreases), group interaction (it is the result of the interdependency among members), and perceptions (members perceive themselves as part of a group because of the mutual interdependency and influence). The point Cartwright and Zander make about interdependency is worth repeating—individuals in a group influence and are influenced by the other members.

Even with this definition, there is still disagreement about groups. One question related to this problem is, "How real are groups?" From a psychological perspective, the only objective reality is the individual. The social psychological perspective also focuses on the individual, but emphasizes the individual in society. The sociological perspective views the group as a conceptual reality, i.e., it may be described without reference to the individual members. The group must be analyzed at the group, not the individual, level. Anthropologists view groups in terms of cultural forces, and developmental stages common to all primates. The writings of Levi-Strauss (1964) and Ardrey (1970) are examples of this approach to the group.

There is difficulty in working from extreme positions. Viewing the group as *only* the sum of its individuals, or as meaningful *only* when studied as a conceptual entity, or as *only* the result

West Side Story

Jet's Song

When you're a Jet,
You're a Jet all the way
From your first cigarette
To your last dyin' day.
When you're a Jet,
If the spit hits the fan,
You got brothers around,
You're a family man!
You're never alone,
You're never disconnected!
You're home with your own—
When company's expected,
You're well protected!
Then you are set
With a capital J,
Which you'll never forget
Till they cart you away.
When you're a Jet,
You stay
A jet!

When you're a Jet,
You're the top cat in town,
You're the gold-medal kid
With the heavyweight crown!

When you're a Jet,
You're the swingin'est thing.
Little boy, you're a man;
Little boy, you're a king!

The Jets are in gear,
Our cylinders are clickin'!
The Sharks'll steer clear
'Cause every Puerto Rican
'S a lousy chicken!

Here come the Jets
Like a bat out of hell—
Someone gets in our way,
Someone don't feel so well!
Here come the Jets:
Little world, step aside!
Better go underground,
Better run, better hide!
We're drawin' the line,
So keep your noses hidden!
We're hangin' a sign
Says "Visitors forbidden"—
And we ain't kiddin'!
Here come the Jets,
Yeah! And we're gonna beat
Every last buggin' gang
On the whole buggin' street!

On the whole!

Ever—!
Mother—!
Lovin'—!
Street!

of cultural forces, greatly reduces our understanding of the group as an individual and social phenomenon. Campbell (1958) has taken a middle-of-the-road position by admitting that groups vary in the degree to which they have a real existence. One of his most important considerations is the degree to which all the components (individuals) of the entity (group) share a *common fate*, that is, the extent to which they experience similar outcomes. If individuals are perceived as constituting a group, and they appear to be bound together in a relationship where each person shares a position relative to each other person, then the group is seen as a viable entity, something capable of independent existence. A second factor Campbell notes is *similarity*. Perceived member similarity affects whether they will be perceived as a group. Motorcycle gangs may be perceived as a group because members possess the same type of motorcycles and they dress similarly (leather jackets, emblems, or hats). The last consideration, less important than the other two, is *proximity*. The degree to which the members of a unity occupy a common space, or are in close proximity, affects the degree to which they are perceived as a viable entity. It is easier to attribute "groupness" to individuals who share physical environments than to individuals who are physically separated. Whether or not a group is perceived as an entity varies with the strength of these three perceptions. When common fate, similarity, and proximity are perceived, the individuals will be perceived as a group. When none of these are perceived, a group will not be perceived. Between these two points lies a range of responses.

A group is a highly complex

structure. It consists of individuals, with all their personal characteristics, interacting with one another in a given environment on a particular task. McGrath and Altman (1966), synthesizing and critiquing small group research, found that the research is concerned with three levels of reference: the *individual*, the *group*, and the *environment*. On the level of the individual, the concern has been with the personality characteristics, abilities, attitudes, and group position of each of the group members. On the group level, group abilities, training, experience, interpersonal relations, and structure have been studied. On the environmental level, the concern focuses upon conditions imposed upon the group, such as the task, operating conditions, and, possibly, the social conditions.

Information provided on the level of the individual is insufficient to predict the level of group performance; information provided on the level of the group alone also is insufficient to predict the level of group performance. Group capabilities may serve to set an upper limit on a group's performance potential. Likewise, information about the environment is insufficient to predict group performance, although it obviously affects it. Therefore, it is necessary to see the combined perspectives of all three approaches to help us better understand small group phenomena.

The component parts of small group interaction are interdependent; they share a relationship in which change in one part produces changes in the others. Studying the *parts*, such as members' personality characteristics and interpersonal relations, without some picture of how these parts fit into a *whole*, is a sure way to develop a false picture

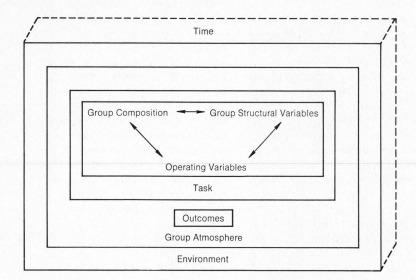

Fig. 1.1. *A graphic model of small group interaction*

of group interaction. Figure 1-1 depicts the relationships among the component parts of small group interaction. Group process takes place over *time*, and with the passage of time change occurs. Group interaction, then, is dynamic – the relationships among component parts are in constant flux.

Group composition includes a host of variables pertaining both to individual group members and how they interact with each other. Individual characteristics include each member's personality, attitudes, beliefs, self-concept, and perceptions of the other members. Interactive variables include group size, combined problem-solving skills, and how well different members can work together. Although it seems that group composition is a "given," such is not necessarily the case. For instance, group procedures which maximize individual usefulness may serve to increase friendly attitudes.

Two group *structural variables* are of concern: the communication network and the attraction network. Communication networks can differ according to type of structure, tightness (how flexible that structure is), and effectiveness (the relationship between the structure and task requirements). The attraction network includes not only who likes whom, but also the formation of cliques and subgroups, and their effects on social-emotional and task development.

Operating variables include the kinds of procedures the group uses in its deliberations, the roles enacted, and the norms and standards set under which the group functions. Deliberation procedures are highly varied. A group may decide to research a problem before discussing it, to divide the problem into small parts which individuals may attack separately, or any one of an infinite number of other procedures. The roles enacted in a group also affect its operation. The number of roles and the willingness and abilities of members to assume necessary roles constitute only three aspects of role enactment which affect the group's

behavior. Because norms prescribe the limits of acceptable behavior, they too must be considered in an analysis of group interaction. Group standards are another aspect of interaction. The extent to which members agree on norms and other evaluative criteria (of task solutions, for instance) will affect the degree to which value conflicts are avoidable.

The *task* provides the general framework within which the group operates. It is the prime reason, the rationale, for the group's existence. Aspects of the task which affect the other components of group interaction are critical task demands, that is, those aspects of the task which make certain abilities and procedures crucial to task solution; the complexity of the task; its difficulty; and the goals.

The *outcomes* of group interaction may be analyzed in terms of the quality, quantity, appropriateness, and efficiency of the solution or decision, and member satisfaction with the outcomes. It is important to note that a group's outcomes affect its subsequent interaction; outcomes are not simply the result of group interaction. A solution, for example, does not develop during the last minutes of discussion. The last minutes of discussion result from a decision to accept a certain solution. Last minute interaction is aimed at reinforcing the decision, and insuring that the members are in agreement. According to Collins and Guetzkow (1964), member satisfaction is a function of task success, success in solving interpersonal problems, and member position in the group. Both high power and a position of centrality produce member satisfaction.

The *group atmosphere* is the emotional framework within

which the group operates. The group atmosphere or climate may be hostile, it may be conducive to work, and it may be affected by the task, the environment (which can create pressures under which the group must operate), and group composition.

Group interaction, structural and operating variables, atmosphere, task, and outcomes take place within a given *environment*. The environment places limitations on the group, and may serve as a facilitative or debilitative agent for task accomplishment. The environment includes such things as the physical area in which the group meets, the materials it either does or does not have, and other groups with which the group may or may not be in competition. Time limits are also an environmental restriction.

Proficiency in small group interaction is enhanced by experience and knowledge. The aim of this book is to provide you with both. Knowledge of the various dimensions and perspectives of small group phenomena, combined with both supervised and unsupervised experiences, should increase your effectiveness and satisfaction as a group member. If this were the only rationale for studying small group behavior, it would be sufficient, given the increasing use of groups in our society. But another, possibly more important, rationale is that the small group can, and usually does, function as a microcosm of the larger society. Consequently, the study of small group dynamics will help group members view and, hopefully, understand their social behavior better. . . .

Groups Versus Individuals

Although it may sound like heresy in this age of "group think," it should be quite obvious that under many conditions groups are *not* useful. Before considering the conditions which affect the decision of whether to employ a group or an individual to solve the particular problem at hand, take time to do the following. Divide your class into small groups with four to six members each. Select several individuals to work alone.

Ask each group and each individual to generate test items for an examination on small group dynamics. Groups should follow a brain-storming procedure, that is, each idea generated should not be subject to discussion until all ideas have been exhausted. The object, for both the groups and individuals, is to generate as many items for the examination as possible.

Ask each group member, as well as each individual, to estimate the temperature of the room. Group members should add their estimates together, then divide by the total number of members to obtain a group average. Now obtain a class average for all the groups.

Solve the following problem: A farmer must cross a river but he has a problem. He has a bale of grass, a wolf, and a lamb with him, and the boat can hold only the farmer and *one of the three at a time.* If he leaves the lamb alone with the grass, the grass will be eaten. If he leaves the wolf with the lamb, the lamb will be eaten. How can he transport the wolf, the lamb, and the grass safely to the other side?

Develop a short crossword puzzle on any topic. Each puzzle must have at least ten words.

Complete a crossword puzzle. Do not use any of the puzzles generated during the fourth problem; use one from your daily newspaper or a magazine. . . .

The following are important aspects to consider in deciding whether to use an individual or a group to solve a particular problem. Depending upon the particular circumstances, some will be more important than others. Which are most important can only be determined by the task and socio-emotional functions your group must perform. A yes response indicates that a group should be used to solve a problem; a no response indicates that an individual should be used.

1. Are many steps required to solve the problem?

2. Are there many parts to the problem?

3. Will the solution be difficult to verify?

4. Are the individuals involved likely to perceive the problem as an impersonal one?

5. Will the problem be of moderate difficulty for the individuals who constitute the group?

6. Is a great deal of information required to solve the problem? Would a single individual be unlikely to possess it?

7. Does the problem demand a division of labor?

8. Are many solutions desired?

9. Are many man-hours required for the problem's solution?

10. Will individuals have to assume a great deal of responsibility for the solution?

11. Are the proposed solutions likely to be diverse?

12. Are the attitudes concerning the problem likely to be diverse?

13. Is it unlikely that group members will engage in nontask-oriented behavior?

PROBE 28. The climate of a group can develop defensively or supportively, depending upon the verbal and nonverbal behaviors of its members.

Group Climate

Jack Gibb

The Supportive Atmosphere

When the new observer comes into a group for the first time, he is able to sense a feeling about the group which we might call an atmosphere or a climate. Even a highly sensitive observer may have difficulty in describing these feelings. It may be helpful to select one of the many *schema* that have been offered for describing climates and use that example to show the distinction between a supportive climate and a defensive climate.

There is some evidence that a supportive climate maximizes the learning in the classroom. Certain kinds of behavior on the part of the teacher and of the students in a classroom tend to produce supportiveness. Because the teacher is such a critical member of the group, her behavior will be most important in the climate setting, particularly in the early stages of the development of the group. As indicated in Figure 1, the behaviors that produce what has been called a "supportive climate" are a shared problem-solving attitude, feelings of acceptance, empathy toward other group members, and listening to the remarks of others. Creative, active listening is a difficult process. People can sit quietly and take a bodily attitude of attending but can, in reality, be formulating their next speech or devising a strategy for some later movement in the group. Perhaps a more active and difficult process is one of attempting to empathize or "feel into" the behavior of other members of the group. Many writers have talked about the significance of acceptance of the person and his attitudes. Here again, the teacher's behavior is critical in determining norms of acceptance of a wide range of student attitudes.

Perhaps the key determiner of the supportive climate is the attitude of willingness to share in a problem that the group holds in common. Here the group member communicates the willingness to enter with the other persons into a

Fig. 1. *The supportive climate*

SOURCE: J. R. Gibb, *Factors Producing Defensive Behavior within Groups*, IV, Annual Technical Report, Office of Naval Research, Contract Nonr-2285 (01), November 15, 1957.

advice giving →
censoring →
defense →   **Defensive Climate**
persuasion →
controlling →
punishing →

→ + defensiveness
→ + responding behavior
→ − growth
→ − perceptiveness
→ − empathy

Fig. 2. *The defensive climate*

SOURCE: As for figure 1.

relationship in which they jointly explore the problem that confronts them. This willingness may occur at fairly deep levels of the personality. In occasional classes, one finds the teacher and the students engaged in a kind of joint inquiry in which all members of the group are trying to find answers to their problems. Learning is seen as a common quest in which many members of the classroom group can serve as resource persons. Learning to learn from others is one of the necessary skills for implementing such a climate.

On the right-hand side of Figure 1 are listed some of the effects of such a climate in the classroom. When such a climate exists, students and teachers feel less need to defend themselves from others, to protect their own attitudes and ideas from attack. Self-initiated activity occurs more readily under supportive climates. Members grow and develop as autonomous persons. When people listen to others, the individuals who are speaking get a chance to achieve a kind of catharsis or purging of their own emotions and feelings. This release is probably a necessary step in the reduction of the normal tensions that occur in all interpersonal relationships. When people feel supported and comfortable, they are able to perceive better. People who sense that they are accepted and understood tend to be released from their own defensiveness and tend to reach out in

counteracceptance and counterempathy toward the other members of the group. A supportive climate exists only in degree. The observer of the classroom will wish to be sensitive to diagnostic signs in the development of such a climate.

The Defensive Atmosphere

A contrasting climate is described in Figure 2.

As indicated in Figure 2, certain behaviors tend to produce and heighten the defensive level of the group. Because of the nature of our classroom activities, most teachers tend to engage in a considerable amount of persuasional activity. They give advice, control the activities of the students in many ways, try by subtle influence to persuade and "guide" the behaviors of the students that come under their tutelage. Less subtly, the teacher may use punishment, evaluation, and censoring as mechanisms for keeping the group in line. These behaviors tend to produce similar behaviors in the class, the total end product of which is a defensive climate. This persuasional and selling climate is characteristic of our culture and tends to be carried over into the schoolroom. The dynamics of competition for extrinsic rewards are such as to produce defensiveness. Most of the strains of the schoolroom tend to promote defensive climates. The teacher is usually under

strong pressure from within himself and from those administratively above him to cover a certain amount of ground, to mold the students in certain prescribed patterns, to reward what is accepted as good behavior, to guide and counsel students who deviate from accepted patterns of behaving. By administering extrinsic rewards for conforming behavior and by attempting to control the behavior of members, the teacher inevitably builds resistance and defense in the schoolroom.

As is indicated on the right-hand side of the figure, certain kinds of behavior inevitably result when defensive climates are produced.

Oftentimes behavior tends to reproduce itself in kind. Thus, defensiveness tends to produce more defensiveness. As classroom members become threatened by extrinsic reward systems, competition, and discipline, there is an increased feeling of necessity to defend one's own image. As people defend themselves, they engage in the kinds of behavior which produce counter self-preserving feelings in others. Accompanying this feeling of increased defensiveness is an increase in responding behavior. Students and teachers are responding to and, in a sense, controlled by the behavior of others. It is less possible for people to grow in defensive climates than in climates where they feel less need to protect their own images. People see the world less clearly. There is less tendency to feel one's self into the position of the other person. When there is less empathy, there is less understanding and countersupport. When climates become largely defensive, they tend to reproduce themselves. Thus, it requires a major educative act on the part of the teacher to counteract the defensiveness of the group.

Andy Capp by Reg Smythe

PROBE 29. **Leadership in a group involves the interaction between a person and the members of the group, all of whom assume various roles at various times.**

You Can Be a Better Leader

Louis Cassels

The average executive spends about 60 percent of his time in meetings and conferences. This recent survey finding points up the fact that ability to work in and through small groups is one of the most useful skills a manager can have.

Like most management skills, this one has to be developed. Managers who are adept at human relations on a man-to-man basis may be clumsy at working with groups.

Here are six suggestions for improving your performance as leader or member of a business work group. They come from Dr. Gordon L. Lippitt, a professional psychologist who is program director of the National Training Laboratories.

Dr. Lippitt's organization has done pioneering research in group processes for twelve years. Founded in 1947, NTL concentrated initially on training leaders of educational, religious, and civic groups. But in recent years managers have constituted a large proportion of its clientele.

To work more effectively in group situations a businessman needs to develop:

1. Awareness of his own impact on a group.

2. Insight into the needs, abilities, and reactions of others.

3. Sincere belief in the group approach to problem solving.

4. Understanding of what makes a group tick.

5. Ability to diagnose the ailments of a sick group.

6. Flexibility as a leader or member.

The first two qualities are closely related. Both require what Dr. Lippitt calls sensitivity.

Awareness

Many people who are alert to human responses in their ordinary business and social contacts become quite insensitive when they are functioning in a group. They plow ahead, intent on their own role or contribution, and never pause to observe the effect of their behavior on the others. People tend to act this way for at least two different reasons.

Some feel vaguely insecure in a group situation. Their nervousness causes them to develop calluses on their mental antennae which would normally pick up the nuances of response from others. Some are born actors who are so exhilarated by the opportunity to impress several people at once that they can be brought down to earth only by the most blatantly negative reaction from the captive audience.

You probably know already which of these types you are. If not, a little self-analysis should enable you to find out. In either case, the antidote is to make a conscious effort at future meetings to observe how you are acting, how much or how little you are talking, how attentively you are listening when others talk, and how your behavior is affecting the rest of the group.

Unless you are a remarkable fellow, you will probably be surprised at what you learn about yourself when you become a participant-observer rather than merely a participant. You may find, for example, that the sense of humor which you always considered to be a welcome relief from tension is actually an irritant and a distraction to others. Or you may learn that some of your colleagues regard your habit of doodling as a sign of boredom rather than concentration.

Sensitivity is doubly important if you are leader of the group. Your status means that your impact on the proceedings, for better or worse, is likely to be greater than anyone else's. It also means that you are less likely to be told, by any overt word or gesture, when you are rubbing the group the wrong way. You will have to rely on much subtler forms of feedback—the expression on a man's face, the tone of his voice, the tense or relaxed atmosphere of the meeting itself, the apathy or enthusiasm which the group exhibits when you call for ideas.

As a group leader, and to only slightly less extent as a member, you need also to recognize the effects of other people's behavior on you. You don't have to like a man in order to work effectively with him in a group, but it is important that you realize that you don't like him—and to differentiate between his personality, which irritates you, and his ideas, which may be extremely valuable.

For example, you may have a violent prejudice against people who chew gum. It is not necessary that you abandon this prejudice if you find yourself in a group that includes an incurable gum chewer. But it is necessary that you recognize the existence of your prejudice and make allowances for it in appraising or responding to a statement which your gum-chewer has made between chomps.

Insight

Insight into the needs and abilities of others is another form of sensitivity that pays big dividends in group leadership. All human beings share certain basic needs—for affection, acceptance, recognition, a sense of belonging, a sense of achievement.

If an individual finds that some or all of these needs are being satisfied through his participation in a group, he will be an enthusiastic and constructive member. On the other hand, if the group consistently ignores or frustrates his needs, he is likely to become hostile or apathetic. He may have no idea that these subconscious psychological drives are affecting his group performance. But a sensitive leader can learn to spot the symptoms and take corrective action.

One highly effective way to satisfy an individual member's psychological needs—and at the same time improve the effectiveness of the entire group—is to probe constantly for unexpected abilities. You call a man into a meeting to serve as an expert on some particular phase of the business that is assigned to him. But if you give him a chance to participate broadly, you may find he has a lot of wisdom to contribute on some entirely different matter.

Tom Tracy

leader n. a person who makes an important decision,

then sits back,

and answers stupid questions for the rest of his life.

Am I a Good Group Participant?

Leland P. Bradford

All during our lives we find ourselves sharing in group activity. We belong to our family, the Scouts, the softball team, the Spanish club, or the church choir. Sometimes we belong to groups just for short periods of time. We go to camp, or we attend a special discussion meeting, or we are on the Valentine's Day party committee.

By the time we get to high school we feel that we know a lot about groups. But now and then we come away from our group activity feeling dissatisfied with the way things are going. There is apparent lack of interest, or there is bickering among the members; the group seems to be growing away from its common relationship and goal.

This sometimes happens because we are not functioning well as units in our group. Since it is we who make up the group, we must always be conscious of our contribution to it. To get at the root of our common group problems, we must first ask ourselves, "Am I a good group participant?"

Below are indicated some of the roles of a good group member. You may play several or all of these roles in your group at some time; in fact, the more roles you play, the better. You should not feel that your place in the group is determined by one role only. If you find that you have not been participating enough, resolve now to be a better group member, and watch how your group will come alive, both for you and for everyone else in it.

1. *Do I propose new ideas, activities, and procedures?* Or do I just sit and listen?

2. *Do I ask questions?* Or am I shy about admitting that I do not understand?

(continued on page 185)

Abridged from "Am I a Good Group Participant?" by Leland P. Bradford in TODAY'S EDUCATION: NEA Journal, March 1956. © 1956 Leland P. Bradford. Used by permission of the author and TODAY'S EDUCATION.

That helps his ego—and adds a valuable human resource to the potential of the group.

The Group Approach

Many executives appoint committees, call meetings and go through the motions of consulting others because that is the way they are expected to act. But they never really delegate decision-making powers to any group. They walk into a meeting with their minds made up, and manipulate the group until it arrives at—and rubber stamps—the decision already reached. To such executives, group procedures are a sham—a device for persuading people they are participating when in reality they are not. To use a group in this way is worse than a waste of time. People know when they are being manipulated, and they always resent it.

There may be times when an executive will want to call a group together simply to announce a decision. That is perfectly legitimate provided it is made clear that the meeting was called purely to communicate a decision for which higher management accepts full responsibility. But you should never pretend that the group itself is taking part in the decision.

There are also occasions when it is far wiser for a manager to turn a problem over to a group for solution, with no strings attached. Many of the problems that arise in modern business are so complex that no one man, however brilliant, can possibly have all of the expert knowledge required to solve them correctly. The group approach enables you to bring a wide variety of experiences, backgrounds, viewpoints and technical competences to bear on a problem.

Group procedures also tend to lead to more creative solutions. It is remarkable how many people have their best thoughts when they are stimulated by the thoughts of others.

Another important reason for letting a group solve a problem is that people feel committed to a decision which they have helped to reach. If you must rely on others to implement a decision, you will do well to let them participate genuinely in the decision-making process. Even if you feel compelled to dictate the basic policy, you can usually delegate to an appropriate group the task of working out details of its implementation.

Understanding

An understanding of what makes a group tick will enable you to follow several basic rules for releasing the group potential.

The first step is to define clearly the problem about which a decision is to be made. Try to get a single, sharply focused question before the group. More time is wasted in meetings because of failure to pinpoint the problem than for any other reason.

The next step is to clarify the jurisdiction of the group. How much latitude does it have for reaching a decision? Is it serving merely in an advisory capacity, or is it fully responsible for a binding decision? Uncertainty on these points will cause members to be wary about giving their opinions.

Try to create a relaxed, permissive atmosphere. Let it be known that you want contributions—and candor—from all participants, that no one is there just to listen and nod.

(continued from page 184)

3. *Do I share my knowledge when it will prove helpful to the problem at hand? Or do I keep it to myself?*

4. *Do I speak up if I feel strongly about something? Or am I shy about giving an opinion?*

5. *Do I try to bring together our ideas and activities? Or do I concentrate only on details under immediate discussion?*

6. *Do I understand the goals of the group and try to direct the discussion toward them? Or do I get off the track easily?*

7. *Do I ever question the practicality or the "logic" of a project, and do I evaluate afterwards? Or do I always accept unquestioningly the things we do?*

8. *Do I help to arrange chairs, serve refreshments, and even clean up when the session is over? Or do I prefer to be waited on?*

9. *Do I encourage my fellow group members to do well? Or am I indifferent to their efforts and achievements?*

10. *Do I prod the group to undertake worthy projects? Or am I happy with mediocre projects?*

11. *Am I a mediator and a peacemaker? Or do I allow ill feeling to develop?*

12. *Am I willing to compromise (except where basic issues such as truth and justice are involved)? Or do I remain inflexible?*

13. *Do I encourage others to participate and to give everyone else a fair chance to speak? Or do I sit by while some people hog the floor, and do I sometimes dominate it myself?*

Tom Tracy

Withhold your own ideas about a solution, if you have any, until late in the session. If you put them on the table too early, you may give the group the false impression that you have already made up your mind and are merely looking for yes men.

Elicit as many ideas as possible before beginning to evaluate or criticize any particular solution. If you let the evaluation process begin too soon, it will choke off the production of alternative solutions and rivet attention on the first few ideas advanced.

Dissociate ideas from the men who put them forward. Never refer to "Jack's plan" or "Jones' proposal." Keep personalities and personal rivalries out of the picture as far as possible by giving each proposal a neutral designation—"plan A" or "suggestion No. 1."

Don't ask the group to guess when it's possible to get facts. If it is difficult to weigh the relative merits of one or more solutions without further investigation or testing, postpone a decision until a later meeting.

Aim for a consensus of the group, rather than take a vote. A consensus is usually not too hard to obtain if you allow skeptics to record their misgivings, and if you make it clear that the decision will be subject to revaluation later if necessary.

Diagnose the Ailments

Sometimes you can impanel a group of highly competent men,
follow all of the right procedures, and still the group won't come alive and produce. That's when you need diagnostic ability.

If you have developed self-insight and sensitivity toward others, you may be able to figure out what's wrong. You don't have to psychoanalyze the members. Just look a little below the surface of their conduct. Try to detect the unexpressed feelings and motivations that are causing them to fight among themselves or to run from the problem.

Watch for "hidden agendas"—the real interests that a group member is trying to further while professing to talk about the problem at hand. It may be necessary to bring some of these hidden agendas into the open—to lay aside the official problem until you have dealt with the distracting troubles.

Generally, it is best not to rely entirely on your own diagnostic powers, but to enlist the help of the group itself in analyzing its difficulties. A good technique for doing this is to distribute simple mimeographed forms—usually called "post-meeting reports"—to be filled out anonymously by all participants immediately after adjournment. How did you think today's meeting went? What did you like best about it? What did you dislike most? What should we do differently next time?

After you have used this blind questionnaire technique a few times, you may find that the members of the group are prepared to do the evaluating out loud at the close of the meeting.
When you thus succeed in making a group conscious of its own procedures, and of its own responsibility to criticize and correct its inadequacies, you are on your way to mature and fruitful group activity.

Flexibility

The final piece of advice to those who have to participate in a large number of group meetings is: Try being flexible.

Many different roles must be played in a group other than leader and member. For example, a group needs idea givers and idea evaluators, question askers and information providers, critics and supporters, challengers and summarizers, stirrer uppers and peacemakers.

Most people tend unconsciously to cast themselves in the same role or roles at every meeting they attend. But it is much better for the group—and for your relations with the group—if you vary your role from time to time.

Try out a new role and see how you feel about it, and how the others react to it. If you've always been an idea giver, see how well you can function as a supporter, or vice versa. You'll be amazed at how much more you can accomplish in a group through a little versatility.

Group Problem Solving

John K. Brilhart

Focus on the Problem before Solutions

What would you think if you drove into a garage with a car that was running poorly and the mechanic almost immediately said, "What you need to fix this buggy is a new carburetor and a set of spark plugs." If your reaction is like mine, you would get out of there as fast as your ailing auto would let you. A competent mechanic, after he asked questions about how the car was acting and observed how it ran, would put it on an electronic engine analyzer. After gathering information by these means he would make a tentative diagnosis, which he would check by direct examination of the suspected parts. Only then would he say something like, "The problem is that two of your valves are burned, and the carburetor is so badly worn that it won't stay adjusted properly."

Our two hypothetical mechanics illustrate one of the most common failings in group (and individual) problem solving: solution centeredness. Irving Lee, after observing many problem-solving conferences and discussions, found that in most of the groups he studied there was "a deeply held assumption that because the problem was announced it was understood. People seemed too often to consider a complaint equivalent to a description, a charge the same as a specification.[1] Maier, after many years of studying problem-solving discussions in business and industry, stated that "participants as well as discussion leaders focus on the objective of arriving at a solution and fail to give due consideration to an exploration of the problem."[2] Groups tend to act like a surgeon who scheduled an operation when a patient complained of a pain in his abdomen, like a judge who handed down a decision as soon as he had read the indictment, or like the hunter who shot at a noise in the bushes and killed his son. Solution-centeredness has harmful effects:

1. *Partisanship is encouraged.* Participants spend a lot of time arguing the merits of their pet proposals. The group often becomes hopelessly split, or negative feeling is aroused which will affect future discussions.

2. *Ineffectual solutions tend to be adopted.* There is a tendency to spend much time debating the first and most obvious solutions, which are usually taken bodily from other situations and are not based on the facts of the present case. New, innovative ideas are not considered.

3. *Time is wasted.* Solution-at-once methods often result in a sort of pinwheel pattern.

PROBE 30. **Problem solving in your group will be more efficient if you follow a pattern or sequence.**

Brainstorming Triggers Ideas

An agent recently came to us seeking help. She wanted an idea. We didn't have the idea she wanted, but we suggested a technique we hope will help her come up with the idea. The technique is called brainstorming. Maybe you can use it sometime. Here's how it works.

Start with a problem. (In the example above it was a title for a newsletter.) Appoint a small committee—three to five persons—and let it meet in a place where there are no distractions. State the problem as a question. Ask each member to answer with the *first* thought that comes to his mind. Appoint a recorder and begin.

There are probably only two hard and fast rules for a brainstorming session.

1. If you have a thought, get it out of your head and on paper. Speak out without hesitation. If you leave the thought loitering around in your mind, it will just clutter up the path of other ideas. Write down every brainstorm—no matter how silly or trite or foolish it may sound at the moment.

2. Don't rush it. Give the session time to work. We think a half hour would be a bare minimum and it may run a half day. Brainstorming is not likely to be effective if the committee members have to leave for another meeting in five minutes.

When all the committee members feel satisfied that they have exhausted their ideas, put the list away and let it simmer for a few days. *This is important!* When you look at it again, one of the brainstorms may seem just right—the idea you have been seeking. On the other hand, one of the "silly" ideas may trigger a brand new thought which is just what you wanted.

(continued on page 189)

Reprinted from "Brainstorming Triggers Ideas" in *Inside Information*, November, 1966. © 1966 *Inside Information*. Used by permission of the Information and Publications Department, University of Maryland.

The problem is mentioned; someone proposes a solution which is argued at length; someone points out that an important aspect of the problem has been neglected; someone then goes back to the problem to see if this is so. This problem-solution cycle may be repeated indefinitely, wasting time on solutions which do not fit the facts of the case. At first, focus on what has gone wrong rather than what shall be done about it.

Begin with a Problem Question Rather Than a Solution Question

Consider the following situation: A student leader asks his group, "How can we get rid of a club president who is not doing his job, without further disrupting the club?" Such a statement of the problem appears insoluble, like how to eat a cake and have it too. The apparent dilemma is the result of incorporating a solution (get rid of the president) into the statement of the problem. The better procedure is to separate the solution from the problem, then focus on understanding the details of the problem. Once this has been done, appropriate solutions will usually emerge. Our student leader might ask, "How might we get good leadership for our club?" Then the group can dig into what is expected of the president, how the incumbent is acting, what members are complaining about, what is wrong, and why. Answers to these questions about the problem may lead to tentative solutions: "Send him to a leadership training laboratory," "Have the sponsor instruct him in his duties," "Ask him to resign," "Temporarily assign part of his duties to the executive committee members" and the like. See if you can distinguish between the following problems which include solutions (solution questions) and those which focus on what is wrong:

How can I transfer a man who is popular in the work group but slows down the work of others?

What can be done to alleviate complaints about inadequate parking space at our college?

How might we reduce theft and mutilation in the college library?

How can we get more students to enroll in physics?

What action shall we take in the case of Joe Blevins who is accused of cheating on Professor Lamdeau's exam?

Map the Problem Situation

To help develop problem mindedness, think of the problem as a large uncharted map with only vague boundaries. The first task facing the problem-solving group is to make the map as complete as possible (in other words, to fully diagnose the situation). The leader of the group should urge the members to tell all they know about the situation: facts, complaints, conditions, circumstances, factors, details, happenings, relationships, disturbances, effects. In short, what have you observed? What have others observed? What have you heard?

At best the "map" of the problem will be incomplete, with full detail in some parts, but gaps or faint outlines in others. Members will disagree on some details. Some observations may be spotty and fleeting. Sometimes the members will admit they do not know enough about the problem to deal with it intelligently. The author remembers a group of students concerned with recommending solutions to a severe shortage of parking space at a large university. The discussants soon decided they did not have enough infor-

(continued from page 188)

Take the naming of *Inside Information* as an example of how the technique works. We (the Information and Publications staff) wanted to develop a "tip sheet," "communication guide," "house organ," or some kind of newsletter. The organizing committee met and made some decisions about format, content, publication dates, etc., and then went into a brainstorming session to find a name. We came up with the following in the first session:

Sign Posts	Flashback
For Public Information	Inside Information
Information Quotient	Show and Tell
Focal Points	Oriole Oracle
Pencil Points	Key Notes
Pertinent Points	The Bulletin
Salient Points	Illuminator
The Transmission Line	Quizling
Fishing Cord	Unclassified
Extension Cord	Unclassified Information

As you can see, most of them connote some phase of communication—but not all. After the ideas had simmered for a week, the committee met again and suggested a few more titles. Finally, we selected *Inside Information* because of the double, or even triple, meaning it might convey. This was to be our internal organ for carrying our communcations ideas to you. The title suggested that the newsletter might carry more than run-of-the-mill announcements, and it could be our way of bringing you into our confidence and into our departmental work—our way of introducing ourselves to you.

Next time you are searching for an idea, why not try brainstorming?

Tom Tracy

Spitballing with Flair

Spitballing, or brainstorming, is something like a group-therapy session in which the patient is the product and the doctors are the admen. Recently, Time Correspondent Edgar Shook sat in on a brainstorming meeting at Chicago's North Advertising Inc. The patient: Flair, a new Paper Mate pen with a nylon tip. Among the doctors: North President Don Nathanson, Creative Director Alice Westbrook, Copy Chief Bob Natkin and Copywriters Steve Lehner and Ken Hutchison. The dialogue, somewhat condensed:

Natkin: We have what I think must be the first graffiti advertising campaign, which we've been running in teen-age magazines. The reason I bring this up is that it could be translated into TV and could be very arresting.

Westbrook: I love graffiti.

Natkin (reading from graffiti ads): "Keep America beautiful. Bury a cheap, ugly pen today. Buy a Paper Mate." Some research has been done on this and it looks like it's working. "Draw a flower on your knee with a Paper Mate Flair."

Westbrook: Why not "navel"?

Natkin: They wouldn't let us say it. We are going to compromise. It was going to be "Draw a flower around your genitals with a Paper Mate Flair." Then they'd say "knee" and we'd say "navel," and we'd meet in the middle.

Westbrook: Body paint is going to get hotter and hotter.

Nathanson: Did you read that memo I sent out about the bosoms? God, I think bosom makeup is going to be big.

Westbrook: I do too. I know just the color for it too.

Nathanson: You know, you can do a fantastic industrial campaign on the idea of a silent pen. Because just think of the noise level. I mean, nothing is noisier than these competitor's pens. Everybody quiet. Just listen. (*He scratches first with the competitor's pen, then with a Flair.*)

Westbook: Boy, that really moves me.

Lehner: Picture the kind of thing you would get if you were awarded the Legion of Honor. Real parchmenty, with a great big heraldry and wax and stamps. And on the certificate it says, "The American Anti-Noise League." And you hear the announcer say with great . . .

Hutchison: Flair.

Lehner: . . . "From the American Anti-Noise League, for exceptionally smooth writing without scratching or squeaking." You hear a trumpet. Tah-Tah! We dissolve to another document. "To Flair from the United Cap Forgetters Council: for having a new kind of ink that won't dry out if you leave the cap off overnight." And a couple of trumpets. Bum-Bum! And on to a third document. "To Flair from the National Pen Pounders Association: for having a smooth, tough,

(continued on page 191)

From "Spitballing with Flair" in TIME, July 12, 1968. Reprinted by permission from TIME, The weekly newsmagazine; Copyright Time Inc.

mation to make wise recommendations. They tried to list the types of information they would need before proceeding to talk about solutions. Soon investigating teams were out interviewing, getting maps, collecting records and reading. The subsequent discussions led to a clear description of the many problems involved, and ultimately to a set of recommendations with which the entire group was pleased. These recommendations were presented to proper authorities, and most of them put into effect within three years. When a group gets into a discussion of what must be done to get needed information, the spirit of teamwork is something to behold! And the solutions usually work.

Perhaps the greatest obstacle to problem-centered thinking is the leader or other member who comes to the group with the problem solved in his own mind. Needed is the spirit of humility, which does not know too much and realizes all of us know only a part.

Agree Upon Criteria

Many times there is a lack of "reality testing" before a decision is made final. Other times, a group cannot agree on which of two or more possible solutions to adopt. If the problem has been fully explored, the most likely source of difficulty is a lack of clear-cut standards, criteria, or objectives. In many discussions there is a need for two considerations of criteria: first, when formulating the specific objectives of the group; second, when stating specific standards to be used in judging among solutions. Until agreement (explicit or intuitive) is reached on criteria, agreement on a solution is unlikely.

From the beginning of the dis-

B.C. by permission of Johnny Hart and Field Enterprises, Inc.

cussion, the group needs to be clearly aware of the limitations placed upon it. This is sometimes called the group's area of freedom. The group which tries to make decisions affecting matters over which it has no authority will be both confused and frustrated. For example, the area of freedom for a group of university students includes recommending changes in teaching methods, but students have no authority to make or enforce policy governing such changes. A committee may be given power to recommend plans for a new building, but not to make the final decision and contract for the building. Any policy decision or plan of action must be judged by whether or not it fits into the group's area of freedom. Thus, if a committee is authorized to spend up to $500, it must evaluate all possible ideas by that absolute criterion.

It is important to rank criteria, giving priority to those which must be met. Ideas proposed can be rated yes or no on whether they meet all the absolute criteria, and from excellent to poor on how well they measure up to the less important criteria.

Single words, such as *efficient*, are not criteria, but categories of criteria. Such words are so vague that they are meaningless when applied to possible solutions. They can be used to find specific criteria. Criteria should be worded as questions or absolute statements. For example, the following criteria might be applied to plans for a club's annual banquet:

Absolute — Must not cost over $400 for entertainment.
Must be enjoyable to both members and their families.

Questions —How convenient is the location for members?
How comfortable is the room?

(continued from page 190)

nylon point that won't push down." And you've got three trumpets going, and an announcer comes back in and says, "Flair even looks like a better way to write." We would play it very straight. Very pompous. Like Robert Morley's voice when he says these words. You get a kind of electricity between the silliness.

Westbrook: Let's face it. People just don't get emotionally involved with their pens. I think there's the danger of taking yourself too seriously when you're talking about a thing like that.

Lehner: We have other ideas that we think would be stronger at this point in time. For instance, one thing that we're playing with now is a guy sitting at his desk . . .

Westbrook: A big, snappy executive.

Lehner: And his secretary is with him and this guy is making notations like a guy would. Writing. "Yeah." "No." "See me . . ."

Westbrook: "You're fired." Stuff like that.

Lehner: And when the girl goes out of the room, he takes a leather portfolio, looks around, opens it up and starts doodling some very silly, funny little things. And the announcer says: "Introducing a new executive status symbol — Flair. To the casual observer, Flair is a dignified, serious, executive pen. But when you're alone, Flair reveals its true identity as the executive play pen. The greatest doodler in the world. This Christmas give him the executive play pen, Flair."

Westbrook: That's a great line! I think we ought to pretend like we got some new colors and see what we can do with it.

Nathanson: What a television color commercial it could be, with fuchsias and, oh, I don't know, you name them. You know, orchid colors. You'll get women to write letters wih orchid . . .

Westbrook: You could have a black pen with white ink or a white pen with black ink. Sort of an integrated pen, you know. (*Laughter.*) It could be called "the soul pen."

Nathanson: Black paper!

Westbrook: With white ink! That's groovy!

Nathanson: With blue paper!

Westbrook: Purple paper with pink ink! Pink paper with purple ink!

Nathanson: Brown ink! We present them with a whole slew of marvelous ideas. Sealskin and alligator pens!

Westbrook: Phony fur pens! Wouldn't you love a fur pen? A mink pen? How about a tiger pen? Or a leopard pen? Would you believe an alligator pen?

Natkin: How about a grey flannel pen?

Westbrook: Grey flannel is out. How about a turtleneck pen?

(*To learn what, if anything, resulted from this meeting, watch your TV set.*)

Defer Judgment When Finding Solutions

Instead of evaluating each possible solution when it is first proposed, defer judgment until a complete list of possible solutions has been produced. Much of the research already quoted indicates that the process of *idea getting* should be separated from *idea evaluation*. Judgment stifles unusual and novel ideas. New ideas come from a minority, and do not have the support of experience or common sense. It is a good idea to list the proposed solutions on a chart or chalkboard. Encouragement should be given to combine, modify, or build upon previous suggestions. Get as many ideas as you can, and permit no criticism of them until after the list is complete.

Plan How to Implement and Follow up

Many times a group will arrive to no avail at a policy decision, a solution to a problem, a resolution or some advice. No plans are made for putting it into effect or to see if the ideas are received by the proper authorities. Every problem-solving discussion should terminate in some plan for action; no such group should consider its work finished until agreement is reached on who is to do exactly what, by what time, and how. If a committee is to make recommendations to a parent body, the committee should decide who will make the report, when he will make it, and in what form. If this report is to be made at a membership meeting, the committee members may then decide to prepare seconding or supporting speeches, may decide how to prepare the general membership to accept their recommendations and so forth. A

neighborhood group that has decided to turn a vacant lot into a playground would have to plan how to get legal clearances, who to get to do the work, where to get the materials (or at least from whom), and how to check on the use children get from the playground. No good chairman or leader of a problem-solving group would fail to see that the group worked out details of how to put their decisions into effect.

Creativity will improve your problem-solving ability.

Brainstorming

Occasionally a problem-solving group may want to engage in a full-fledged brainstorming discussion. Brainstorming depends on the deferment of judgment; many auxiliary skills and techniques can be used to advantage. Brainstorming can be applied to any problem if there is a wide range of possible solutions, none of which can in advance be said to be just right. The process of brainstorming can be applied to any phase of the discussion: finding information (What information do we need? How might we get this information?), finding criteria (What criteria might we use to test ideas?), finding ideas (What might we do?), or implementation (How might we put our decision into effect?). In addition to what has been said about creative problem solving, the following rules of brainstorming should be presented to the group:

1. *All criticism is ruled out while brainstorming.*
2. *The wilder the ideas, the better.* Even offbeat, impractical

Tom Tracy

suggestions may suggest practical ideas to other members.

3. *Quantity is wanted.* The more ideas, the more likelihood of good ones.

4. *Combination and improvement are wanted.* If you see a way to improve on a previous idea, snap your fingers to get attention so it can be recorded at once.

It is often advantageous to have in the discussion group both people with experience and people quite new to the specific problem (for a fresh point of view). A full-time recorder is needed to write down ideas as fast as they are suggested. Sometimes this can be done with a tape recorder, but a visual record that all can see is best. Be sure the recorder gets all ideas in accurate form.

The flow of possible solutions can sometimes be increased by asking idea-spurring questions. One can ask: "How can we adapt (modify, rearrange, reverse, combine, minimize, maximize) *any general solution*?" A concrete suggestion can be used to open up creative thinking in a whole area. For example, someone might suggest: "Place a guard at each door." The leader could then ask, "What else might be done to increase security?" When the group seems to have run out of ideas, try reviewing the list rapidly; then ask for a definite number of additional suggestions to see if you can get more ideas. Usually you will get many more, including some very good ones.

1. Irving J. Lee, *How to Talk with People* (New York: Harper and Brothers, 1952), p. 62.

2. Norman R. F. Maier, *Problem-Solving Discussions and Conferences* (New York: Mc-Graw-Hill Book Company, 1963), p. 123.

Making a Decision as to the "Best" Solution

R. Wayne Pace and Robert R. Boren

The culmination of the selection process arrives when the actual decision is made to adopt a particular solution for the problem. Although in any given case there may be several ways of reaching this decision, it is of utmost importance that the group members *agree* on the method to be used. Again, this need for maximal agreement can prove to be a difficult communicative task in a small group. The group's goal in this regard must be *to reach a level of acceptance where each individual is committed to abiding by a decision arrived at in a particular way*. To achieve such an objective is often time-consuming and likely to engender a considerable amount of conflict. Nevertheless, the decision-making process cannot be completed unless a systematic way of resolving differences or overcoming indifferences can be accepted by all. Paradoxical though it may seem, even a refusal or failure to make a choice involves the making of a decision. The following is a brief, descriptive summary of some of the most commonly used strategies for the making of choices in the culminating phase of problem-solution interaction:

1. Decision through bypassing. An idea is offered; but before it can be discussed or brought before the group for formal action, another idea is presented. The first idea is simply bypassed and allowed to fail through inaction.

2. Decision through power. The most important, prestigious, authoritative, or otherwise powerful person in the group actively supports the idea and acts on the assumption that all others agree. Holding the power, the holder is able unilaterally to make the choice.

3. Decision through vocal coalition. A vocal minority of the group creates the impression that widespread support exists for an idea. Because the other members of the group fail to offer their objections, the seeming strength of the vocal coalition makes the choice.

4. Decision through majority vote. Through the procedures of a poll (show of hands, voice vote, or secret ballot), the idea that is supported by more than one half of the group is accepted.

5. Decision through plurality. On occasion, although a choice must be made, a majority cannot be developed in favor of a particular idea. Plurality allows for the idea having the largest number of supporters to be accepted as the group decision. Political elections, for example, are often determined by plurality rather than majority.

6. Decision through consensus. When communication among members of the group has been genuinely open and receptive, and when each person has been able to express his or her opinion and tender his or her objections, agreement can be reached at the point when members are willing to subscribe to the idea even if they have some reservations about it. Consensus represents support for a majority opinion given willingly and as a consequence of the members' understanding of that opinion and the fact that they have influenced its shaping during interaction.

7. *Decision by unanimity.* Unanimity occurs when all members of the group actually agree on the selection of an idea or a solution. Usually, important group decisions are reached by consensus; but there are times when complete agreement by all members should be sought.

Decisions, we must remember, do not represent the end of the problem-solving process. The group—having decided upon a solution to the problem facing it—must proceed to take whatever additional steps it *can* take to set in motion the machinery necessary to achieve the agreed-upon solution. Always, to be effective and bring about the desired change, ideas must be translated into *workable plans* and *implemented* "on the job"—in the reality of the pertinent situation.

Prods

1. How many small groups do you belong to? Which one is most effective? Why? What specific factors influenced your choice?
2. Chat with a manager of a local company about the number of small groups in his or her unit. In the manager's opinion, which are more effective and which are less effective. Determine why.
3. Could answers to questions 1 and 2 be secured better by a group or by an individual? Why?
4. Think of a group to which you belong. Is the climate primarily defensive or supportive? Cite specific examples to support your answer.
5. Interview a manager of a bank, department store, or theater. Ask the manager questions about his or her leadership style based on Cassels's six points. What kind of leader do you think the manager is?
6. List twenty possible ways to improve national elections, and note how long this task took you. Ask three to five other people to work together on such a list, and note the time they spent. Did the group produce a larger number of better ideas? Explain the results.

4

SPEAKER = AUDIENCE

PROBE 31 A public message deals with matters of concern to a large group or to several small groups.

PROBE 32 Organizing messages around a body of information of interest to listeners will enhance your effectiveness as a speaker.

PROBE 33 The Motivating Process is a way of organizing an effective persuasive speech.

PROBE 34 A public speaker is someone who seeks to inform or influence an audience.

Relationship 4: Speaker-Audience

When a large number of people gather to listen to a speaker, a speaker-audience relationship occurs. This relationship differs from dyads, serial chains, and small groups in a number of ways: the size of the audience limits feedback; less interaction occurs between the speaker and listeners; the language is more formal and less adaptive because of the speaker's need to reach the largest number of listeners; and the speaker generally makes more deliberate preparations for this occasion than for less formal ones.

The speaker-audience relationship may result from such formal circumstances as politicians addressing potential voters, professors lecturing to their classes, commencement speakers expounding to the graduates, entertainers amusing their audiences, businessmen informing their service clubs, or ministers persuading their congregations. It may also result from such less formal circumstances as coaches giving pep talks to their teams, police sergeants briefing their patrolmen, tour guides informing their tourists, street hawkers pushing their products to wary pedestrians, or children selling lemonade to thirsty passersby.

Speaking to an audience allows a person to structure messages carefully and to control nonverbal behavior to produce a specific response in several people at once—perhaps to assert his or her own power. Whatever your purpose, whenever or wherever your occasion, whoever your audience, you will be a better public speaker by following some simple rules for selecting, organizing, supporting, clarifying, and delivering messages to audiences.

Although Aristotle first published many principles to guide effective public speakers in the Greek forum over 2000 years ago, we find most of his advice still relevant today, as the following discussions demonstrate.

Public Communication Today

Roderick P. Hart, Gustav W. Friedrich, and William D. Brooks

Today, communication is not limited to face-to-face situations—we have worldwide electronic communication, television saturation, and packaged entertainment. And it is understandable why some have said that live, in-person public speaking is as extinct as the dodo bird. Nothing could be further from the truth! No only is public speaking alive and well, but it is thriving as it never has before despite—and perhaps because of—the coming of the mass media. *Per person*, public speech consumption is higher today than ever before, including the era of the late 1800s. Even platform lecturing, one small aspect of non-mediated public communication, is a booming, million-dollar industry today. Political figures, journalists, authors, entertainers, business leaders, and proponents of all sorts of "isms" have found the lecture circuit of the 1970s to be a virtual gold mine. More than one presidential loser has paid the campaign bills by going on the lecture circuit. We, as a people, have *not* lost our enthusiasm for in-person public speaking as a significant social institution. Teddy Roosevelt once called the public speaking platform America's fourth great institution, surpassed only by the home, school, and church. This statement remains true today, no matter what has happened, or may be happening, to the other three institutions.

No one knows exactly how many speeches are given each year in the United States, but conservative estimates made by one group, The International Platform Association, run as high as 500,000. Speeches are given by persons representing literally thousands of organizations, groups that are large and small, governmental and private, commercial and philanthropic. For example, Senator William Fulbright (1970) states in his book, *The Pentagon Propaganda Machine:*

> Besides using all of the modern tools for opinion molding, the military makes use also of the oldest—public speaking . . . [using more than] 1000 speakers a month within one Army command alone . . . in an almost steady stream, they have been speaking to Rotary Clubs, Reserve Officers Meetings, at ship launchings, and almost anywhere a responsive audience might be expected to gather. . . . The Navy's Office of Information every two years publishes a booklet titled "Outstanding Navy Speeches." In the preface of one of the most recent, the Navy Chief of Information [says that] "navy men and women are delivering more and better public speeches than ever before." (pp. 128-129, 133)

Indeed according to the CBS special, "The Selling of the Pentagon," the war in Vietnam might have lasted as long as it did because of the "traveling colonels"—military personnel who toured the

---

PROBE 31. A public message deals with matters of concern to a large group or to several small groups.

From pp. 11–14, 23–28 PUBLIC COMMUNICATION by Roderick P. Hart, Gustav W. Friedrich, and William D. Brooks. Copyright © 1975 by Roderick P. Hart, Gustav W. Friedrich, and William D. Brooks. By permission of Harper & Row, Publishers, Inc.

Beetle Bailey by Mort Walker

© King Features Syndicate, Inc., 1973.

Everybody's Talkin'

Fred Neil

*Everbody's talk'n at me
I don't hear a word they're say'n
Only the echoes of my mind*

*People stop'n star'n
I can't see their faces
Only the shadows of their eyes*

*I'm go'n where the sun keeps shin'n
Through the pour'n rain
Go'n where the weather suits my clothes
Begg'n off of the northeast winds
Sail'n on the summer breeze
Skipp'n over the ocean like a storm*

*Everybody's talk'n at me
Can't hear a word they're say'n
Only the echoes of my mind
I won't let you leave my love behind
I won't let you leave my love behind*

chicken-and-peas circuit thumping for continuance of the war.

If ever there was a fear that mass media extravaganzas would run public speaking out of town, that fear has now been buried. Indeed, public speakers are seemingly created and nurtured by the television screen. Instead of killing off the public platform as was at first predicted, TV has actually stimulated the demand for "live" speakers. In 1972 alone, there were upwards of 25,000 professional speaking opportunities in the business and convention fields alone—ranging from closed seminars for a handful of top-echelon executives to the annual open meetings of the National Education Association, which brings out a whopping 10,000 registrants.

The second largest sponsor of paid lecturers is education—from kindergarten assemblies to graduate school forums. About one in five of all elementary and secondary schools have at least one public program annually. The average number of speaking programs is running as high as five per institution. This totals up to 130,000 programs each year. Add to that another 200,000 programs on the junior college, college, and graduate levels, and it seems that the machinery of education is being well lubricated by the juices of eloquence![1]

Such public speaking statistics are staggering. In one week, for example, there were 40,000 paid speaking engagements in New York and 30,000 in Chicago. In addition, some U.S. senators make as much as $35,000 per year on the lecture circuit.

The Social Significance of Public Communication

All this talk—this public talk—with which we are being inundated is not talk for the sake of talk.

There is a reason for it—man has no other means as efficient as public communication for solving his problems, for creating and maintaining organizations, or for collectively making and implementing decisions. On the other hand, public talk is used to start wars, to fester public wounds, and to visit all sorts of social and political plagues on suspecting and unsuspecting publics. Through public communication man deals with his environment-at-large. Thus, whether we like it or not, there are few tools other than public talk with which to maintain the delicate balance between community and jungle.

Public Communication As Problem-Solver

Sociopolitical experts tell us that in the near future a means must be found for bringing newly emerging countries into the contemporary framework, that of a highly developed, technological, and automated world. Methods by which these peoples and states may be integrated smoothly into a world society must be worked out and, most importantly, articulated.

For example, anthropologist Margaret Mead is among those who have pointed out, that great numbers of people are being moved, in the short span of 20 to 30 years, from something akin to the Stone Age into an unabashedly technological era. Soon, young people in such societies may be able to say, "My father was a stone carver, but I'm going into internal medicine!" Satellites, supersonic planes, and telecommunications do not merely make such rapidly changing situations probable, they make them inevitable. These changes can occur smoothly and efficiently *only* if public communication is able to give voice to these unique chal-

lenges that are placed on contemporary humankind.

Another challenge encroaching upon us is that of creating governmental systems which permit diversity and dissent within a semblance of uniformity and majority rule. We are being called upon to build a society for all—not just for the rich and well-educated, but also for the educationally and economically unfortunate. With the rapid change that now characterizes our day-to-day lives, and with the rate of technological innovation being what it is, we must develop a *public* atmosphere conducive to allowing patterns of human behavior to change in pace with the material changes that affect society. Speakers by the hundreds have called attention to the fact that man has inadvertently let the rate of technological change out-pace our more distinctively *human* progress.

Moreover, these technological changes have made the world one. Many of our time-honored boundaries, borders, and rules belong, for the most part, to *pre-technology*. Technology has made many such delimiting artifacts obsolete. The paradox we now seem to be facing is that on the one hand we accept and encourage technological revolutions that inevitably make the world a "global village"; yet on the other hand we are being blinded to the human needs about us created by technological escalations.

It takes no great insight to see that substantial technological changes require prodigious human accommodations, and we, in *public* ways—in our organizations, institutions, and governmental systems are being called upon to provide for such human changes. The vehicle which is increasingly bearing the brunt of such burdens is public communication.

Public communication does not exist in a vacuum but rather is part of the social and political mosaic. It is an essential part of every organization and every society in the world. For that reason, it is essential that we come to understand and to use effectively and constructively communicative ways of making human contact.

Communication at some level and in some form is a process common to all living things. It is found in its most complex and sophisticated form in man. Communication is man's key instrumentality—his primary means—for forming relationships, for understanding his world, and for creating his institutions and organizations. At the risk of sounding philosophical, let us state that our societal evolution and perhaps our collective survival rest on the ever-burdened shoulders of public dialogue.

The Distinctive Features of Public Speech Settings

All salesmanship, all oratory, whether it be a parson in his bloody pulpit boring his audience to bloody death, and making them want to get away from his misery; or whether it's a heckler screeching with all the crowd giggling in front of him, this is hypnosis. And I'm always conscious . . . of deliberately utilizing an audience in this way. For example, I'll pick out one person. He will act as a scapegoat for the whole of the crowd, because then it will relieve the crowd to know that their own anxieties are taken away, piled on him, and they can all insult him through me. And if this is done with sense of humour in order to keep a balance in the crowd, it's pleasing to the crowd, and quite often it's pleasing to the person I pick out because quite often they are masochists. . . .[2]

These remarks were made by one of the dozens of itinerant,

ragamuffin speakers who regularly engage in soapbox oratory in London's Hyde Park. While we can learn many lessons from such colorful ramblings, one message seems to stand out—*there is a rather unique geography and sociology to public speech settings*. As our Hyde Park speaker indicates, there is a unique *gestalt* surrounding public communication. For example, even though individuals make up a group, a group is more than the sum of its individual members. Groups take on their own characteristics, their own standards of behavior, and adopt their own roles and patterns of communication. How else could we explain the differences we all see between the S.D.S. rally and the conclave hosted by the Housewives Against Obscenity?

In public communication, where the concern is with an individual attempting to influence the attitude or knowledge of a public, many principles associated with informal, private, and dyadic settings are relevant; but upon closer inspection we can see that public settings are also unique in some ways. In this section we will examine these distinctive aspects of public communication on the assumption that we can increase our chances of using public discourse effectively if we are intimately acquainted with its special characteristics.

General Characteristics of Public Communication

Public communication occurs, generally, in "public," not in "private" places. This is not as much double-talk as it may first appear. Sociologists such as Erving Goffman (1963) have defined "public places" as any region in a community that is fully accessible to members of that commu-

nity. Private places, on the other hand, are places where only members or invitees gather. Examples of public places might be streets, parks, restaurants, theaters, shops, meeting halls, and dance floors. Private gathering places include, for example, offices, factory floors, kitchens, and living rooms. Thus, one of the unique characteristics of public speech is that it normally occurs in public places, with all that this implies in an institutionalized, organized society.

Another distinction of public communication is that *the event, the communication encounter, is a pronounced "social" occasion.* This is not true, necessarily, in the small group and dyadic settings. The sociologist distinguishes between the more private meeting of two persons or of a small group and the meeting of several persons in a public place. The latter is called a "social occasion" by students of human behavior. Such meetings are bounded in regard to place and time and typically are facilitated by fixed equipment. Examples of social occasions are picnics, a night at the opera, a lecture in an assembly hall, and theater performances. Each such type of social occasion normally possesses its own distinctive *ethos*, spirit, and emotional structure which are carefully created and sustained. Such occasions (1) are usually planned in advance, (2) are guided by an agenda of activity, (3) have an allocation of management functions (some person or persons perform standard roles and do certain things), (4) have clear-cut and agreed-on specifications of what constitutes proper and improper conduct, and (5) conform to a preestablished unfolding of phases—certain things are done at certain times. Clearly, there are accepted roles, ways of behaving, and other constraints

unique to public speech settings, many of which have already been discussed. As we have seen, public speaking occurs in a public place and thus is affected by constraints and expectancies different from those found in the dyadic and small group setting. Thus, when we see the apparent "choreography" of a well-planned political rally, we are seeing the stylized traits characteristic of public, *social* occasions. To test this out for yourself, just make a short list of the "do's and don'ts" you adhere to in your lecture classes. In such a public speech setting, the order, rules, and communicative jobs are all well laid-out ahead of time, and woe to the student who dares violate them!

For another thing, *there are special norms that regulate behavior in the public speech setting*. That is, the public speech situation is part of an "institutionalized setting." It seems true that *social* occasions which must be held in *public* places must also subscribe to some kind of *public order*. Public order refers to the norms or rules that have been created to regulate interaction among those members of a community who may or may not be well acquainted. Public, face-to-face communicative encounters also fall victim to the establishment of norms, or rules of conduct. Goffman (1963) points out that "public communicative influences come under strict normative regulation which gives rise to a kind of communicative traffic order" (p. 24). The norms of behavior for speaker and listeners may vary from group to group somewhat (e.g., you are "permitted" to ask questions in some lecture classes), but many norms are basic enough so that they are shared across all types of groups in a given society or na-

tion. The "funny thing" that has happened to so many speakers "on the way to the speech" may, then, be a function of certain conventionalized rules for speech introductions. Unfortunately, all too often such values are adhered to ad nauseam.

In addition to these three traits which grow out of the "public-ness" of public communication, there are many other defining characteristics of such a communication setting. Rather than go into them at this time, let us consider a list of "distinctive features of public communication" that may serve as a practical summary of what we have said so far. As we move on in this book, we will be stopping back, from time to time, to consider each of the following traits more extensively. Contrasted with dyadic and small group encounters, in public communication we find that:

1. The message must be *relevant to the group as a whole* — not merely to one or a few individuals in that group. In public communications, the "common denominator" must be constantly searched for by the speaker.

2. *"Public" language is more restricted,* that is, it is less flexible, uses a more familiar code, is less personal in phrasing, and is filled with fewer connotations than is "private" talk.

3. *Feedback is more restricted* since it is limited to subtle nonverbal responses in many instances.

4. *There is greater audience diversity* to deal with. In public communication we face the difficulty of entering many "perceptual worlds" simultaneously.

5. As the size of the audience increases, there is a greater chance of *misinterpreting feedback,* since there's so much to look for.

6. The speaker must do a more *complete job of speech preparation* since there is so little direct moment-to-moment feedback by which he can guide his remarks.

7. The *problem of adaptation* becomes paramount since one message must suffice for many different people.

8. *Audience analysis is more difficult* and necessarily more inaccurate when many people are interacted with simultaneously.

9. It is sometimes *difficult to focus attention* on the message because of the great number of distractions a public situation can entail.

10. A *greater amount of change* is possible in public communicative settings since the message reaches more people in a given unit of time.

Intra-audience Effects in Public Communication

No discussion of public communication would be complete without some mention of one of the most distinctive features of public speech settings. Intra-audience effects, *a network of messages sent and received by audience members themselves,* constitute one of the most interesting facets of public communicative acts. As an example, picture yourself in front of the television set ready to watch the "Tonight" show. Johnny Carson makes his appearance and amidst the polite applause, we clearly hear the refrains of

NBC

Loud Clapper and Shrill Whistler. Quite simply, these characters serve to induce their fellow auditors in the studio to respond favorably and to join in the fun. But that's not all. The laughter and clapping of the studio audience serves, *in turn,* to encourage all the folks out there in TV Land to similarly enjoy the proceedings — a kind of rippling effect.

We saw another example of the intra-audience effect in *What Do You Say to a Naked Lady?* (the movie produced and directed by Allen Funt) when four "experimenters" and one "stooge" were brought into a room as five supposed participants in a job interview. On cue, the four experimenters wordlessly began to disrobe. In almost all instances shown, the naive subject also undressed even though he was given no verbal reason to do so.

Desmond Morris in *The Naked Ape* (1967) describes the same phenomenon more precisely when he discusses the responses of teenagers to their idols:

As an audience, they enjoy themselves, not by screaming with laughter, but screaming with screams.

THAT WAS THE LIEUTENANT'S FIRST SPEECH BEFORE AN AUDIENCE

AS FAR AS I'M CONCERNED, IT'S ALSO HIS LAST.

4-1

MORT WALKER

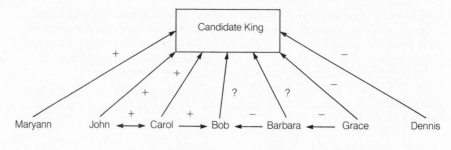

+ = Positive reaction to speaker
− = Negative reaction to speaker
? = Unpredictable reaction to speaker

Fig. 1. *Intra-audience effects in public communication*

They not only scream, they also grip their own and each other's bodies, they writhe, they moan, they cover their faces and they pull at their hair. These are all the classic signs of intense pain or fear, but they have become deliberately stylized. Their thresholds have been artificially lowered. They are no longer cries for help, but signals to one another in the audience that they are capable of feeling an emotional response to the sexual idols which is so powerful that, like all stimuli of unbearably high intensity, they pass into the realm of pure pain. *If a teenage girl found herself suddenly alone in the presence of one of her idols, it would never occur to her to scream at him. The screams were not meant for him, they were meant for the other girls in the audience.* (p. 98; italics added)

A Model of Intra-Audience Effects

As can be seen from these examples, the effects of auditors on one another can be powerful forces in public speech settings. Naturally, such listener-listener interaction does not always operate in a direction favorable to the speaker. The ways in which these intra-audience responses can complicate the speaker's job are represented in Figure 1. A politician, candidate King, is giving a campaign speech to an audience of seven people. The following model indicates some of the communicative reactions *and interactions* which may result from his speaking.

Although in reality intra-audience effects are much more complicated, our model depicts some of the *adaptive demands* forced upon our plucky politician by his very "busy" audience. The following short-hand comments are made available by our diagram:

1. From the speaker's point of view, Maryann is a "good listener." She is totally enthralled with the candidate's speech, hanging onto every word he says and is oblivious to her fellow auditors.

2. John and Carol, on the other hand, are "perfect listeners." Like Maryann, they are really "into" the speech but *in addition* are reinforcing the speaker's remarks (for one another and for Bob) by their approving chatter and applause.

3. From the candidate's viewpoint, Bob is inscrutable. Bob is quite interested in overhearing Carol's positive reactions to the speech and the negative reactions of Barbara, and

hence he may not be paying much attention to the political oratory itself.

4. Barbara's reactions are also difficult to assess. She is being greatly affected by Grace, who appears to be really turned off by the speech. Because she needs immediate social support (she and Grace being members of the same sorority), Barbara is probably tending in Grace's direction. Because her feedback to the speaker is minimal, it's difficult to tell how Barbara will eventually react.

5. Grace is obviously a lost cause, what with her scowls, sarcastic laughs, etc.

6. Dennis is equally disturbed by the speech but is just grimacing, not overtly expressing his displeasure.

How should our speaker adapt to such a set of conditions? He can probably afford to direct his attention away from Carol, John, and Maryann for a while (since they are "with him" for the moment) and concentrate instead on Bob, Barbara, and Dennis. By soliciting their opinions, for example, King might draw them into the conversation and hence discover and adapt to the sources of their disagreement (a technique that grade-school teachers often wisely use with unruly children). The remaining problem is, what is he to do with Grace?

Not all members of an audience have the same social power. There are, for instance, *opinion leaders* who have a great deal of influence on an audience. Thus, if Grace is a person of considerable clout, King might ask for her comments on an issue, hoping that this amount of personal attention will reduce her hostility. If Grace is *not* an opinion leader, the speaker is probably best advised to ignore her and to concentrate instead on more viable possibilities, hoping that the *group* of auditors he has "hooked" will then sway the one he has not yet been able to reach. The tireless, but tiresome, adage "ya' can't win 'em all" seems to be especially true of public communication, a situation in which the *complex, dynamic, social geometry of an audience* can do much to advance and retard the efforts of even the canniest of speakers. The issue of intra-audience effects, although interesting in and of itself, serves better to point up the complex *adaptations* forced upon a speaker by the "publicness" of public communication.

---

1. Allan M. Widen, "TV Ups Lecture Industry," Gannett News Service release, *Journal and Courier*, Lafayette, Ind., July 21, 1972, p. 4.

2. Heathcote Williams, *The Speakers* (New York: Grove, 1964), pp. 142–143.

A Good Talk: C.O.D.
(Content, Organization, Delivery)

Robert Haakenson

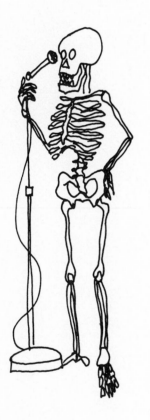

One afternoon a Roman Emperor was entertaining himself at the Colosseum by feeding Christians to the lions. Several Christians were sacrificed and the crowd screamed for more.

The next martyr said something to the lion, and the beast slunk away. Then a second lion; same result. And a third. The amazed throng began to shift its sympathies to the Christian. The Emperor announced that the Christian's life would be spared. He insisted, however, that the martyr appear before him.

"I am sparing your life," said the Emperor, "but before I release you, I demand to know what it was that you said to those beasts."

"I merely said to each lion: 'After dinner, of course, you'll be expected to say a few words.'"

As community-minded adults, each of us faces a pretty good likelihood he will be "asked to say a few words" at least once during the coming year. The audience may be eight or eight hundred—or more likely—forty, a typical community group audience. How do you feel about it? When someone says to you, "Of course, we'll expect you to say a few words after dinner," do you—like the lions—run in dismay? You shouldn't.

You should welcome the opportunity. Here are some helps.

FIMP—For Instances Meat and Potatoes: Content

Speech content, what the speaker says, really consists of two things: the topic and the supporting particulars. The most effective particulars are "for instances"; they become the meat and potatoes that put flesh on the speech outline skeleton.

Topics

The topic may be assigned or it may be left to the speaker's choice. It may be narrowly defined, even specifically phrased, or it may be suggested in the most general sort of way. The speaker may believe the more strictly he limits the topic the more he simplifies his assignment. This is not necessarily true. The decision must be made on the basis of analysis of the audience and commitment to meeting its believed needs.

If the speaker believes a general introduction to the subject is the most useful for the audience, then he will conceive of his topic as a broad survey. He may, on the other hand, determine he will be more helpful if he limits the topic to a narrow aspect and then will develop it in depth.

In the early stages of preparation he should approach the topic comprehensively, but keeping in mind the audience's believed interest. Later on, especially when phrasing his central idea (to be described later), he will sharpen his concept of the topic, covering only what he wishes to cover and taking into account the response he hopes to win from his hearers.

Supporting Particulars

Now, regarding supporting particulars amplifying details, specifics, or FIMP, let us ask: What forms do they take? How do we go about finding them? How do we select them for inclusion?

Types   Following is a list of types of particulars. It is not exhaustive, but illustrates the possibilities:

> Instances
> Case histories
> Events
> Examples, illustrations: real or
>   hypothetical
> Narratives: true or fictitious;
>   serious or humorous
> Definition
> Description
> Contrast/comparison
> Enumeration/listing
> Figures/statistics
> Humor: quip, pun, repartee
> Quotation: witness testimony,
>   authority opinion
> Figure of speech: allegory, per-
>   sonification
> Audio-visual aid

Sources   The speaker should be active in four ways in conducting his research: *reflection* (taking stock of what he already knows); *reading* (reviewing all types of printed material); *conversation*

(formal and informal talks with experts and lay people, informal polls or questionnaires); *observation* (some topics lend themselves to direct investigation, e.g., community improvements, institutions, organizations, landmarks, nature).

Some tips: begin with *reflection*. Almost always we will surprise ourselves on what we already know on any given topic. Jot down notes during this inventory-taking. Second, do at least some or all of the first three, and —if at all possible—the fourth. Varied research activities provide both perspective and riches of specifics. Third, gather materials voraciously. Our speaker should wind up with at least four times as much material as time will allow him to include in the talk.

Criteria   As our speaker sits down with his voluminous notes, he needs guidelines on what to include and what to reject. Here are four standards:

1. Relevance. No matter how dramatic and appealing the narrative may be, how compelling the instance, it is not worthy of inclusion if it does not amplify the point under consideration. This, therefore, must always be the first test: Is it pertinent? Does it apply?

2. Accuracy. When we are satisfied that the specific applies, then we must satisfy ourselves that it serves truth. Is it representative, typical? In argumentation (speaking to convince), we must concern ourselves with documentation, revelation of sources. Information has a way of being as good as its source. Conversely, highly respected sources have a way of giving credence to data, e.g., "If it came from *Encyclopedia*

Britannica it must be true." To that end, we will be careful to note details on printed and spoken sources: person, place, data, time, other circumstances; publication, date, page, etc.

3. Human interest. On a logical basis, relevance and accuracy certainly are the overriding criteria for good speech materials. On a psychological basis, human interest factors rise to the top. "No matter how good your data are," a pragmatist might say, "if they don't capture listeners' attention, they are wasted."

Here are some of the time-honored factors of attention and interest: narrative ("once upon a time . . . "), action, conflict, variety, novelty, the familiar in an unusual context (unexpectedly encountering a neighbor 1000 miles from home), humor, the bizarre or abnormal.

Dr. Russell Conwell, who founded Temple University, was famous for his "Acres of Diamonds" lecture. By giving this talk 7000 times, he earned seven million dollars, many of which were devoted to the education of deserving young men at Temple University. "Acres of Diamonds" is made up of *one story after another*, developing his theme that opportunity lies everywhere about us if we will scratch the surface. Like a skilled composer, Dr. Conwell lost no opportunity to develop his theme.

4. Adequacy. This is a tough criterion. When do we have enough specifics—enough for our listeners' understanding, conviction, motivation? This can only be answered in the crucible of actual speaking.

We can offer a suggestion on the length of a talk, however. A veteran pastor was asked by his new assistant, "How long should I preach when I give my first sermon next Sunday?" "That's up to you," came the reply, "but we feel we don't save any souls after twenty minutes."

Also, we can suggest a formula: "Balance the specific with the general." Use the case history or specific instance, thus providing narrative quality and something with which the listener can identify. Then, lest the listener charge that the specific is atypical or unrepresentative, the speaker advances the appropriate statistic or authority opinion to demonstrate that what is true in the instance cited is generally true. Balance the specific with the general.

Show and Tell: Audio-Visual Aids
A special type of FIMP is audio-visual aids: maps, graphs, charts, tape recordings, phonograph records, flannelboards etc. They are special because they simply present other types of specifics in audible or visual form, e.g., statistics on a graph, description on a photo, authority opinion on a tape recording, etc.

Use of a molecular model in a talk about prescription drugs illustrates many of the principles of effective visual aids. The speaker begins with the octagonal "benzine ring," representing the volatile, poisonous industrial solvent benzine. Then the speaker adds a cluster of red and yellow atoms at the top of the octagon and he has another compound: this time a food preservative for catsup and jellies—benzoic acid. Then the speaker adds another group of atoms and the compound is not volatile or poisonous,

not harmful in ordinary doses, but remarkable in pain-killing properties: *aspirin.*

The molecular model illustrates some "RSVP" principles of effective audio-visual aids usage:

Relevant: The aid visually depicts the exact point under discussion: the significance of tiny molecular changes in pharmaceutical research.

Subordinate: The aid is an aid. Too often audio-visual aids dominate, making the speech an audio-aid to a demonstration. A good test is: the point can be made successfully without the aid, but is better because of it.

Visible (audible): Too often, aids are too small, too faint or too complex to be fully clear to all members of the audience. Simplicity and boldness should prevail. Also, the aid should be in sight only while in use. The red, black and yellow balls of the molecular model made it adequately visible for an audience of 800. Further, it offered the great advantage of the speaker keeping it between the audience and himself, keeping unity in focus of attention.

Portable: Most talks are presented in public meeting places. The speaker must get his aids there and back. Huge billboards, bulky models, weighty devices become big problems. Imaginative use of paper, cloth and slide or filmstrip projections can provide size with minimal inconvenience.

The molecular model also illustrates some of the following desirable practices:

Action: Adding to, or taking away from the aid heightens interest; marking up a map or graph achieves the same.

Use a modest number: A good rule of thumb is one aid per main point. No talk should have more than five main points.

Use a variety of aids: A chart listing main points, a map, a model, a statistical graph, a tape recording.

"Roll your own": Personally-created aids can achieve the simplicity and boldness desired. What they lack in polished artistry may be more than made up for by relevance and impact.

Stow the visual out of sight when not in use. Otherwise it is a distraction, competing for attention. For the same reason, *only in exceptional cases* should aids be distributed to members of audiences. (Handouts may be distributed *after* the talk). (An exception on aids being stowed out of sight is the so-called "organizational visual." This is a card, blackboard, flannelboard or other device listing the main headings of the talk. This visual is introduced when the speaker previews his main headings, kept in sight and referred to as each main point is introduced, and used for the final summary, then put down out of sight before the "haymaker.")

"BUY A CIGAR AND A PAIR OF SPECTACLES."*

*Winston Churchill on how to become an effective speaker

Courtesy of Houghton Mifflin Company.

Tell, Tell and Tell: Organization

Some authorities regard *organization* as the basis of truly versatile eloquence. Let us consider *schema, central ideas, main headings*, and *transitions*.

Schema

We may properly think of almost any communication in this simple schematic:

_____

_____

_____

_____

The long first line represents the *central idea*. If the communication has unity, it should have a single major theme, thesis, controlling purpose or thrust. Then this central idea should be based systematically on appropriate *main headings*, here represented by the three shorter lines. There should be not fewer than two main headings nor more than five, and the most typical number is three.

Central Idea

How does the speaker come up with the central idea? It may be automatic. He is asked to speak on his opposition to a sales tax for his state. His thesis declares itself: "We must defeat the proposed state sales tax."

Equally often, however, his central idea will be elusive. He is asked to speak on state finances. What does he wish to say? Does he wish to praise or find fault? Does he wish to inform, convince, motivate, inspire, entertain? Does he wish to discuss the broad topic or some limited part? Does he wish his listeners to do something about his recommended program?

When the central idea is elusive, the speaker should give long and hard thought. He may ask himself, "After the sound and the fury, the tumult and the shouting have died, and the details have faded, what is the ultimate 'residue' I would like my listeners to retain?" When he can answer that in a simple declarative sentence, he probably will have his central idea.

Incidentally, when the central idea is simple exposition ("The Community College movement is expanding rapidly"), we call it a

theme. When it takes sides on a controversial issue ("U.S. should pull its military forces out of Southeast Asia"), we call it a *thesis.* Theses may be stated in different ways calling for different patterns of main headings (see below).

Even if the central idea pretty well decides itself, give it long thought, especially in terms of the response wanted from the audience.

Main Headings

When the central idea has been declared, it is usually relatively easy to come up with the main headings (main points). We wish to wind up with not fewer than two nor more than five: fewer than two, we are not subdividing; more than five, we are not grouping properly. A major purpose of grouping is to serve memory—the audience's *and the speaker's.* Also, almost any central idea will subdivide itself very nicely into two, three, four, or five main headings that cover the subject and are parallel. The most frequent number, as you will see, is three. Some persons trace this to the religious Trinity; others to the fact that any continuum has two extremes and a middle ground.

Items, events and phenomena in our universe tend to organize themselves into four major patterns. Following are those four with illustrative "stock designs" for each:

1. Chronological or time sequence: past, present, future

   Lincoln's Gettysburg Address, which had its 100th anniversary on November 19, 1964, is a classic example: "Fourscore and seven years ago . . . Now we are engaged in a great civil war . . . It is for us, the living, rather to be dedicated here . . . "

2. Spatial (topographical or geographic)

   federal, state, local
   metropolitan, suburban, rural
   inside, outside
   near, mid-distant, far
   left, center, right
   forward, midships, aft
   top, middle, bottom
   East Coast, Midwest, Rockies, Southwest, Far West
   Cook County, Downstate Illinois
   upper peninsula, lower peninsula
   land surfaces, water surfaces

3. Topical (distributive or classification)

   who, what, where, when, how, why (sometimes)
   theory, practice
   quality, price, service, beauty
   background, problem, methodology, findings, implications
   flora, fauna
   animal, vegetable, mineral

A very useful device both for preliminary analysis of a complex subject and later selection of main headings is the so-called decachotomy: political, social, economic, religious/moral/ethical, philosophical, educational, scientific, cultural/esthetic, military, psychological. If we were to investigate a subject such as electoral college reform, we might use this list to decide that the most important implications are political, social, and philosophical. Later, in making the talk, we might elect the same three as the best main headings.

4. Logical

   problem, damage (consequences), solution
   need, desirability, practicality
   cause, effect

There is good reason to believe that the most used stock design is the chronological (past, present, future). This is not surprising. When we consider almost any topic, it is natural to reflect: "What is the background; how did we get into this? Where do we find ourselves now? What is the next step?"

The most-used stock design probably should be problem, damage, solution. This is because we speak purposefully, to meet needs, to resolve problems, to achieve progress. Damage is included because it is the springboard of audience involvement. If, for example, we develop the problem of the electorate's persistent defeats of proposals to fluoridate the public water supply, and the recommended solution is to enlighten the electorate by a program of education, the listener might nod his head in agreement. "Yes; quite right; good sense"; but all at arm's length. If, on the other hand, the speaker drives home incontrovertibly that while this problem continues, *it is these very listeners* and *their children who pay the consequences* (dental decay, pain, cosmetic unattractiveness, inconvenience, financial cost), the listener not only agrees but is ready to act—no longer arm's length, now shoulder-to-shoulder.

The problem-solution design, of course, is a foreshortening of educational philosopher John Dewey's reflective process: define the problem—nature, extent, cause(s); list all plausible alternative solutions; weigh and evaluate each alternative solution; select the best alternative solution (or best compromise or combination); recommend action to implement the solution selected. Then, at that point, reflection ceases and action begins.

Occasionally we hear of a fifth pattern of analysis, called the "psychological." Here the intent is to match the listener's reaction, meeting his interest (or disinterest) as we predictably will find it, and moving ahead as it (human nature) would. Richard Borden's "Ho Hum" formula is a good example:

Ho hum
Why bring that up?
For instance
So what?

The "AIDA" formula for successful advertising is another: attention, interest, desire, and action. Purdue University's Alan Monroe advanced a "motivated sequence," blending the logical problem-solution with psychological factors: attention step, need step, satisfaction step, visualization step, and action step.

Earlier we referred to central ideas that develop partisan stands on controversial issues being called theses. And we said that when these are stated in certain ways, they call for the development of main headings (contentions or arguments) in corresponding patterns. A thesis may be stated as a question of fact, quality, degree or policy. When we argue whether a thing exists or is real, we declare our thesis as a question of fact. We will find that developing our main headings to establish theory and practice will be wise. ("Cigaret smoking causes lung cancer"; "Extrasensory perception is a fact.")

When we argue whether a thing is good, beautiful, dependable, we state the thesis as a question of quality, e.g., "Television is good entertainment"; "Modern art is ugly"; "The sales tax is unfairly discriminatory." We will find that using criteria as main headings will serve well, e.g., "U.S. compact autos provide fine transportation" (thesis) and quality, price, service, safety, beauty (main headings).

When we argue whether a thing is better or worse than, larger or smaller than, prettier or uglier than something else, we are stating the thesis as a question of degree, e.g., "U.S. compact autos are superior to foreign-made." Again we will be well-advised to develop main headings as criteria, e.g., "Radio news coverage is superior to television's" (thesis) and speed, accuracy, comprehensiveness, clarity (main headings).

When we argue whether something ought or ought not to be done, we state the thesis as a question of policy, e.g. "We should fluoridate the public water supply"; "We must stop the military conflict in Southeast Asia"; "The United Nations should not admit Red China to membership." Main headings here should establish problem, damage, and solution, e.g., thesis: "We should support programs of planned parenthood in all developing nations"; main headings: "1. The problem of world overpopulation is acute. 2. Dire consequences are starvation, grinding poverty and political exploitation. 3. Expansion of birth control programs is a practical and desirable solution."

Transitions

Structure of the speech should emerge boldly. If the listener can visualize the framework he can help the speaker fit the component parts together in their intended relationships. Nonetheless there should be smooth transitions that tie part-to-part and part-to-whole. The best transition is a partial summary, e.g., "Thus we see there is a critical problem of overcrowded classrooms. Secondly, let us consider the consequences while this problem continues . . . " Other transitional

A STUDENT CAN BE CONFIDENT

ABOUT ASSIGNMENTS IN

SPEAKING!

if he knows about

O
RGAN
IZA
TI
ON

Courtesy of Prentice-Hall, Inc., Englewood Cliffs, New Jersey.

devices include enumeration (e.g., "Secondly, consequences"), questions (e.g., "Next we may ask: who is affected by this situation?"), directional phrases (e.g., "Let us move then"), audio-visual aids (e.g., "Consider now, please, this portion of the display").

Model Outline

The following is a model outline, employing the recommendations above, but not including the actual supporting particulars (specifics) that flesh out the skeleton.

 I. Introduction
  A. Icebreaker
   1. Reference to audience's (Olympia Civic Association's) contributions to mental health programs
   2. Reference to the speaker's own service with the Mayor's Committee
   3. Reference to the day's news item on the Committee's proposal
   4. Case history of John D., whose rehabilitation was botched by archaic mental health services
  B. Preview
   1. We must all help in establishing the Olympia Community Mental Health Center
    a. Problem of out-dated mode of treatment
    b. Damages to patients, families and community
    c. Workability, desirability and bonuses of Committee's Plan
 II. Body
  A. We all must help in establishing the Olympia Com-

munity Mental Health
Center
1. Problem of antiquated
    approach to treating
    mental and emotional
    illness
    a. Olympia facilities
        are antiquated
        ("specifics")
    b. Olympia modes
        of treatment are
        consequently archaic
        ("specifics")
2. Damage
    a. Patients suffer long-
        er and more in-
        tensely than neces-
        sary
        ("specifics")
    b. Family is distraught
        and inconvenienced
        unnecessarily
        ("specifics")
    c. Olympia taxpayers
        and citizens gener-
        ally bear the brunt
        ("specifics")
3. Solution
    a. Mayor's Committee's
        proposed plan to im-
        plement Community
        Mental Health Cen-
        ter is practical, deal-
        ing with problem at
        its roots
        ("specifics")
    b. Plan is desirable,
        consistent with
        highest precepts of
        community action
        for local problems
        ("specifics")
    c. Plan offers several
        "extras," bonus
        advantages
        ("specifics")

III. Conclusion
    A. Summary
        1. We must all move di-
            rectly and speedily to
            establish the Olympia
            Community Mental
            Health Center

and understands the purpose

and application of

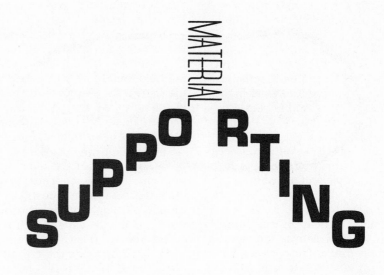

as well as the elements of effective

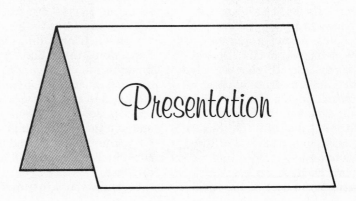

a. The problem of out-moded treatment is a civic disgrace
b. The consequences touch every Olympian, certainly the community leaders here assembled
c. Support of Olympia Civic Association members will help implement Committee's eminently practical and highly desirable plan.
B. Haymaker
1. Recall case of "John D."? Never again need this tragedy occur if we will act now.

From the foregoing it can be seen that the heart of this outline is the schema: central idea and main headings. The speaker will "tell 'em what he's gonna tell 'em, tell 'em, and tell 'em what he told 'em"—preview, body and summary. Then to this basic pattern he adds an icebreaker to begin, and a haymaker to conclude. The purposes of the icebreaker are two: (1) to call attention to, and arouse interest in the speaker and his topic; and (2) to create common bonds and warm rapport between speaker and audience.

Chief icebreaker items are narratives (preferably of the case history type); references to the audience, topic and/or occasion (latter includes "outside world," e.g., news of the day); humorous anecdotes; participation, such as show of hands, rhetorical questions; sensational "shocker" statements; definitions; quotations of Scripture, maxims, poetry; audio-visual aids, and the like.

If time is plentiful the speaker may wish to use several of these items to arouse interest and build rapport. Perhaps the best icebreaker is the case history type of narrative. It attracts attention (we never outgrow the magic of "let me tell you a story") and arouses interest. Properly selected it creates mutual ties among speaker, topic, audience and occasion—definitely identifying the speaker with topic—and clarifies the talk's theme.

The purposes of the haymaker are to bring the talk to a climactic finale, and for the speaker to land his final blow for his central idea. (Ancient orators made much of the *peroration* in which the speaker made his final eloquent plea for his central idea.)

The speaker may use for his haymaker many of the selfsame items he uses for the icebreaker: quotation, rhetorical question, humor, participation. It is particularly esthetically satisfying if the haymaker can revert back to the icebreaker, bringing the talk full-circle. Possibly the best combination, therefore, is, for an icebreaker, a case history type narrative that illustrates the talk's central idea, and, for a haymaker, another reference to that narrative, possibly completing the story or bringing it up to date.

Animated Conversationality

Can you recall a recent experience when you went all out in friendly persuasion? You wished to persuade some friend of yours to a point of view or action not for your good, but for his good as you saw it. These things were happening—all intuitively: You brought into play every reason, contention, emotional appeal, instance, description, story, comparison, quotation, figure and statistic that would build your case. You thus employed all the substance or *content* at your disposal.

Secondly you structured your persuasion. You may have said, for example, "All right, we are agreed up to here, are we not?" Then you would venture off into no-man's land, penetrating as deeply as you thought you could before experiencing rebuff. Then you would fall back and regroup, consolidating your gains, then venture off on another tack into no-man's land. Thus you were structuring, adding *organization* to your persuasive armamentarium. Thirdly, your personality ran its gamut and all the techniques of effective presentation came into play as you pled your case.

You were alternately friendly and stern, forceful and humble. Your voice ranged from shouting to whispering and the inflections varied persuasively. Your enunciation was crisp, biting out the syllables of key words with telling precision. You moved about freely, sometimes towering above your friend, sometimes almost on bended knee before him. You gestured freely. Your face was expressive, characterized chiefly by alertness and a friendly smile. Your eyes rarely left those of your friend as you studied and adapted to his responses. Your language was eloquent; you expressed yourself dynamically in compelling words, phrases and sentences.

If you deliver a speech with animation and enthusiasm, your audience will receive it better.

In short, you were intuitively bringing into play every facet of personality and every aspect of *delivery* (psychological set, voice, articulation, bodily expression

"Well, I see my time is up . . ."

and language) that would enhance your persuasiveness. And equally important, you were totally unselfconscious as you immersed yourself in the project of *eliciting the desired response*, winning your friend over to believe and act as you know best for him. These are the selfsame things that should characterize our platform presentations: a lively, communicative personality; a rich, varied vocal expressiveness, with accurate pronunciation and distinct enunciation; bodily expression that is plentiful, meaningful and spontaneous: movement about the platform, stance, gesture, facial expression and eye contact; and language that is accurate, vivid, appropriate for the conceptual and vocabulary level of the listeners, action-oriented and rich in imagery.

When our speaker takes the platform we wish him to achieve the following:

1. A lengthy focal or initial pause, with a friendly facial expression (preferably a smile) as he looks out over the audience. This pause enables listeners and speaker to settle down in preparation for their respective "duties," and also builds suspense.

2. A rather full, and certainly genial and spontaneous salutation: "Thank you, Program Chairman Ellery Webb, for a sparkling sendoff; Mr. President Montgomery, Reverend Young, Judge Cloud, officers, guests, and members of the Olympia Civic Association." The most important parts of the salutation are the ac-

knowledgment of the introduction and addressing the members by their organization's name. The speaker's salutation can virtually simulate his response if he were being introduced to these folks around a living room in a social setting.

3. "Parry and thrust" ad lib remarks to achieve a smooth transition into the text of the talk itself. At best these remarks will call attention to the speaker and his topic, arouse interest in them, and create common ground and rapport among speaker, audience, and topic. References to the audience, the occasion (including news of the day), the speaker himself, and the topic all can be effective.

4. Impressive presentation of the talk itself: "situation well in hand" authority; "think the thought" involvement; "elicit desired response" communicativeness; "persuasive vitality" in vocal expressiveness (with crisp enunciation); "plentiful, meaningful, spontaneous" physical expressiveness; and felicitous language, alive with action and rich in imagery.

5. Triumphant finale: knowing his closing sentences "cold," our speaker brings the talk to a resounding climax. He concludes with a terminal pause, holding eye contact, and avoids (as he would the plague) limping off on the weak crutch of "Thank you."

Tom Tracy

PROBE 33. The Motivating Process is a way of organizing an effective persuasive speech.

The Motivating Process

John A. McGee

The history of the Motivating Process deserves brief comment. Books on the psychology of business had long used the functional terms, attention, interest, desire, and action, to describe the process of selling merchandise. Professor G. R. Collins applied this sequence to the public sales talk. In 1926, Dr. P. H. Scott and the author conceived the idea of applying this method to all speeches which sought to influence belief or action. In 1929, Mr. J. A. McGee, then at Purdue, published a book containing a statement of this approach.

A. H. Monroe
January 15, 1935

Organizing a Persuasive Speech

The greatest homage we can pay to truth is to use it. Emerson

An architect might design a house with the kitchen in the basement, the dining-room in the attic, the bedroom on the front porch, and the laundry where the living-room usually is. But, quite obviously, he does not do so. Customers would be rather scarce if this were his practice. Experience proves that it is more convenient to place the kitchen and the dining-room close together than it is to locate them on different floors of the house. Likewise, experience has shown us that to make a man act in a certain way, you must lead his mind through certain natural steps. *To be most effective, a persuasive speech should be organized in a particular manner.*

The Motivating Process

Imagine yourself with twenty other people in a room on the third floor of a building. Some one smells smoke, and it is discovered that the building is on fire. Immediately, every one in the room is confronted with the very practical problem of finding a way to escape. A glance proves that the stairs are enveloped in flames. The way to the fire escape, also, is cut off. Three stories is quite a distance to jump. Somebody suggests that the only logical way to get out is by tying together a number of coats and using them for a rope. The solution appears to be the logical one, and the group, visualizing what will happen unless they take immediate action, proceed to carry out the plan.

This illustration discloses the essential steps through which the human mind goes in arriving at any conclusion and acting upon it. Since the object of persuasive

---

speaking is to secure this sort of definite response from an audience, we may conclude that there are five steps which a speaker should use, under most circumstances, to gain his end. *First,* he must compel an audience to listen to him; *second,* he must make them feel a strong need for solving some problem; *third,* he must point out the logical solution; *fourth,* he must make the solution appear so attractive that a strong desire for it is aroused; *fifth,* he must invite definite action by pointing out practical ways of arriving at the solution. These are the five steps in organizing a speech. The entire series of steps is called the *motivating process.*

The good speaker gains his end by:

(1) Securing attention;
(2) Stating a problem [*need*];
(3) Offering a solution [*satis faction*];
(4) Visualizing its desirability;
(5) Inviting definite action.

Each of these steps is as indispensable to purposeful speaking as each ingredient is to the making of a good cake. Conditions may modify the various steps somewhat, or even dictate the omission of one or more of them, but most effective speakers under most circumstances secure their total effects by leading the audience through these fundamental steps.

A brief statement of the purpose of each step in the organization of a persuasive speech, and certain practical suggestions as to procedure in building each phase are in order at this point.

Attention Step

It is scarcely necessary to point out the fact that gaining and holding attention is the speaker's first and most vital problem. Attention may be defined as a state of readiness to respond, and the attention phase of a speech is that introductory part of your address that is calculated to focus all the faculties of your listeners upon the problem that you would discuss with them.

It must not be assumed that because we designate the first portion of a speech as the attention phase that the speaker is relieved of the responsibility of gripping his auditors' attention after he has disposed of his introductory remarks. *To dominate the attention of your listeners is your primary job during the entire course of time that you spend on the platform.* But, as the old saying goes, "First impressions are lasting ones"; and so we emphasize the gaining of attention at the outset of a speech by designating the opening as the attention step.

It is enough to notice that the attention step of a speech should lead the audience naturally into a consideration of the problem that the speaker wishes to present. This may be done in various ways. The speaker may tell a story or recite an incident or make a striking statement that leads up to or suggests the situation which he wishes to visualize for the group.

Below is printed an example of one method successfully employed to catch the attention of an audience and focus that attention upon a situation that demands a remedy:

"A pale, thin moon looked down and grinned. The pert, young coupé stood lifeless, its hood stuck up like the broken wing of a bird. The girl bit her lips to keep from crying. The boy was stern, his shirt ruined — likewise his temper. And November didn't explain all of the frost in the atmosphere.

"The boy said, 'Never again!'
The coupé said, 'Never again!'
The girl said, 'Never again!'

"The girl meant, 'Never again will I go out with this man!' The girl was right. She never did. The coupé meant, 'Never again will I be able to run!' The coupé was wrong. $80.00 worth of repairs and it did run again. The boy meant, 'Never again will I be such a fool about my motor!' The boy was right, but a trifle late."

Use your own ingenuity and strive to secure unusual and vivid openings that will grip the attention of your listeners and compel them to listen to you. The first duty of the public speaker is to secure and hold the undivided attention of his audience.

Problem Step [*Need*]

You will recall that in our illustration of the steps which the human mind takes in arriving at a conclusion, that occurrence which followed immediately upon the smelling of smoke was the realization that the group was confronted with the very practical problem of escaping from the burning building. In other words, a situation was revealed to them that alarmed them and impelled the conclusion that something must be done. Now it is precisely this thing that a speaker who wants to get a definite response from an audience must do after gaining attention. *A persuasive speech should give an audience some definite problem to solve.* Or, to put the matter in a different way, an address calculated to gain a definite response must make the audience visualize a condition of affairs that is completely unsatisfactory and about which something must be done. Abraham Lincoln, throughout the course of his famous debates with Judge Douglas, spent a large portion of his time arousing his listeners to a sense of dissatisfaction with prevailing conditions. He made them see the dangers that confronted the Union, half slave and half free. "A house divided against itself must fall." This was the burden of Lincoln's anti-slavery campaign.

In a general way, all human actions may be traced to one of two attitudes of mind: desire for a change; fear of a change. Either a man is dissatisfied with his business methods, with his social life, with political affairs in his community, and wishes to do something to change these conditions, or he is eminently contented with these affairs and is afraid that some one will "throw a monkey wrench" into the wheels. His course of action with regard to his business life, or his social life, or his community life will be dictated by his satisfaction or dissatisfaction with affairs as he finds them.

For example, Mr. Jones, the hardware man, has been handling a certain line of radios for the past two years. He does not feel that they are selling as well as they ought to. He observes that his nearest competitors are outstripping him in the sale of radios, and he is completely dissatisfied with the profits that he is making in this branch of sales. One day the agent for a new line of radios comes into Mr. Jones's store. Because of the attitude of mind in which he finds Mr. Jones, this agent is very likely to be able to convince this hardware dealer that he should change from the old line of radio equipment to the new line which this particular salesman offers. Thus, a feeling of dissatisfaction with prevailing conditions is behind this action upon the part of the hardware dealer.

On the other hand, Mr. Smith across the street has had remarkable success in selling a certain line of radios. He is well satisfied with the profits he is making in this branch of sales. The salesman for the new line of radio equipment enters Mr. Smith's place of business and is unable to make a sale, because Mr. Smith is perfectly contented with the results he is getting from the line of radios he is already handling. When it is time for him to restock, he will buy the same product that he has bought in the past, because he fears that a change might result in a loss of profits. Thus, his action is the result of the opposite state of mind from that which produced Mr. Jones's action.

It is the duty of a speaker either to arouse a longing to change existing conditions or a desire to maintain those conditions in the face of impending change.

In the problem phase a situation is visualized—one that is quite alarming in its possible consequences to the audience. This problem is personalized. *It is this personalization of the problem phase that should be emphasized particularly.* We have endeavored to keep constantly in mind the necessity of the public speaker being objective—he must think in terms of the audience. And no place is this quite so necessary as in the problem phase. It is not enough for you to demonstrate that some alarming misfortune is about to overtake the human race in general, but it is imperative, if you want to get a response from a particular group, to show that group that they, themselves, are likely to suffer as a result of failure to act. In developing the problem phase, do not neglect to avail yourself of the methods discussed in a previous lesson, by which the thought is made concrete and striking.

When the speaker wishes to protest against an impending action, rather than urging a change, his procedure in the problem phase will differ somewhat from that described above. Suppose that you want your schoolmates to take action to prevent the resignation of an athletic coach. In such a situation, your job is to arouse contentment with conditions under the present coaching régime, and to alarm the group with the probable consequences of the impending action, at the same time making it apparent that the thing will happen unless they take steps to prevent it.

Two simple formulae will assist you in learning to develop the problem phase:

(1) When you seek action to change conditions:
   A. Illustrate the situation; the more detailed the picture the better;
   B. Make that situation seem extremely undesirable to the particular audience before you.

(2) When you seek action to prevent a change:
   A. Illustrate the present situation briefly;
   B. Make it appear desirable to the audience before you;
   C. Alarm them with the probable consequences of altering the situation;
   D. Demonstrate the imminent danger of such change occurring.

This problem phase, like the preceding one of attention, will be modified by the situation under which you speak. An audience of striking miners requires little persuasion on the part of a speaker to be aware of a deep feeling of dissatisfaction with existing conditions. A speaker may very easily develop this essential basis for action with such a group; yet, even here the step may not wisely be omitted. Sometimes a mere recital of grievances already felt

The Motivating Process Applied to Various Types of Audience

	(1) Favorable to Proposition	(2) Interested but Undecided	(3) Apathetic to Situation	(4) Opposed to Proposition
Attention	Intensify interest: 1. Vivid illustrations. 2. New aspects of the situation. 3. Challenge.	Direct attention toward basic elements of the problem: 1. Definition. 2. Narrowing question. 3. Historical data. (Seek clarity; avoid dullness.)	Overcome inertia: 1. Startling statements. 2. Hit vital spots. 3. Vivid illustrations.	Secure common ground: 1. Emphasizing points of agreement: a. Attitude. b. Beliefs. c. Experiences.
Problem *(need)*	Make problem more impressive: 1. Vivid illustrations. 2. Startling disclosures. 3. Personalize; arousal of personal responsibility.	Demonstrate basic causes of problem: 1. Make certain that audience is aware problem exists. 2. Why does the situation exist?	Demonstrate existence of problem: 1. Powerful evidence. a. Facts. b. Figures. c. Testimony. 2. Hook up with common experiences.	Overcome opposition to change: 1. Seek agreement on general principle; then apply principle to specific problem. 2. Overpower objections: a. Facts. b. Testimony.
Solution *(satisfaction)*	State solution definitely: 1. Don't argue. 2. Be brief. 3. Command, if conditions warrant.	Demonstrate that your plan is best solution: 1. Explain the plan. 2. Offer proof that it removes causes of problem. 3. Expert testimony. 4. Examples of successful operation.	(Audience should now be interested but undecided. Follow technique in first column to the left.)	Demonstrate that your plan is the best solution: (Follow technique for solution step in column No. (2). In addition, relate the solution to the general principle agreed upon above.)
Visualization	Make results of solution more vivid: 1. Imagery. 2. Impelling motives. 3. Projection of the audience into the future. 4. Mild exaggeration.	Same as column No. (1). Beware of exaggeration.	Same as column No. (1). Beware of exaggeration.	Same as column No. (1). Beware of exaggeration.
Action	Request definite action: 1. Specific means by which individuals may help.	Request definite action: 1. Specific means by which individuals may help.	Request definite action: 1. Specific means by which individuals may help.	Request definite action: 1. Specific means by which individuals may help. 2. Appeal to habit.

is the quickest way to gain the response desired. For the present, develop the problem phase fully; later lessions will demonstrate modifications of it for varying conditions.

Solution Step [*Satisfaction*]

No very deep process of reasoning is required to conclude that the logical next step in the building of a persuasive speech is to offer some answer to the question which the problem phase brings before the audience. What shall be done? What is the best method of getting out of the unfortunate situation in which we find ourselves? *Very frequently, this is the most important part of a persuasive speech, because while many persons may agree with a speaker that something should be done, there is frequently quite general disagreement as to what remedy should be tried out.* After the group realizes that the building is on fire, they are keenly anxious to find the best and quickest means of escape. But not infrequently there is disagreement as to what constitutes the most desirable method. It is your job in the solution phase to prove to the group that the particular solution which you have to offer is the one for them to adopt. In other words, at this point, invite the particular response that you have had in mind from the first for the audience to perform. Having shown that political corruption is bankrupting the government and bringing untold hardship upon every man in the audience, propose the election of your candidate as the logical means of relief.

The necessity of this solution stage in a speech is so apparent that little space need be devoted to showing why it is used. The step is not, however, a simple or inconsequential one. Many good speakers have called it the most critical point in a speech: that time when you bring forward the new idol to replace the one torn down.

Without entering into a detailed discussion of the methods of developing this part of a speech under varying circumstances, it may be suggested that there are certain general questions about your proposition that it is well to answer for the audience. *Does your scheme supply a remedy for the major defects that you have alleged are prevalent in the present system?*

In addition to the question of the power of the proposed solution to remedy the defects of the existing system, *it is necessary to show that there are no vital objections to it.* Will it introduce new evils into the situation?

It will be apparent from the above discussion of the solution step that it is concerned in no small measure with logical demonstration. It seems to produce conviction in the minds of your auditors: to have them admit "this is what ought to be done."

To produce in a man's mind the conviction that your ideas are sound, it is almost always necessary to offer real evidence: facts, figures, and authentic testimony of men who are in a position to know the facts about the question you are discussing.

An example of one sort of solution step is printed below. The difficulty of presenting a really adequate sample of this lesson is almost insurmountable, but the selection from an address by William Jennings Bryan, delivered in Chicago on September 13, 1899, will serve to illustrate the general method of building the solution step. Mr. Bryan had already portrayed in his majestic fashion the grip which corporations and trusts had on the American people. This portion of the speech in which the problem is developed is, obviously, omitted, as is also a part of the solution step, because space does not permit their inclusion.

> "Let me suggest one thing that I believe will be a step in the right direction. The great trouble has been that, while our platforms denounce corporations, corporations control the elections and place the men who are elected to enforce the law under obligations to them.
>
> "Let me propose a remedy—not a complete remedy, but a step in the right direction. Let the laws, state and national, make it a penal offense for any corporation to contribute to the campaign funds of any political party. Nebraska has such a law, passed two years ago. Such a measure was introduced in the state of New York, but so far it has not become a law.
>
> "You remember the testimony taken before a Senate committee a few years ago, when the head of the sugar trust testified that the sugar trust made it its business to contribute to campaign funds, and when asked to which one it contributed replied that it depended upon the circumstances.

> " 'To which fund do you contribute in Massachusetts?' was asked. 'To the Republican fund.' 'To which fund in New York?' 'To the Democratic fund.' 'To which fund in New Jersey?' and the man replied, 'Well, I will have to look at the books; that is a doubtful state.'
>
> "If the people are in earnest, they can destroy monopoly, and you never can do anything in this country until the people are in earnest. When the American people understand what the monopoly question means, I believe there will be no power, political, financial, or otherwise, to prevent the people from taking possession of every branch of the government, from President to Supreme Court, and making the government responsive to the people's will."

Visualization Step

The fourth step in a persuasive speech—that of arousing intense desire for the particular solution you offer to a problem—might be thought of as a part of the solution step. *But this process that we term visualization is essentially one of emotional arousal.* It is a projecting of the audience into the future and portraying for them the successful realization of their desires as a result of adopting your proposal. The solution step, just discussed, is more concerned with logical demonstration. It seeks to produce intellectual conviction in the minds of your hearers. *But mere demonstration of a new and better plan of action than the one now used may not arouse an active desire to take the step.* Emotional arousal is an essential part of the process used to gain action. Picture for your audience how much more satisfactory conditions are likely to be if they will adopt your scheme; make them fear what may happen if they fail to act as you want them to.

As we shall see later, imagery of all kinds enters into this projection of the group into the future. We speak of it as visualization, but the process is not limited to the arousal of a visual image. It may be expedient to appeal to the sense of hearing, smell, and the like. But for the present, strive merely to paint a word picture of some sort showing your remedy in operation, meeting the demands of the audience.

Congressman William C. Dawson, speaking in the House of Representatives on March 3, 1852, furnished an excellent example of the visualization step. He had discussed at some length the proposed Homestead Law, the object of which was to permit easy acquisition of land by settlers. After discussing the various features of the bill, Mr. Dawson said:

> "Pass this bill and it will provide homes, and happy ones, for a vast number of meritorious persons, and teach them the full value of a government which desires to fulfil the first of its duties—that of promoting the happiness and prosperity of its citizens.

> "What a useful lesson would such a plan prove to the governments of Europe, and what an example would it furnish of republican care for the good of all, thus promoted by our happy institutions. It would present a spectacle at which the patriot, in the full exaltation of his heart, might rejoice; at which the honorable gentleman from Tennessee (Mr. Johnson) might rejoice, as Lycurgus did when returning through the fields just reaped, after the generous provisions that he had made for the citizens of Sparta and Laconia; and seeing the shocks standing parallel and equal, he smiled, and said to some that were by: 'How like is Laconia to an estate newly divided among many brothers.'"

Action Step

The final step in the securing of any action is that of summation and conclusion. *The importance of one final turn of the wheel cannot be overemphasized.* Notice the particularly effective conversationalist, when you have passed a pleasant evening with him. He does not say merely "good night," and then retire. That would be distinctly a "let down" from the congenial plane upon which the evening has been spent. Instead, he tells one final anecdote more interesting, perhaps, than any he has yet related, thus leaving you with the impression that there are many more pleasant evenings in store for you in his company. The successful salesman, too, not infrequently saves his choicest bit until the decisive moment—that moment when his prospect is about to sign on the dotted line. Public speakers from Demosthenes to Beveridge have devoted no little attention to what we term the action phase of the speech. In the final moment of a talk, it is imperative that you make a good impression to leave in the minds of your audience.

Precisely how does one go about building this step of a speech? What should it contain? What methods are used to develop it? Only general directions will be indulged in at this point; more specific directions will follow in a later lesson.

In general, let your action phase sum up what has preceded, and invite definite action from the group. Notice the method employed by Senator James A. Reed in concluding a political speech at Sedalia, Missouri:

> "Let us demand the honest administration of government; the swift and sure punishment of all public plunderers, bribemongers,

"That's not fair! I listened to the others."

Reprinted from *The Saturday Evening Post.* Used by permission of Chon Day.

and other malefactors; the equalization of the burden of taxation; the repeal of all laws creating special privileges; the dismissal of an army of spies, snoopers, sneaks, and informers, the liberation of honest business from oppressive interference by governmental agents; the prosecution and punishment of those who, by trusts, combinations, and restraints of trade, make war on honest business and despoil the people."

Gaining attention, stating a problem [*need*], offering a solution [*satisfaction*], making that solution appear highly desirable, and inviting specific action, then, are the five essential steps in the development of a persuasive speech. It is usually unwise to omit any of these steps.

Read carefully the complete speech that is printed below, noticing particularly each of the five steps as shown by the boxes surrounding each one.

Ship-Shape Condition

Attention

> "The last cable is off—the whistle blows—and the great liner starts on another long voyage. As the shore line fades away, veterans and inexperienced travellers, alike, can only guess what the future holds in store. But they know that before the ship sailed, every vital part was given painstaking inspection. Hour after hour throughout the voyage, the same watchfulness will be continued. The captain is ready to meet heavy seas, for in fair weather he has prepared for storms.

Problem [*Need*]

> "Each of us, during the autumn, bears a strange resemblance to a ship leaving port. Some, sturdy and sound, ready for what may come; others, weak and unfit for a crisis; still others needing only a slight overhauling to qualify them to meet the added hazards which the winter months bring.
>
> "January claims more deaths than December, and February more than January. Year after year, the same thing occurs—because men and women and children have not fortified their bodies to meet the rigors of winter. Then follows March—March called the 'danger month,' because it is then that neglected colds suddenly change from seemingly unimportant affairs to deadly menaces. Tired hearts and racked lungs make only a feeble fight for life. The plain truth is that all too many people live an abnormal life in the winter time. They eat too much. They do not get enough exercise or enough fresh air. Too heavy a diet and too little sleep make a bad foundation on which to build health and strength.

Solution [*Satisfaction*]

> "So now, during the crisp, autumn weather, exercise in the open whenever possible. And during the winter, if you have no time or opportunity for outdoor exercise, you will find that intelligent daily indoor exercise in a properly ventilated room is a fine substitute—a daily tonic.
>
> "But, first of all, have a thorough physical examination. If there are any defects which can be corrected, see that they are given immediate attention.

Visualization

> "It is a real cause for thanksgiving that this is only November, and there is still plenty of time to make preparations for sailing safely through the 'danger month.'

Action

> "You who are wise will fit yourselves to meet the approaching winter months in ship-shape condition."

New from <u>Time-Life Video</u>: a communications course no profit-conscious company can afford to pass up.

Executive talk: the better it is, the better your business.

Course Lesson #1: How to Make a More Effective Speech. Including the confidence to stand on your own two feet and get an audience off their hands.

Course Lesson #2: How to Give a More Persuasive Presentation. And give it the personal wallop it needs to become a vivid, forceful sales tool.

Course Lesson #3: How to Conduct a More Productive Meeting. One that results in decisions leading to action, not just more meetings.

Many an executive who thinks clearly and imaginatively on paper tends to be less successful when communicating these ideas to an audience.

The price your company pays? Dead-end meetings. Ambiguous presentations. Perhaps a critical corporate speech that wanders off the mark.

It all adds up to bad talk. And bad business. Because bad talk wastes time. Costs money. And reflects no credit on anybody.

Happily, help is here from TIME-LIFE VIDEO. We've just created and completed a delightful-to-take executive course designed to change bad talk into friendly persuasion.

The complete course is entitled "Communicating Successfully"—and consists of three multimedia lessons that combine your choice of video tapes or films, coordinated exercise books, and both prerecorded and blank audio cassettes.

All three video tapes (16mm film if you

prefer) feature Robert Morse, the noted stage and screen star, and they are among the brightest, most entertaining, and most helpful "how to" training aids ever conceived. The course was designed by a select group of behavioral scientists and allied experts…and offers any executive clear and attainable guidelines for making a better speech, giving a stronger presentation, and leading a meeting that *gets* somewhere.

Here, at last, is the definitive communications course from the definitive communicators: TIME-LIFE. For more detailed information about it, write to us on your company letterhead. Better yet, talk to us via a collect call.

A MULTI-MEDIA SERVICE

Time & Life Building, Rockefeller Center, N.Y. 10020 (212) 556-4554

TLV

OF TIME-LIFE FILMS, INC.

PROBE 34. A public speaker is someone who seeks to inform or influence an audience.

Characteristics and Organization of the Oral Technical Report

Roger P. Wilcox

Main Purpose of Oral Technical Report: to Inform

A speaker may attempt to secure any one of three basic responses from his audience. He may want them to be entertained or interested (as in the case of the after-dinner speaker); to believe or act differently (as in the case of a safety talk); or to understand (as in the case of directions on how to operate a machine). Basically, the oral technical report is expository or informational. The speaker should strive for all three basic responses, but his main purpose is to advance the audience's understanding of the topic under discussion.

If the main purpose of the oral technical report is to inform, the speaker must be objective and impartial towards his material. Even though he may present strong advantages in favor of some recommendation, he scrupulously presents its disadvantages as well. The speaker stops short of playing the role of the advocate arguing for the adoption of a special point of view. He is more like a scientist reporting his latest findings to a group of fellow scientists.

In keeping with the objective point of view, the development of the oral technical report is primarily factual. Although an occasional anecdote may be valuable for illustration or enlivenment, the body of the report should consist of such objective data as explanations, descriptions, definitions, statistics, and expert opinion. Any conclusions offered should be based strictly on the facts available.

Yet, the speaker must take care that emphasis on the data does not obscure understanding of what the data support. An example of this is the speaker who is so preoccupied with explaining certain equations employed in his study that he never makes clear what his equations were intended to prove, nor what results they produced.

Although an oral technical report does not necessarily need the use of visual aids, they are usually recommended. Graphs, diagrams, models, and samples are employed freely for such purposes as explaining mechanisms and processes, presenting statistics, and stating objectives or listing main points. Because it is so easy to use visual aids ineptly, a few suggestions are:

- Charts and diagrams should normally be prepared before instead of during the presentation, when valuable time may be needlessly consumed.
- Aids should be kept simple, focusing only on what is most pertinent.

- Each drawing or chart should be adequately titled and labeled.
- Diagrams and labels should be large enough to be fully legible to those seated farthest away.
- Charts should have a professional look. Drawings and lettering not neat in appearance detract from the report.
- Normally, materials should not be distributed during the presentation since they divert attention from the speaker.
- Aids should not be revealed until they become pertinent in the presentation.

Proper Organization Important for Effective Report

As in any form of communication, the pattern of development is very important. The organization of the oral technical report can be most conveniently discussed in terms of the three major divisions of the report: body, introduction, and conclusion.

The *body* is normally organized in terms of the steps involved in the problem-solution sequence. They include (a) an analysis of the problem to show what is wrong (the evidences of effects of the problem), the conditions which brought about the problem (the causes), and a statement of what is desired (the criteria or expectations); and (b) an explanation and analysis of one or more solutions in terms of their advantages and disadvantages in solving the problem and meeting the criteria.

The report need not always follow the entire sequence. Sometimes it may only analyze the causes of a problem or explain and evaluate a solution to a problem.

The discussion of each phase of the analysis should close with a statement showing the sub-con-

Evaluation of the Oral Report

YES NO

Introduction
_____|_____ Did the speaker effectively capture the interest and attention of his review group right from the start?
_____|_____ Did the speaker give the necessary explanation of the background from which the problem derived?
_____|_____ Did the speaker clearly state and explain his problem?
_____|_____ Did the speaker indicate the method(s) used to solve the problem?
_____|_____ Did the speaker suggest the order in which he would report?

Organization
Was the plan of organization recognizable through the use of:
_____|_____ (a) Sufficient introductory information
_____|_____ (b) Successful use of transitions from one main part to the next and between points of the speech
_____|_____ (c) Appropriate use of summary statements and restatements?
_____|_____ Were the main ideas of the report clearly distinguishable from one another?
_____|_____ Was there a recognizable progression of ideas that naturally led to the conclusion?

Content
_____|_____ Did the speaker have adequate supporting data to substantiate what he said?
_____|_____ Was all the content meaningful in terms of the problem and its solution? (Avoidance of extraneous material.)
_____|_____ Did the speaker present his supporting data understandably in terms of the ideas or concepts he wasy trying to communicate?
_____|_____ Were the methods of the investigation clearly presented?

(continued on page 226)

Source: "Characteristics and Organization of the Oral Technical Report" by Roger P. Wilcox in *General Motors Engineering Journal*, Oct./Nov./Dec. 1959. © 1959 General Motors Corporation. Used by permission.

(continued from page 225)

Visual Aid Supports

_____ Did the speaker effectively use charts, graphs, or diagrams to present his statistical data?
_____ Did the speaker use clear drawings, charts, diagrams or blackboard aids to make his facts or explanations vivid to the review group?
_____ Did the visual aids fit naturally into the presentation?
_____ Did the speaker give evidence of complete familiarity with each visual aid used?
_____ Did the speaker clutter his report with too many visual aids?

Conclusion

Did the speaker conclude his report with finality in terms of one or more of the following:
_____ (a) The conclusions reached
_____ (b) The problem solved
_____ (c) The results obtained
_____ (d) The value of such findings to the corporation or industry at large
_____ (e) Recommendations offered?

The Question Period

_____ Did the speaker give evidence of intelligent listening in interpreting the questions?
_____ Were the speaker's answers organized in terms of a summary statement, explanation, and supporting example?
_____ Did the speaker show freedom in adapting or improvising visual aids in answering questions?

Delivery

_____ Did the speaker use a natural, communicative delivery?
_____ Did the speaker use adequate eye contact in maintaining a natural, communicative delivery?
_____ Did the speaker use sufficient movement and gestures?
_____ Did the speaker use good clear diction to express himself?
_____ Could the speaker be heard easily by everyone?
_____ Was the speaker confident and convincing?
_____ Did the speaker display enthusiasm when communicating his ideas?

clusions arrived at during that phase.

The *introduction* prepares the audience for the body of the report. This is done by motivating the listener to want to hear what the speaker has to say and orienting the listener as to what the report contains.

You can develop an effective informative speech by following the pattern of an oral technical report.

Motivating the audience depends on two steps. First, the speaker should dwell briefly on the importance of the problem so the listener will have the feeling, "Here's something I want to find out about." Second, the speaker should establish the distinct impression that he has something worthwhile to offer on this subject. This can be done indirectly by referring to the speaker's interest and background concerning the problem and particularly to the amount of time spent and methods used in his investigation. Another way is to create an impression of competence, both in the introduction and throughout the report.

Orienting the listener is accomplished by (a) identifying and defining the problem by showing its relationship to the area from which it was taken, making clear what phases of the problem will be included in the report, and being explicit as to the exact purpose of the report; (b) providing whatever background is necessary concerning how the problem arose; and (c) giving a preview of what the main divisions of the report will contain.

When the introduction is completed, the listener should be motivated to want to listen to the report and should know what it will cover and in what order.

The *conclusion* normally fulfills three main functions. First, the various subconclusions presented during the report at the close of each unit are summarized. Second, general conclusions, in the form of generalizations drawn from the subconclusions, are presented. And finally, any recommendations, arising from the general conclusions are offered.

How Not to Speak at a Meeting

Few meetings produce, nor do they require, much golden-throated oratory. But the ability to stand up and talk—lucidly, convincingly and sometimes persuasively—is a must at any meeting. The rambler, the mumbler, the man who doesn't really know what he's talking about or *how* to talk, how to communicate, is worse than a nuisance; he's a dead loss.

These visuals depict a few of the all too common mistakes unpracticed speakers are likely to make.

The Fumbler: The Fumbler, at the podium, is about as popular as the fumbler on the football field. A good many speakers now use visual aids regularly. Their first rule is: Know thy equipment.

The Preening Peacock: He never gets his tie quite straight or his coat adjusted or his hair smoothed to his satisfaction. Chances are he's nervous. Chances are he doesn't know he's repeating these nervous gestures. But his audience knows it—and his audience is distracted.

(continued on page 228)

(continued from page 227)

The Moving Target: This fellow walks off his nervousness. Listening to him is like watching a tennis match. He detracts from his own talk and, more important, may well "walk himself" away from some of the principal points he planned to make.

The Comedian: A joke is fine . . . but don't begin to mistake yourself for a scintillating night club comedian.

The Deadly Sleeper: This man is simply dull. He sometimes looks as if he might drop off to sleep . . . and his audience does.

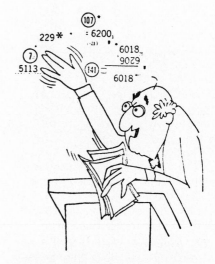

The Musician: This fellow accompanies his talk with a rendition on the change, keys and so on in his trouser pockets . . . and in short order his audience is busy trying to recognize the tune he's playing instead of listening to him. Many practiced speakers take their change and keys out of their pockets before they approach the podium.

The Nearsighted Note Nibbler: Most speakers use notes . . . but the best ones don't act like it. Usually, over-reliance on notes simply means the speaker is ill-prepared. But if he doesn't find his material important and interesting why should his audience?

The Great Scientist: He may be a brilliant speaker. Unquestionably, he's a brilliant man. Unfortunately, he's as abstruse as he is brilliant: there may be only nine other men in the world who fully understand him— and none of these are in his audience. Translating *technicalese* into laymen's language is one of the toughest problems many speakers face today.

A Politician's Guide to Success on the Stump: Hire a Heckler

John P. Keating

When President Nixon took to the campaign trail in last year's elections, a small but vocal group of hecklers seemed to show up at every rally. These hecklers probably were unaware that their mere presence may have given the President his biggest dividends of the campaign. A series of studies in the last decade shows that the distraction that hecklers create could be the catalyst to swing the votes of the uncommitted or wavering.

Vaccine

In the early 1960s William McGuire attempted to explain how people resist persuasive arguments against their dearly held beliefs. Seeing an analogy with the way the body resists an attacking virus, he put forth the inoculation theory ["A Vaccine for Brainwash," *P.T.*, February 1970]. Just as inoculation wards off an attacking virus, McGuire maintained, people persist in their positions by developing antidotes that counterattack arguments against them. If people practice and develop counterarguments, they remain secure with their old convictions, and attempts to change their opinions are futile.

To demonstrate his theory, McGuire worked with such cultural truisms as "Everyone should get a yearly chest X-ray." Because these truisms rarely are challenged, people have little chance to develop counterarguments, and resistance to an attack is poor. When white prospectors carried the tubercle bacillus to Alaska, Eskimos had no resistance to it because the bacteria had not previously existed among them, and tuberculosis became a plague. Similarly, as McGuire suspected, when without warning subjects heard an attack on the cultural truism about chest X-rays they could not counterattack; they wavered in their belief, thinking that radiologists had hoodwinked society into the dangerous practice of once-a-year chest X-rays. But given a little practice at resisting arguments against truisms before attack, subjects developed their own resistance and continued to beatify time-honored cultural practices.

It seems that the tool employed to conserve opinions in the heat of attack is the counterargument. In political campaigns counterarguments are readily available. The favored campaigner will provide inoculation against opposing views. He may not cover the whole gamut of possible arguments, but he primes his constituents to manufacture their own antibodies and remain inoculated against the possibility of defection. The more concentration they exert at the time of the attack, the more efficiently they will produce counterarguments and the more firmly they will remain ensconced in their old positions.

Din

The inoculation theory piqued the curiosity of other psychologists. What would happen if people were distracted during an argument and could not devote all their attention to the attack and to the production of counterarguments? Would they still hold to their comfortable positions? Or would resistance lessen, enabling the persuasion to raise doubts or change their convictions?

You can develop an effective persuasive speech by following the pattern of political speaking.

Leon Festinger and Nathan Maccoby sought an answer. Fearlessly walking into a bastion of loyalty to tradition, they exposed a group of fraternity brothers to an attack on fraternities. At the same time, they showed an amusing film to some of the men. As expected, all the men rejected the message. But the ones who had their attention divided by the film accepted more of the points made by the attack than did the ones who merely listened to the attack.

These investigators concluded that people counterargue, actively but subvocally, when they encounter disagreeable messages. When distraction interferes with this process of counterargument, it weakens resistance to the persuasive communication.

But commentators disagreed with the interpretation. Some suggested that the amusing nature of the film made the attack more palatable, provoking less animosity and more acceptance. Some thought that the novelty of the situation may have resulted in more learning and thus more

attitude change. Others argued that in order to justify the greater energy expended in listening to the message through the distraction, the men gave the communication more merit than they normally would have.

Distractions from hecklers can increase the acceptance of a politican's arguments.

Machine

Though the explanation was hazy, the result—greater acceptance of the negative communication—was certain. To clear away the haze, Robert Osterhouse and Timothy Brock went a step further. They reasoned that if they could (1) remove the amusement factor from the distraction, and (2) equalize the novelty and the energy that subjects expended in listening to a negative communication while they were distracted or not distracted, then explanations contradictory to Festinger and Maccoby's would be discounted.

Osterhouse and Brock constructed a distraction machine—a black wooden panel, similar to those used in airplanes, with four numbered lights that could be flashed at varying intervals. They told their subjects, students at Ohio State University, that they would hear a faculty member present a report that advocated doubling tuition. Some were distracted while they listened to the report—they were instructed to monitor the panel by calling out the number of each light as it flashed. With this simple distraction device, students who monitored more lights tended to agree much more with the tuition in-

crease proposal than did those who had less or no distraction. Osterhouse and Brock concluded that calling out the numbers on the panel hindered the ability of the students to counterargue with the professor and led to greater agreement. Even though the students had bags full of arguments against increased tuition, they needed time to subvocalize these arguments and counterattack. Interference with their concentration debilitated their resistance.

Mix

It seemed clear from this study that if the counterargument mechanism could be shut down or interfered with, a person would be much less immune to disagreeable communications. But one last question remained. Osterhouse and Brock had designed their distraction study to interfere with the subvocalization of counterarguments. Would resistance to persuasion be equally broken down by distractions that did not call for vocalizations?

At Tim Brock's suggestion I attempted to answer this question in an experiment using the same kind of tuition-increase message that Osterhouse and Brock had used. While exposing some students to no distraction whatsoever, I had other students monitor either 10 or 25 light flashes each minute by one of three methods: I asked some to respond to the panel vocally, others to monitor the board by pushing the flashing light with their fingers to extinguish it, and still others to do both at the same time. I found no appreciable difference in acceptance of the communication between those who called out the numbers and those who monitored the panel manually. Those who performed both operations simultaneously were the most accepting. And, as expected, those who were the most distracted – with 25 lights each minute in each of the operations – agreed more with the communication than did either of the other two groups.

I undertook this experiment somewhat timorously, since the tuition issue was a hot one at the time; frequent advertisements in the campus newspaper condemned any proposed increase. But even though the students were aware of the issue and were forewarned of the nature of the communication, they still needed uninterrupted concentration and time to produce adequate counterarguments to buttress their resistance. It was also apparent that they did not have to contribute to their own distraction by actively vocalizing. And surprisingly, those who were most distracted retained as much information from the communication as did those who were less distracted.

Stump

But how do distraction machines in a university laboratory relate to the campaign trail? We know that people resist change in thought by counterattacking any disagreeable message. The campaigner trying to swing votes to his side by persuasive arguments would be well advised to prevent his audience from launching reasoned counterattacks. The distractions and confusion inherent in campaign rallies can provide such interference. Instead of engaging in repartee with hecklers, a wise politician would continue with his stock speech, hoping for the distraction to grow louder – though not so loud that his voice could not be heard above the clamor. The dissident demonstration would distract potential voters at the rally or in front of television sets. And as we have seen in the series of studies starting with McGuire's, distraction would make these potential voters less defensive against the candidate and more accepting of his arguments, whatever they might be. These studies, of course, used communications whose ideas were diametrically opposed to the audience's views. In political campaigns, where the issues are more complex and ambiguous, politicians could anticipate even more success than the laboratory psychologist would predict for them.

I had a dream the other night about what I fancy would be the acid test of this theory. Jerry Rubin was addressing American Legionnaires while the Iron Butterfly performed its loudest music and a claque of paid hecklers shrilled in the audience. And Rubin won the Legion's endorsement.

How to Listen to Campaign Oratory If You Have To

Robert Bendiner

To help voters make their choices this year, enough words will be spoken to fill three thousand books, each the size of *Gone with the Wind* and each rating that title. Fortunately, most of this outpouring will not get into print. But you will probably catch two or three volumes' worth, and maybe you will want a guide through the verbiage.

The first rule for penetrating the underbrush of words is to keep always in mind that a candidate is not out to explain anything to you. It is not your mind he is after: it is your glands. He is out to show you, above all, that he is *your* kind of man — only more so. For this reason, a good campaign talk always starts out with the speaker finding a link to his listeners — no matter how hard he has to stretch for it. Here is the same candidate addressing three different audiences:

To a veterans' convention — "I am proud to be here, among my former comrades in arms. I was not 'big brass,' but I think I know the thoughts and feelings of a humble soldier . . ." (He was, in fact, at Camp Yaphank in World War I, when the Armistice happily cut off his military career.)

At a county fair and ploughing contest — "My Grandfather Richards, on my mother's side, had a small farm, like most of you folks here, and many's the day I spent getting to know the backbreaking work that makes the farmer this country's forgotten man . . ." (He

spent three summer vacations there as a growing, eating boy.)

In a trade-union hall — "I am delighted to be here, because this is where I belong. I am proud to have in my pocket right now a membership card in one of the great trade unions of this country . . ." (An honorary card bestowed on him by a bricklayers' union when, as an alderman, he laid the cornerstone for a new local.)

Where the audience is a mixed group, the speaker finds a quick kinship in geography. He will always have a soft spot for Devil's Gulch, Ariz., because his mother was born 18 miles from there. Or for East Overshoe, Ill., because his Uncle Henry ran a poolroom there in 1912. At worst, he can always call a town his "second home" on the ground that he once stayed overnight at the local hotel and had his laundry done.

Once past the amenities, our man is ready to plunge into serious matters, equipped as he is with a life belt of ready-made phrases to keep him afloat. The kind he chooses depends on whether his party is in or out of office. If he belongs to the "out" party, government expenditures are *criminal waste and extravagance*. And all members of the executive branch of government automatically become *bureaucrats*.

If our man belongs to the "in" party, government expenditures are *the best return on his dollar the American taxpayer has ever had.* As for executive personnel, they are *dedicated public servants,* who daily sacrifice themselves for you and me when they could be making millions in some other job.

There are, of course, turns of phrase that are common to both the "ins" and the "outs." In this category are the diminutives— *little man, common man, small businessman, small farmer* and the like. In an election year, we seem to have an enormous population of midgets. The candidate's immediate audience, however, is never made up of these wee folk; it is made up of *the great people of this great state.* That's you. The little people are your relatives and neighbors. They don't happen to be there, but on their behalf, you will no doubt appreciate this unselfish champion of the underdog.

Having mastered these semantic twists, the student of campaign oratory is ready to move on to those tags that politicians hang on each other in the hope that voters will treat the wearer like a medieval leper. In this category are the various Red labels, ranging from *pro-Communist* to *fellow traveler* to the newest variants, *soft on communism* or *soft on Russia.* Every candidate has to run against two opponents— the other party's candidate and Nikita Khrushchev. It might be assumed at this stage in history that every American politician is against communism, just as he is against barracuda in the bath. But unless his views are the exact opposite of the Russian leader's on everything from astrophysics to the can-can, he may be put down as *playing into Khrushchev's hands.* In common with certain head-hunting natives of Borneo both John F. Kennedy and Richard M. Nixon relish a

They Say	*They Mean*
My opponent is making a political football out of this grave and complicated issue.	He has a good thing going for him there. If my party was on the paying end of that issue, I'd sure know what to do with it.
Let us return to spiritual values.	Let's put my party in again and see what happens.
Clean up the mess in Washington (or Boston or Albany).	Clean up their mess in Washington (or Boston or Albany). It will take a few years before we have a mess of our own.
We will conduct a vigorous, fighting campaign.	We will smear them.
They are trying to smear us.	They are conducting a vigorous fighting campaign.
It is time to close ranks.	It is time to close ranks behind us. (If the opposition wins, it is time for honest criticism.)
I am not here to make a speech.	I mean to talk for another 40 minutes. Don't anyone leave.
I am not suggesting that my opponent is personally dishonest.	He is a willing dupe.
This is the speech *they* wrote for me, but I'm going to throw it away and speak from the heart.	They slipped me tomorrow's speech, which would lay an egg with this audience.
I cannot go into the details now, but I think I may say without fear of contradiction that our policies have proved to be sound.	All sound.
We will take the American people into our confidence.	We will let them in on all the opposition's scandals we can uncover.
They are playing into the hands of our country's enemies.	They are criticizing us again.
You may hear talk that they have reformed, my friends, but the leopard doesn't change its spots.	We haven't been able to get anything new on them lately.
We have had enough of their defeatist talk.	Let's forget the facts for awhile. Things are tough all over.
They have made a tragic blunder, for which we must all pay the price.	They have had a nasty break, and it looks as though we can cash in on it.

good meal, but it would probably be wrong to assume on that evidence that either of them is soft on cannibalism. Unless this particular trick is held in check, anyone who lights a match may be put down as soft on arson.

In a milder category are the hundreds of clichés, rubber stamps and warmed-over metaphors, mixed and unmixed, that make the padding of campaign oratory. Most of them are so washed out by waves of repetition that they call up no pictures at all and are intended only to get the speaker from one sentence to the next with the least resistance. He thinks it sounds good to work in references to *our Founding Fathers, Old Glory, hearths and homes, our children and our children's children.* These are not really words at all. They are red-white-and-blue cement.

Now that you have been warned, how are you to get through the next few weeks? Here are a few rules that may help:

1. Spend a preliminary month in a Trappist monastery, so that the sound of even a politician's voice, no matter what he says, will have a certain welcome freshness.

2. Decide in advance on three or four questions that a candidate ought to deal with in this year of 1960. If he dodges or skirts all four of them the first time you hear him, ignore him the next time and go back to Bat Masterson.

3. If he answers even one of these questions to your satisfaction, give him a second try. If he answers two or three, vote for him. And if he successfully answers all four, go out and work for him.

4. Try listening to a candidate in the company of someone who generally opposes your views. If the two of you can't get up a good row about the talk afterwards, the chances are that the speaker didn't say anything.

5. No matter how frighteningly the campaigners warn you that the salvation of the world depends on their winning, remember that on November 9, half of them will be wiring congratulations to the other half on their great victory and promising to co-operate fully in the predicted disaster.

Nick Pavloff

June Is Speakers' Month

Howard Mumford Jones
Harvard's Abbott Lawrence Lowell Professor of Humanities, Emeritus

In the month of June the voice of the commencement orator is loud in the land. The commencement speaker is, I think, a purely American invention, like chewing gum and baseball.

He inhabits no other country, and he comes in four sizes.

(1) He may be a Very Important Personage, who might conceivably announce a Very Important Policy Change in foreign affairs, or business, or religion, or the income tax, theoretically to the graduating class but actually to the newspapers, all to the glory of dear old Siwash.

(2) He may be the recipient of an honorary degree. The recipient of an honorary degree is of course a Very Important Person but he is not necessarily a Very Important Personage, and commonly all he is expected to do is to point with pride on the one hand and to view with dismay on the other.

(3) The father (or uncle) of somebody in the graduating class may serve. He is usually unequal to the task, and embarrasses his young relative.

(4) Anybody. I think I have heard better commencement speeches from Anybody than I have from any member of categories (1), (2), and (3).

Commencement oratory suffers from some built-in difficulties. The first is that as nobody sug-gests a topic, a theme, or a proposition, the orator is like a blindfolded man sailing a boat on a sea without shores to a port he never arrives at.

The second is the miscellaneous and conflicting interests of his audience — or audiences. To the graduating class he is simply delivering another required lecture. The college president hopes for the best. The main hope of the trustees is that the guy won't talk too long and that he won't say anything "radical." They don't want to embarrass the current fund drive.

As the parents think that everything is just too wonderful, they would be quite as pleased if the orator recited "Alice in Wonderland" until it came time for John to cross the stage. The newspaper boys already have copies of the speech and couldn't care less.

As for the general public, what with graduating classes getting larger, alumni associations growing bigger, and the faculty becoming more numerous, not to speak of the inability of the college gymnasium to expand in our space-time world, it mostly isn't there.

Over the decades commencement orators have developed a number of gambits that sometimes lend certainty to their undertaking but do not improve it as oratory. One is to congratulate the graduates and then tell them that their education is just begin-

Courtesy of the Boston Globe: June Is Speakers' Month by Howard Mumford Jones, June 1966

ning – a reflection that would annoy the faculty, except that they have heard it so often, it no longer stings.

A second is to admit the complete failure of the older generation, represented by the orator, and to turn the world over immediately to the graduating class. Despite the universal rebellion of individuality in the graduating class, symbolized by their universal long hair and their universal short skirts, the graduates commonly do not want the world – they want to know about the draft and a job and matrimony.

A fourth ploy is Leadership. The seniors are informed they are the Leaders of Tomorrow's World. As we graduate some thousands of students from all sorts of institutions annually and semi-annually and quarterly, it seems clear that the Future is going to be filled up with Leaders who will have nobody to lead.

The commencement orator is part of a ritual, a rite of passage, and perhaps it doesn't make any difference what he says, just as it would be simpler to mail the diplomas to the graduates. But they come to the platform and get them. It is all part of a show. The show at least allows parents to glory in what they think they have paid for, and substituting tape recordings won't do.

Still, commencement is a climactic point in education. It is the last, and sometimes the first, occasion when the graduates as an organized group confront the world they are about to be catapulted into. I think somebody ought to build a better bridge between the campus and the world outside than that offered by the usual American commencement speech, even if it is only a Bailey's bridge.

Somebody might indicate clearly and passionately what you can and what you cannot do with a liberal education, now that you have got one. Somebody might reasonably assess the place of the college in a world in tension. Somebody might indicate that, higher education being an exposure to a world of ordered intelligence, other persons have found ordered intelligence of this kind to be in some limited degree use- ful, or enriching, or annoying, or stabilizing in business or matrimony or the entertainment world or Madison Avenue. In such a case the commencement speaker would have to address the graduates and not the universe at large. This is probably asking too much. It is far easier to address the universe.

Prods

1. Think of two large organizations (e.g., university, state government, business, city police, hospital) with which you are familiar. To what sector of the public are they responsible? Is it likely that speeches by representatives of these organizations would be different? Why?

2. How does a political scandal affect the credibility of the President of the United States? In what ways would it affect what he says in a public speech?

3. If you were speaking to a group of publishers about laws governing pornography, what would your central idea be? Using the chronological pattern of organization, state three main headings for your talk. State three others for the topical pattern.

4. Watch and listen to a public speaker deliver a speech before a live audience. Describe his or her delivery. Was it animated? Did the speaker have any problems in delivery? Did you think he or she was more or less effective because of delivery?

5. You are to speak to an audience of oil company executives about industry research for alleviating the energy crisis. State two main ideas you might include in this report. What kinds of visual aids could you use?

6. Listen to a political campaign speech. How did the speaker try to win over his or her audience? Were there any hecklers? What would you have done differently from what the speaker did?

". . . Furthermore . . ."

From *The Saturday Evening Post* courtesy of Reg Hider.

The Ending

I had a friend one time.
He died.

— a prison inmate

Many relationships wither under the strain of misunderstandings, thoughtlessness, and even cruelty as well as differences in status, location, and experience; and yet people persist in seeking to share understanding. We cannot deny that some people seek advantage over others or deliberately try to hurt them. If such designs were the rule rather than the exception, surely we would see the end of human cooperative behavior. As you seek to improve your relationships with people, we can promise only a fierce struggle and the possibility of occasional peace and happiness.

You will be wise to ponder your new knowledge. With caution and humility, approach each communicative event as a new experience, honestly trying to do your best. Only in that way will you find it possible to narrow the communication gap.

Throughout this book we have sought to present some basic ideas about human communication — its personal, message, and environmental components and the four fundamental relationships in which people interact. Taken together, these components and relationships comprise a fairly complete picture of human communicative behavior, which may help you analyze and comprehend human interaction and to develop specific skills to improve your communication with others. We hope that from our presentation you have gotten a sense of what it means to communicate with others as well as a good feeling about the subject of human communication. Aware of our strengths and weaknesses as human beings, we can at least resolve to do better next time. Nevertheless, the only reality we can offer is the challenge of improved communication in a world in which perfection is a lie.

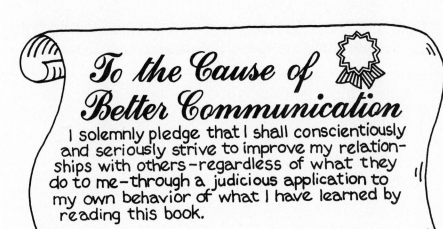

To the Cause of Better Communication
I solemnly pledge that I shall conscientiously and seriously strive to improve my relationships with others — regardless of what they do to me — through a judicious application to my own behavior of what I have learned by reading this book.

There Will Never Be a Gap Gap

We suffer from, among other things, gaposis, or a plethora of gaps. Among them are the Credibility Gap, the Communication Gap, the Culture Gap and the Missile Gap, the Sputnik, Power, Credit, Technological and Ecumenical gaps. And what household is not familiar with the ever-present Financial Gap?

Long before there were any of these gaps, of course, there was a Delaware Water Gap. God gave us that gap, but it is relatively small, dividing only the states of New Jersey and Pennsylvania. The great gaps are man-made, and we lead the world in producing them. We are also rich in headline writers grateful for a three-letter word to cover them all. Last week the New York *Times* garden section even produced a Skilled Plantsman Gap, which it called nationwide. Washington alone has created more gaps than all the other world capitals put together (although this statistic must be hedged because Moscow does not make figures of this kind available). Washington also produces a ceaseless flow of Stopgaps.

The greatest of all gaps, because it is one of the oldest and grows exponentially, is the celebrated Generation Gap. It has been the subject of much confused interpretation. To set this straight, it is necessary to understand what a gap is and what a generation is.

A gap, of course, is an interstice, an absence. It separates this from that, I from Thou. The last man to experience existence without an interpersonal gap was Adam. As soon as Eve made her appearance, the Communication Gap was born. Neither knew how ignorant they both were. From the first bite of apple they started to find out. In the attempt of each to convey a vision of reality to the other, the gap widened, and it has been widening ever since. Ours is the most abyssal Communication Gap ever achieved, because in an age of specialization we have uncovered such a vast number of things to be ignorant about. The only way to halt that widening would be to stop learning. The Generation Gap came with Cain. A generation is the space between father and son, the smallest and the greatest distance the universe knows. Of one blood and bone, they are achingly alike; of different times, they can be galaxies apart.

(continued on page 239)

(continued from page 238)

Generation is one of our most abused terms. A generation's span cannot be stated in years. Fathers—and mothers—have been as few as five and as many as 90-plus years older than their offspring. A school generation may be six, eight or nine years, depending on the school system. A college generation (undergraduate) is usually four years. Generations of computers (we're into the third now), of space capsules, missiles and antimissile defense systems get shorter all the time.

President Kingman Brewster of Yale was referring specifically to students in the colleges as of 1968 when he labeled their generation the Cool Generation—using the adjective in its inverted, McLuhanesque sense of committed, motivated. Who, though, qualifies to be included among their predecessors, the so-called Silent Generation, those unquestioning, uncaring Bachelors of Arts who are alleged to have strolled out of Academe during the Eisenhower years? Where did they leave off and the Cool Generation begin? With the class of '61 (three and a half years under Ike, one semester under Kennedy)? The Class of '65 (no Ike, about 800 of Kennedy's thousand days and a year and a half of L.B.J.)? After what cutoff birthdate is a parent of today declared ineligible for membership in the Depression Generation? The Postwar Generation?

Since human beings are born every second, it is glib and often dangerous to label generations. Each man knows he is his father's son, and that is his generation. Oh, he may have a way of identifying with coevals: seeking out others who fell in love to the melody of *Star Dust*, or *I Left My Heart at the Stage Door Canteen*, or *Rock around the Clock*. But contemporaneity is not generation: there is no genesis in it. Generations flow from specific fathers to specific sons. Each newborn infant is a tiny piece of the future and however much he and his father are alike, they are as different as two tenses. To decry it is to protest against time itself.

To call it a Generation Gap gives it an impolite burden of meaning. To the young it's what separates them from those committed to hypocrisy and false values. To their elders it's the separation from those who don't appreciate the nuances of life, the complexity of motives and the arts and necessities of compromise. Trouble is, once people blame their differences on age, they feel it useless to argue them out. And so what they call a Generation Gap becomes the worst Communication Gap of all.

We've Only Just Begun

LYRIC BY PAUL WILLIAMS   MUSIC BY ROGER NICHOLS

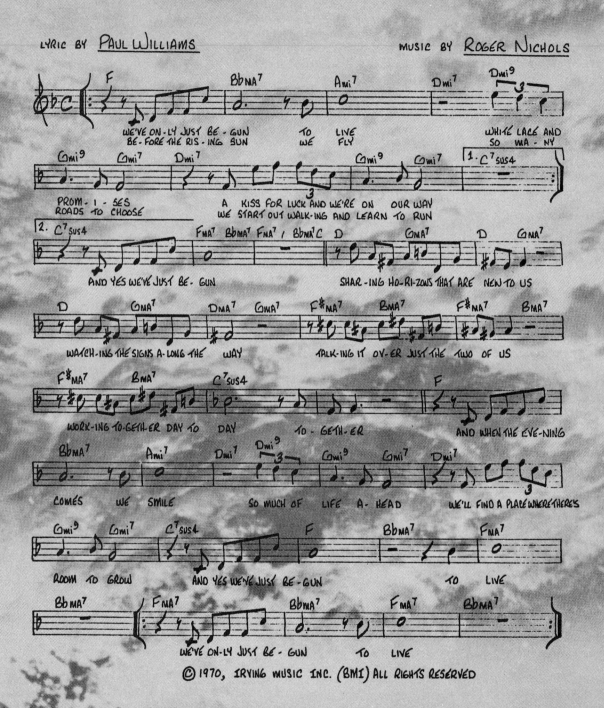

© 1970, IRVING MUSIC INC. (BMI) ALL RIGHTS RESERVED

Other Message Forms:
Illustrative Materials and Minor Articles

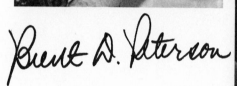

Brent D. Peterson

Gerry Goldhaber

R Wayne Pace